Jonathan Edwards for the Church

The Ministry and the Means of Grace

Edited by:
William M. Schweitzer

ЄP

EP BOOKS

1st Floor Venture House, 6 Silver Court, Watchmead,
Welwyn Garden City, UK, AL7 1TS
web: www.epbooks.org
e-mail: sales@epbooks.org

EP books are distributed in the USA by:
JPL Fulfillment, 3741 Linden Avenue Southeast, Grand Rapids, MI 49548
orders@jplfulfillment.com
Tel: 877.683.6935

First published 2015

British Library Cataloguing in Publication Data available
ISBN: 978-1-78397-116-9

All royalties from the sale of this book will be donated to the Evangelical Presbyterian Church in England and Wales Church Planting Fund.

Printed and bound in the UK by 4edge Limited

Commendations

In recent years there has been a resurgence of interest in the life and work of Jonathan Edwards. It is not always appreciated that Edwards labored within and for the church. His writings offer tremendous help and encouragement to those who, like Edwards, are called to serve the people of God. One challenge to modern readership is that Edwards' output is both voluminous and diffuse. *Jonathan Edwards for the Church* has done our generation the invaluable service of compiling and distilling Edwards' wisdom on the ministry and the means of grace. The essays in this volume will challenge, refresh, and invigorate as they place us at the feet of one who committed his life and energies to the glory of the church's Head, Jesus Christ.

Guy Prentiss Waters, James M. Baird, Jr. Professor of New Testament
Reformed Theological Seminary, Jackson, Mississippi, USA

The context and times in which Jonathan Edwards ministered the Word of God were very different to ours, yet, as this volume shows, his life is a fruitful field in which his modern day evangelical successors may glean. This collection of essays does more than apply lessons from Edwards' ministry, however: it is a much needed corrective to the current idea that the gathered church, worshipping God around God's Word week by week, is somehow inadequate to the needs of contemporary society. On the contrary, the knowledge of God is ministered precisely through the local church, and Edwards is a guide to recovering that vision. The authors have done a great service in helping us catch it.

Iain D Campbell, Free Church of Scotland, Isle of Lewis

Jonathan Edwards spent his life working in, and writing for, the local church. While the academic guild plays an important role and can teach us much, Edwards himself would cringe at the detached dissecting of his work by many specialists today. *Jonathan Edwards for the Church* is a refreshing read because it reminds us that Edwards belongs first to everyday Christians—pastors and their flocks—and that the ultimate value of reading Edwards is not greater knowledge but, through greater knowledge, warmer worship.

Dane Ortlund, PhD, Senior Vice President, Bible Publishing at Crossway

Jonathan Edwards is remembered throughout church history as a pre-eminent theologian, scholar, and philosopher. However, as a pastor, his greatest contribution is to the church. Edwards' ministry is a bastion of light and joy for all those called into gospel ministry providing hope and perseverance to press on in the race. The scholars brought together for this project paint for us a clear portrait of a man giving his life in full measure for the advance of God's people in the gospel of grace.

Steven J. Lawson, *President, OnePassionMinistries, Dallas, Texas, USA*

While there has been an increasing insistence that we view Jonathan Edwards in the context of his main focus in life—namely, the church—there have been relatively few genuine attempts to apply Edwards to the life of the church. In *Jonathan Edwards for the Church*, a collection of pastors and ecclesially-oriented scholars take on the task of putting Edwards' first things first with valuable results: a book that actually demonstrates how this 18th century pastor can help 21st century pastors fulfill their callings to God's glory.

Sean Michael Lucas, Senior Minister, The First Presbyterian Church, Hattiesburg, Mississippi, USA
Associate Professor of Church History, Reformed Theological Seminary, Jackson, USA

Dedication

To the faithful ministers who pursue the reformation and revival of Christ's church through the ordinary means of grace

Contents

Contributors

Revd Nicholas T. Batzig
  Church planting minister of New Covenant Presbyterian Church in Richmond Hill, GA

Revd Dr Michael Bräutigam
  Minister of the Free Church of Scotland, residing in Melbourne, Australia

Revd William Macleod
  Minister of Knightswood Free Church (Continuing) in Glasgow, Scotland

Revd Dr Gerald R. McDermott
  Teaching Pastor of St John Lutheran Church in Roanoke, VA

Revd Roy Mellor
  Minister of the Church of England, residing in Durham, England

Revd John J. Murray
Retired minister of the Free Church of Scotland (Continuing) residing in Glasgow, Scotland

Revd Dr Stephen R. C. Nichols
Senior Minister at All Souls, Langham (Church of England) in London, England

Revd Dr Jon D. Payne
Church planting minister of Christ Church Charleston (PCA) in Charleston, SC USA

Revd Dr William M. Schweitzer
Church planting minister of Gateshead Presbyterian Church (EPCEW) in Gateshead, England

Dr Douglas Sweeney
Chairman of the Board of Elders and adult Sunday School teacher at St. Mark Lutheran Church in Lindenhurst, IL

Revd Dr Jeffrey Waddington
Minister of Knox Orthodox Presbyterian Church (OPC) in Lansdowne, PA

Acknowledgments

The first order of grateful acknowledgement goes to Roy Mellor, Chris Schröder and Gerry McDermott, three men who believed there ought to be a conference on Jonathan Edwards in England and were willing to make it happen. I am also thankful for the directors and editors of Evangelical Press who thought there ought to be a book conveying Edwards' insights on the ministry and the means of grace to the church. Of course, this book could not have been produced apart from the authors who contributed their chapters—Nick Batzig, Michael Bräutigam, William Macleod, John J. Murray, Stephen Nichols, Jon Payne, Doug Sweeney and Jeff Waddington—thank you for your zeal for truth, pastoral concern and gracious spirit. Others who were of particular help on this project were Nathan Hilton, Alun Lewis, Benjamin Mitchell, Josh Rieger and Benjamin Wontrop. None of this would have been possible apart from the elders and congregations of Gateshead Presbyterian Church, Durham Presbyterian Church and Sheffield Presbyterian Church. Having neglected to do so in my previous book on Edwards, I would like to thank Kin Yip Louie and Kris Lundgaard for their generous gifts of books. Finally, if we have learned anything from Edwards, we should be careful to give all glory to God alone.

Foreword

J onathan Edwards (1703–1758) is perhaps the greatest theologian
ever to walk on American soil. Today the study of Edwards'
thought has flowered into a publishing industry unto itself.
Researchers all over the world now probe the writings of Edwards
for his keen insights into the most vexing of theological and
philosophical questions.

Yet we must not forget that Edwards' primary calling was to
serve the church as a pastor. To this work he gave his life, devoting
a quarter of a century to the church in Northampton, and several
more years in Stockbridge. He agreed to leave the pastorate to
become the president of the College of New Jersey (Princeton)
only when urged to do so by a council of ministers. He stood in
the theological tradition of William Perkins (1558–1602), who wrote
in the flyleaf of his books, 'Thou art a minister of the Word; mind
thy business.'[1] Therefore, this excellent book on Edwards *for the
church* brings us close to the heart of Edwards' greatest concerns
and deepest desires. Reading the following chapters will both help

you to understand Edwards better, and present you with a glorious view of the Christian ministry.

Edwards took his pastoral calling very seriously. As he explained in an ordination sermon preached at the height of his own controversy with the church in Northampton, he saw ministry as a calling to follow Jesus Christ in washing the feet of the saints (John 13:15–16).[2] It is a vocation that thus demands humility, diligence, suffering, and hearty zeal in seeking the salvation of men. He said he was preaching 'to myself, and others in this sacred work of the gospel ministry' when he called ministers to follow the example of Christ, promising that in it they find honor 'in some respects greater than that of the angels' and walk in 'the way to enjoy the sensible, joyful presence of Christ with us.'[3]

At the center of the minister's calling is his responsibility to submissively receive and boldly preach the Word of God. The Word is the great means of grace by which Christ washes His church from its sins. Edwards urged another man being ordained for the ministry, 'Sir, I would now humbly and earnestly recommend to you that Holy Book which God is about to commit into your hands, and containing that message which you are to deliver to this people in his name ... humbly submitting your reason as a learner and disciple to that, renouncing all confidence in your own wisdom.'[4]

Edwards' words help us to understand his incredible self-discipline as a student of the Bible and theologian. They also remind us that the ministry is a calling to suffer reproach and opposition precisely because it is the ministry of the Word. Edwards said,

God is now about to deliver to you [in the Scriptures] a summary of doctrines already discovered and dictated to your hand, which you are to teach and be zealous to maintain. And if the time should come that you should be reproached for so doing ... and you should be called a bigoted zealot, one whose zeal runs before your knowledge, one that durst not indulge a freedom of thought, one that dare not presume to think otherwise then your forefathers thought, one of those that judge of God by themselves, that think that God is a morose, ill-natured sort of being because they are so, one that is a person of little sense or reason—if such proud contemptuous reproaches are cast upon you, merely because you rely more on God's testimony than the dictates of your own reason, the time will soon come when they will be wiped away. Your Lord and Master, that commanded you to preach these doctrines, will defend you.[5]

Pastoral ministry must always set the Word against the world. Perseverance in ministry is only possible when our afflictions are counter-balanced by the eternal weight of glory. May God use the following chapters on the ministry and means written by these Edwardsean pastor-scholars to raise up and strengthen the ministers of the Word to fulfill their precious calling, and to encourage all who love the truth.

Joel R. Beeke

Introduction

Edwards For the Church

Not so long ago, there was an academic conference in which a paper on Jonathan Edwards was being discussed. After some high-powered discussion between professors at prestigious institutions, an unfamiliar voice spoke up from the back. It was *an ordinary evangelical pastor*. He protested that if we really wanted to learn from Edwards, we should focus on things that actually matter to the church rather than academic hair-splitting. The audience seemed somewhat embarrassed but, after a brief pause, the show went on. This incident did not change anything on that day but, years later, it serves as a point of departure for us.

Although everyone affirms that Edwards has important contributions to make to both the church and the academy, somehow all the conferences and the books that come from them end up serving the latter much more than the former. In the minds of many, the evangelicals already have Edwards; we need to get him into the academy. Yet, while we could never say that the work is done, the academy of today actually knows something about Edwards, certainly more than it ever has before. On the other hand, the church has not necessarily kept pace and it may well be that ground has actually been lost.

Yet it was the church that employed Edwards for all but a few years of his career and it was the church that was the intended audience for the vast majority of his output. It is where his writings have already proven time and again to be of great use (see chapter six) and we pray that it is the place where they may yet again be used of God to bring needed reformation in our day. Edwards is of the church and *for* the church. This volume self-consciously imitates his church-wards orientation.

What do we mean when we say this is for the church rather than the academy? We do not mean a low standard of research or writing; we think that the church should actually set the standard for such things. We do not mean fluffy or sentimental; the church should be the place where one comes to hear eternal truths in a straightforward way. We do not even necessarily mean *easy*. Although we have tried to communicate clearly, this is not always an 'easy' book nor should it be; the Bible itself is not always so (2 Peter 3:16). No, a book is 'academic' not because of any superficial feature but because it aspires to contribute to the academy. *This* book is intended to inform and to prompt change in the contemporary church.

Not surprisingly, this means that our primary audience is ministers. We want ministers to gain from Edwards a clearer vision for their vocation in both theory and practice. If, for instance, some do not currently rely upon God's ordinary means of grace—the Word, the sacraments and prayer—we want them to start. However, they are not the only audience we have in mind. We also want lay elders to know about these things, in order to rightly guide their churches and to find good men to serve in their pulpits. And finally, we want God's people to know what it is that Christ has ordained for their blessing. If they already benefit from such things, they should encourage their elders to continue in doing good. If not, they should respectfully request improvement. Too often, compromise and departure from God's ways are justified on the basis of 'this is what the people want.' May the day come when decisions to focus more on the ministry of the Word, sacrament and prayer are made because 'this is what the people demand.'

With two exceptions, the chapters in this book began as lectures given at 'Jonathan Edwards for the Church,' a conference held in Durham, England in 2014. Given the worldwide proliferation of Edwards centres and events it was with some disbelief that we learned from conference chairman Roy Mellor that there had never previously been such a conference on English soil. This is rather ironic, since contemporary Reformed evangelicalism in England would hardly be recognisable apart from God's providential use of a certain American theologian (see chapter 6). In keeping with the overall vision articulated above, the speakers for the conference— and thus the authors for this book—were selected as much for their ministerial as for their academic credentials. They are all ordained elders; ten are ministers and one is a ruling elder. They are all evangelical and Reformed in the sense that they all subscribe to a Reformation confession; seven to the Westminster Confession, three to the Thirty-Nine Articles and one to the Formula of Concord.

On the Ministry

The first part of the book relates Edwards' advice, in precept and example, regarding the Christian ministry. In 'Directing Souls: What Pastors Today Can Learn from Edwards' Ministry,' Gerald

R. McDermott relates Edwards' guiding principles for the ministry. He frames these principles as exhortations which Edwards might have made had he preached a sermon on 'What you must do as a pastor to endure faithfully to the end.' For that is what ministers are called to do; not to triumph nor even 'succeed' but to endure faithfully to the end. The final of his exhortations, 'you must be willing to suffer,' comes on the basis of McDermott's own experience as well as his research. However, we are not to suffer as Stoics but as joyful Christians; Edwards '… was able to keep his focus—during all of his times of conflict and suffering—on the beauty of God. And because of his vision of God's beauty he was able to walk in joy—while suffering all the same.'

William M. Schweitzer, noting that there is widespread confusion in the contemporary church, wants to recall the church to Edwards' clear vision of the ministry. He begins by summarising some relevant aspects of Edwards' theology, such as the fact that God's purpose in creation was for Him to communicate His own knowledge, love and joy using certain means. The minister's job, then, is to convey the means of God's communicative grace to His people. Edwards employed various paradigms to elucidate this very high calling, such as stewards working on Christ's behalf, looking glasses displaying Christ, interpreters speaking for Christ and instruments conveying Christ to the church. Schweitzer offers six contemporary applications, including 'make the ordinary means of grace your great business' and 'don't try to change the message.'

Roy Mellor uses as a springboard an issue that recurs at various points throughout the book: Edwards' perplexing dismissal from Northampton. In his chapter, 'When the Road is Rough: Staying with what Matters Most,' Mellor points out that it was Edwards' convictions not his performance that got him fired, and that the possibility of this happening to good men did not end back them. He points to three convictions in particular—the necessity of conversion, the church's identity as the Bride of Christ (or the purity of the church) and the importance of discernment—that would probably undo any faithful man in such a situation. He closes with these words '... Edwards' commitment to his convictions even in the face of vicious opposition came from a more basic commitment: faithfulness to God's Word. This is the standard by which Edwards, and all ministers, must be judged.'

The next two chapters deal with what might be considered 'specialist' aspects of Edwards' career, but they are elements which our authors argue were integral to Edwards' comprehensive understanding of the ministry.

Jeffrey C. Waddington writes on the subject of 'Jonathan Edwards: Pastor-Apologist.' The point of this title is to emphasize that, although Edwards made significant contributions to apologetics, he did not consider this to be a diversion from his ministerial calling but an aspect of it. What today's church urgently needs is for ministers to imitate Edwards by taking on the role of pastor-apologists, to be resident theologians and apologists for their own congregations. Moreover, Waddington reminds us that Edwards did not defend some generic version of Christianity but rather full-bodied, experiential Calvinism, seen in his defence of the first Great Awakening and several key Reformed distinctives as well as his work on some more basic issues of the faith. We are likewise called to 'defend the whole of the Christian faith, not concede the difficult parts in order to gain a hearing.'

Jon D. Payne then considers Edwards' service as a missionary to the American Indians. The modern missions movement probably owes more to Edwards than to any other man. Sadly, however, the church of our own day has forgotten what she once knew and has become preoccupied with 'cultural transformation' rather than verbal proclamation and 'message contextualization' rather than orthodoxy. Payne relates that, while Edwards never turned a blind eye to the Indians' hardships, his unwavering focus was to deliver them from the wrath to come by preaching. And while Edwards' was highly sensitive to his audience, his first question was not, 'What does this culture require?' but rather, 'What does the Bible say?' Payne closes with an exhortation for the church to '… renew its commitment to identify, call, and support qualified, trained, gifted, and ordained men to plant churches.'

The last chapter in this section is John J. Murray's 'The Influence of Jonathan Edwards on the Church in Britain.' In order to gain an appreciation for the usefulness of appropriating Jonathan Edwards for the ministry today, it is useful to understand something of the amazing influence he has already had. Murray thus chronicles the various aspects of Edwards' influence in Great Britain starting with his own contemporaries. He goes on to highlight the effect that Edwards' writings have had on the great leaders of more recent church history, including Thomas Chalmers ('My theology is that of Jonathan Edwards'), Robert Murray M'Cheyne ('Bought Edwards' Works … Tonight more set upon missionary enterprise than ever') and Dr D. Martyn Lloyd-Jones ('It is certainly true they helped me more than anything else;' 'Their influence upon me I cannot put into words').

And the Means of Grace

The second section concerns the wonderful tools that God has put into the hands of ministers to save and to perfect His people: the ordinary means of grace.

The most fundamental of the means of grace is the Word of God. It is for this reason that the enemies of Christ have long sought to undermine its authority. Such efforts were well underway in Edwards' own day among the Deists and other sceptics, who wanted the Bible to be treated as an ordinary, non-essential human book. In chapter seven, Douglas Sweeney explains how Edwards argued not only for the absolute necessity of Scripture but also for its fullest divinity and supernatural power. He presents 'the fruit of Edwards' thought and preaching on the character of Scripture based on years of careful gleaning through the whole of Edwards' corpus.' His object in doing this is so that, 'as ministers in mostly non- or post-Christian cultures,' we might follow his example to 'stem the tide of unbelief and apathy, encouraging instead a robust biblical supernaturalism.'

It is not enough that the church recognise that the Bible is supernatural and divinely authoritative, we also need rightly to understand it. The academy's concept of Scripture seems designed mainly to fragment and relativize it. In 'Jonathan Edwards and the Bible: Christ, the Scope of Scripture,' Stephen R. C. Nichols points us instead to an account that is 'breath-taking in its unified scope yet utterly comprehensive in its detail.' Nichols follows Edwards' plan 'A Harmony of the Old and New Testament' as his structure, working through the Christological scope of prophecy, typology and 'doctrine and precept.' He closes with some practical benefits of adopting Edwards' approach today, including that Edwards' idea of the Bible as 'God's grammar book of a typological language offers … a way of connecting the everyday world' to the things of eternity.

A special application of this principle is to be found in Nicholas T. Batzig's 'Christ in the Song: How Edwards Can Help Us Recover the Song of Solomon.' Batzig reminds us that the Song of Songs has long been 'one of the most important texts for preaching and theological reflection in the Reformed church' but laments that 'many contemporary Christians will live and die without hearing a single sermon' on it. This is largely because modern canons of biblical interpretation make it out to be ordinary love poetry. Batzig relates to us Edwards' main work on the Song, detailing how Edwards 'preached the *Song* as a Divine love poem depicting the love between Christ and the church.' He concludes that 'It would do the church a world of good if her ministers would seek to emulate Edwards and avail themselves of the rich redemptive-historical treasures of the *Song*.'

It then remains for the minister to communicate, effectively and powerfully, the great message of Scripture. This is the thought behind of Michael Bräutigam's, 'Our God is an Awesome God: Communicating Jonathan Edwards' Vision of God's Excellencies.' As opposed to contemporary ideas of 'seeker sensitive' preaching, Bräutigam urges ministers to emulate Edwards by summoning people into the presence of an awesome, holy God. We should always remember that we want to communicate God's love and joy to our hearers as well as mere knowledge. Indeed, Edwards 'wants to introduce to us the glorious God who communicates himself in all of reality.' As application, we should think of preaching as a momentous occasion, as the point when 'Christ is magnified and listeners are satisfied with their vision of an excellent God' and theology brings them into wondrous doxology.

Finally, in a day in which revivalist churches need to be reformed and Reformed churches oppose the idea of revival, we have included William Macleod's stirring sermon, 'Wilt Thou Not Revive Us?' as an appendix.

The Means of Grace

1. Directing Souls: What Pastors Today Can Learn from Edwards' Ministry

Gerald R. McDermott

Introduction

The older I get, the more I think that being a pastor, especially being a senior pastor of a sizeable congregation, is one of the toughest jobs in the world. Every Sunday morning a pastor faces scores or hundreds of critics who are quick to think or say that he has missed the mark in the sermon or the way he dealt with a pastoral problem. It is often a lonely calling, and there are recurring periods of discouragement. Jonathan Edwards knew all of these things very well. After a honeymoon period that lasted longer than for most pastors, he endured years of opposition from leaders in his own congregation. Finally, in one of the most mysterious events in the history of American religion, they threw him out of the biggest church outside Boston. His own recurring melancholy didn't make it any easier.

Yet in the midst of it all, he kept a holy calm and fierce

determination to keep fighting the good fight. How did he pull it off? I want to present eight principles that he believed central to the pastorate. I think they helped him see his ministry through thick and thin. I find them personally inspiring, and they have encouraged pastors with whom I have shared them. I have turned each principle into an exhortation, which he probably would have done if he had preached the sermon, 'What you must do as a pastor to endure faithfully to the end.'

1. Embrace an Exalted Vision of the Pastoral Calling
The first principle is an exalted vision of the pastoral calling. Edwards proclaimed in an ordination sermon that a minister of the gospel is 'a burning and a shining light.'[1] God sent Christ as the 'Sun of Righteousness' to a fallen dark world. To convey Christ's light to human beings, God uses the means of 'appointed ministers in his church to be subordinate lights, and to shine with the communications of [Christ's] light, and to reflect the beams of his glory on the souls of men.'[2] They are the principal progenitors of the expansion of the history of the work of redemption. More important than presidents and prime ministers, more crucial than decisive wars, more helpful than economic recovery, is the work of pastors. Their preaching and pastoring bring Jesus Christ to the world, and expand the size and influence of his body in history. All the rest of history is determined, finally, by the life of that body.

Now Edwards didn't want this to go to pastors' heads, as it does sometimes to the heads of those who have not been out on the battlefield long. He reminded them that they are 'feeble, frail, sinful worms of the dust, in this work, who need redemption themselves.' Their glory is 'in some respects' greater than that of the angels, and they are the more dignified of the two classes of creatures, but 'in themselves [they] are utterly insufficient' for the work of ministry. They are like physicians trying to raise the dead: they are 'utterly unable to deliver the souls of men out of' the power of darkness, apart from a miracle of God. But with divine enabling they can be like the twelve apostles, who were 'poor fishermen' who yet became 'the conquerors of the world.' They must remember that God could have conquered the whole Roman Empire at once without their ministry, but graciously decided to use them and share his glory in the process. As a result, they did greater works than Christ himself on earth. 'Christ's preaching and miracles on earth converted but few. But the apostles turned the world upside down.'[3]

In the post-Christian West where the majority think Christian orthodoxy is unintelligent or immoral, pastors can hardly imagine what it would be like to turn their corner of the world upside down. They find themselves sometimes second-guessing the value of their ministry. In these moments Edwards would remind them that God has committed to them what is of more value than anything else in the world—the souls of men and women he created. When God commits their souls to the care of ministers, he said, it is like a prince who commits to the care of a subject 'some great treasure, consisting of most precious jewels' to carry for him through an enemy's country and bring home safe to his palace. Edwards also compared the minister to a watchman over a city during a time of war, and to shepherds who lead their flocks 'through a great and howling wilderness, full of hungry wolves and roaring lions.'[4] There is no more important calling in the Kingdom than bringing eternal life to God's human creatures and then helping nourish that life.

2. Have Clarity Regarding the Ministerial Task

Second, Edwards had a keen insight into how ministers nourish spiritual life. Pastors, he said, are 'guides' and 'teachers' with three functions. First, they 'discover' or reveal glorious things to their hearers, enabling them to see what angels see. Second, they '*refresh* and delight the beholders,' since light is refreshing to those who have sat in darkness. This new light provides the healing salve required to 'bind up the broken-hearted.' Third, they 'direct' souls through this dark world to 'regions of eternal light.' In a word, 'the work of ministers is to rescue lost souls and bring them to eternal happiness.' Pastors are 'guide[s] to lead them to an understanding of what we are taught in the Word of God of the nature of grace, and to help them apply it to themselves.'5

This pastoral guidance would not only lead souls out of darkness into light, but in the process 'wash and cleanse the souls of men.' Part of the washing and cleansing involves teaching and correcting, which God uses to mature the body of his son. 'God deals with his church in this respect as parents do with children. They gradually instruct them as they can bear, that they may grow in knowledge as they grow older, till all their childish mistakes are corrected.' God uses ministers as his primary agents in this celestial pedagogy. Their role is 'to correct the mistakes of his people and gradually introduce an increase of light.'6

But Edwards made this more personal. The principal task of ministers, he said, is to *care for souls*. Not to preach *at* them, but to come alongside them and build up their souls—which are more important ultimately than the health of their bodies. Edwards was not (finally) a dualist on the human person—separating in some ultimate sense body and soul—but for pastoral reasons he said God is more concerned with human souls than bodies because souls 'are in a special and more immediate manner his workmanship.' Bodies came from earthly parents and pre-existent matter, but 'the souls of men are by God's immediate creation.' This is why Scripture refers to earthly fathers as the 'fathers of our flesh' but God as the 'father of our spirits' (Hebrews 12:9). Souls are 'in a higher, more direct and immediate manner from God,' and it is by them that God gains glory from all his creatures. For 'they are the eye of the creation to behold the glory of God manifested in the other creatures, and the mouth of the creation to praise him and ascribe to him the glory that is displayed in them.'7

Caring for souls calls for all the Christian virtues in a pastor. Ministers should be patient under affliction, meek toward men, eager to forgive injuries, and ready to 'pity the miserable' and 'weep with those that weep.' They ought to be tender and gentle toward the weak, and loving toward their enemies. They need to pray regularly for those under their care. This kind of prayer and practice will show 'to all that behold them, the amiable, delightful image of the beauty and brightness of their glorious Master.'8 I have found in my ministry that if people know I care about them, they receive more easily what I have to say. If I weep with those who weep when tragedy comes to them, later on they will want to hear how to build up their souls. And if I forgive and pray for those who oppose me, sometimes even they will be open to my spiritual direction.

Caring for souls sometimes means being willing to defy convention. Edwards' relationship with teenagers was a departure from customary pastoral practice. Instead of leaving them exclusively to their parents for religious instruction, Edwards gathered teens into groups for study and prayer under his supervision. He was also willing to defy cultural norms by advocating their participation in congregational singing.[9] I have learned from Edwards and my own pastoring that when I regularly pray for those under my care, God will give me ideas of how to help them in ways that are sometimes new and different. It is often exciting to see the results.

There are two other ways in which Edwards shows ministers how to nourish eternal life in the Kingdom. The first is by proper administration of the sacraments. Both Luther and Calvin made this one of the two marks of the true church. Many Edwards scholars have suggested that Edwards slighted the sacraments; as one claimed, he was 'no proponent of evangelistic sacramental piety.'[10] In fact, Edwards had a robust sacramental theology that eclipsed that of his seventeenth-century Puritan forebears. While for them 'the primary value of the sacraments' was to provide seals of the covenant, Edwards exalted communion with God so as to see the sacraments as ordinances 'at which Christ is peculiarly present to his people.'[11]

Edwards agreed with his Reformed predecessors that the sacraments are visible words of God's grace, seals of the covenant of grace. He said they are means of grace that, like the Scriptures and 'instructions of parents and ministers,' supply the mind with ideas of the things of religion so that grace has an 'opportunity' to act on the soul, 'when God shall infuse it.' Edwards likened this to the way 'Elijah, by laying fuel upon the altar, and laying it in order, gave opportunity for the fire to burn, when God should send it down from heaven.' The more these ideas are true, fully fleshed out, lively and often revived, 'the greater opportunity [will be] for the Spirit of God to infuse grace.' Strictly speaking, God doesn't *need* these means in order to impart grace, for 'grace is from God as immediately and directly as light is from the sun,' but in his wisdom he 'don't [sic] see meet to infuse grace, where there is no opportunity for it to act, or to act in some measure suitably.' He chooses to use the sacraments' vivid pictures of the gospel because they help remove prejudices of reason by providing sensory images that move the heart to action. Frequent use of them tends to restrain sin and provide further impetus to use these and other means. In a word, the sacraments—like the other ordinary means of grace—are ways of 'waiting upon God for his grace, in the way wherein he is wont to bestow [it]; 'tis watching at wisdom's gates, and waiting at the posts of her doors.'[12]

Yet, as William Danaher has argued, for Edwards a sacrament is not just an emblem or pedagogical aid. Far more, it is a type of Christ in which Jesus Christ is present, offering the gift of himself afresh with all of his benefits—as he speaks to and communes with believers. Sacraments, in other words, are re-presentations of Christ.[13]

In my own ministry, the sacraments are crucial. I tell my parishioners what countless others in the Great Tradition have taught—that while the sermon *tells* the gospel, the sacraments *show* the gospel. What is more, the sacraments communicate the Triune life in tactile ways and with tangible beauty that enrich the ministry of the Word. In this postmodern age that prizes multiple dimensions, the sacraments present Christ to all five senses and not just one. In a day when both believers and unbelievers are drawn to beauty and mystery, the sacraments provide both. I tell my religious studies students that if they are looking for mystical experience, there is greater mysticism in Christian orthodoxy than in

Buddhism or Daoism, and the location of much of that mysticism is the sacraments. Luther thought that the principal organ for the Christian is the *ear*. Edwards complemented that by suggesting the *eye* is even more so. The sacraments bring the Son of God to believers' eyes and ears and tongues and flesh and noses. They help show that the gospel brings life to every part of us.

The last way I want to mention that Edwards shows us how to nourish the life of God in the church was his practice of training the next generation of ministers. Edwards trained many ministers in his home, and he preached ordination sermons at a growing rate as he became older. One of my sons was taken aside by his minister and told he might have a calling to the ministry. That was a few years ago. Now my son is being trained largely by this minister right in the parish, and is beginning theological training in the summers and online—while he holds a 'secular' job and raises a family. My point is that Edwards' own example suggests that we should do more of what my son's pastor is doing—going out of our way to discern a calling on young men, and helping train them to lead the next generation in the history of redemption.[14]

3. Understand That Preaching is the 'Main Business' of Ministers

Third, Edwards lifted up preaching as the 'main business' of ministers. This is the chief way, after personal pastoral guidance, that brings washing and cleansing to the souls of men and women. Edwards considered preaching of paramount importance for the work of redemption, which was at the center of his ecclesiology and historical vision.[15] He eagerly awaited the onset of what he forecast as a 'glorious work of God's Spirit,' a 250-year period of revival and persecution that would be followed by the millennium.

This outpouring of the Holy Spirit would come by nothing else but Spirit-anointed preaching. Preaching is the 'principal means' God uses to bring all good to the souls of people, and the greatest good is 'bringing [these] poor sinners to Christ and salvation.' Preaching will not only save but sanctify, by both putting people on the road to heaven and making them holy as they walk the road.[16]

Edwards used noble images to illustrate the premier significance of preachers in the work of redemption. They are like the trumpets blown by Old Testament priests at the great Jewish feasts, like farmers who go forth to sow seed in the earth, like burning and shining lights, and like mirrors that convey and reflect beams of the light of the world. When they preach the gospel rightly, they are the very 'voice of the great God.' Using earthier comparisons, he compared them to Samson's jawbone of the ass, teeth that a nurse uses to chew food for babies, saliva ('spit') that Jesus used to mix with dirt and open the eyes of a blind man, David's sling that helped kill Goliath, and the ox that treads out the corn.[17]

The principal task of the preacher is to make what is true become real in the perception of hearers. Edwards had noticed that lack of spiritual experience and frequent repetition of religious maxims can obscure recognition of what is real. When he was only nineteen years old, he preached on the doctrine, 'When man dies, he is forever stripped of all earthly enjoyments.' He told his hearers that while all the world 'knows the *truth* of this doctrine perfectly well' it nevertheless 'don't [sic] seem at all *real* to them.' Five years later he said two things are required in order for something to seem real to us: 'believing the truth of it, and having a sensible idea or apprehension of it.' I have written elsewhere on this Edwardsean notion of a simple idea imparted by a 'divine and supernatural light,' that makes what was previously a mere notion become a vivid reality by means of something like a sixth sense. In his private notebooks Edwards wrote that this is 'a light cast upon the ideas of spiritual things ... which makes them appear clear and real which before were but faint, obscure representations.' What was previously only thought becomes seen, tasted and felt. It takes on a tactile dimension that forever fixes its reality in the apprehension of the believer.

Edwards believed this new seeing and tasting of the reality of divine things comes principally, if not exclusively, through preaching.[18] But if preaching is to continue to be a means of such grace, it must stick to the 'pure word of God' that tells of the 'excellency and glory' of the Savior, 'how great his love is, what he has done and suffered for poor sinners,' and 'what we must do.' Just as cattle are not to mix with a 'diverse kind,' preachers should sow the holy seed of the gospel 'without any mixture of the doctrines and inventions of men, or wild notions of their own.' They must 'not preach those things which their own wisdom or reason suggests, but the things already dictated to them by the superior wisdom and knowledge of God.' These things are 'inexhaustible' in number and depth, since 'that Divine Being, who is the main subject of [divinity] is infinite, and there is no end to the glory of his perfections.' His works, 'especially the work of redemption,' are marvelous and 'full of unsearchable wonders.' Therefore the task of the preacher is difficult. He must explain doctrine, unravel difficulties by reason and argument, but in an easy, clear and orderly way.[19] To do this effectively would take years. That is, Edwards devoted most sermons to particular points that he considered essential to Christian thought and practice. But since no one sermon or even series of sermons could fill out those essentials, Edwards thought of preaching in terms of long cycles of teaching. It would take several years or more of preaching several sermons a week to complete a cycle of instruction which Edwards thought necessary for proper Christian education. Thus some scholars have wrongly thought they could capture Edwards' vision in one or even a handful of Edwards' sermons.

4. Study Hard

The fourth principle of Edwards' vision of ministry was the importance of study. Although Edwards said the preacher's sermon must penetrate the affections of his listeners and not simply change their thinking, he was emphatic about the necessity of cognitive content. In a 1739 sermon on 'the importance and advantage of a thorough knowledge of divine truth,' he taught that Christians must not be content to remain babes in knowledge of divine things, or to be satisfied with spiritual experience alone. They must seek 'not only a practical and experimental, but also a doctrinal knowledge of the truths and mysteries of religion.' He explained that there are two kinds of knowledge of divine things—the speculative or natural that pertains to the head, and the practical and spiritual that is sensed in the heart. While speculative knowledge without spiritual knowledge is worthless, speculative knowledge nevertheless is 'of infinite importance' because 'without it we can have no spiritual or practical knowledge.' There is no other way that we can benefit from means of grace except by knowledge. 'Therefore the preaching of the gospel would be wholly to no purpose, if it conveyed no knowledge to the mind.' This assertion was based on Edwards' understanding of the human person: 'The heart cannot be set upon an object of which there is no idea in the understanding.' He would explicate this at much greater length in the fourth positive sign in his *Religious Affections* seven years later, but here he summarized as follows: 'Such is the nature of man, that nothing can come at the heart but through the door of the understanding: and there can be no spiritual knowledge of that of which there is not first a rational knowledge.' The upshot was that the 'sense of the heart' that is at the heart of true religion is normally impossible without doctrinal understanding:

> A man cannot see the wonderful excellency and love of Christ in doing such and such things for sinners, unless his understanding be first informed how those things were done. He cannot have a taste of the sweetness and divine excellency of such and such things contained in divinity, unless he first have a notion that there are such and such things.

Hence the way to deeper spiritual experience was through greater cognitive understanding of divine things: 'The more you have of a rational knowledge of the things of the gospel, the more opportunity will there be, when the Spirit shall be breathed into your heart, to see the excellency of these things, and to taste the sweetness of them.' Therefore, the Christian preacher is obliged not only to preach but also to teach more and more of the infinite and unsearchable wonders of God and his redemption.[20] He must be *'pure, clear and full in his doctrine.'* 'He must not lead his people into errors, but teach them in the truth only.' He must teach 'that same religion that Christ taught.' But in order to reach this point, ministers 'should be diligent in their studies.' They should be 'very conversant with the Holy Scriptures, making it very much their business, with the utmost diligence and strictness, to search those holy writings.'[21] He also instructed pastors and serious laypersons to read other Christian books of history and theology.

Edwards of course was a model of study. He labored indefatigably to produce searching sermons and lectures. Those productions probably took up the better part of his working weeks—typically preparing two sermons for each Sunday and a Thursday lecture for his congregation of 1300 souls. No wonder that, with his more scholarly work added to these efforts, he averaged thirteen hours per day in his study. This was after rising at four in the summer and five in the winter, followed at some point by prayer alone and then family prayer. Just before retiring at night, he and Sarah prayed together.[22]

These days churches demand that the pastor be all things to all men—chief administrator, social worker, counselor, facilitator, PR agent, party host, man about town, member of every church committee, janitor, evangelist, public apologist and theologian, and—when he has time—scholar in his study. My advice to pastors, especially when they first take a church, is to tell the church that your principal task is to bring the Word of God in preaching and teaching, and that therefore you need to spend at least twenty hours of week in your study. That means reading theology and not just the Bible, scholarly works and not just devotionals or books of sermons by others. Some will fight this, but your devotion to this will make you a better preacher and minister to souls.

5. Remember that it Demands Piety Bathed in Serious Prayer

Fifth, Edwards said none of this will work without piety bathed in serious prayer. If the minister is to be successful watching over his flock, he must be a man of 'holy ardor.'[23] It is not enough to have 'speculative knowledge or opinions, or outward morality or forms of religion.' True faith is 'an ardent thing' with 'true spiritual comfort or joy.' The good minister is fired in his heart with 'divine love or charity' which is 'a holy flame enkindled in the soul.' He will probably suffer reproaches and defeats if he preaches the true gospel, but he will still have an inner power that comes from '*participation of the divine nature*,' which is a divine principle—'the life of a risen Savior, who exerts himself in the hearts' of all true saints and their ministers. The Savior within will inspire a love to both Christ and human souls. That love will produce a fervor or zeal that animates the minister's prayer, preaching, exercise of church discipline, and counseling.[24]

A life of secret prayer is what keeps the inner flame glowing brightly. Ministers 'should be much in seeking God, and conversing with him by prayer, who is the fountain of light and love.' They will be 'sensible with Isaiah that they are men of unclean lips' and so will 'seek that their lips may be as it were touched with a live coal from the altar, as it were by the bright and burning seraphim.' This sense of need will move Christ's ministers to follow his example of prayerfulness: 'We read from time to time of [Christ's] retiring from the world, away from the noise and applauses of the multitudes, into mountains and solitary places for secret prayer, and holy converse with his Father; and once of his rising up in the morning a great while before day, and going and departing into a solitary place to pray (Mark 1:35); and another time, of his going out into a mountain to pray, and of continuing all night in prayer to God (Luke 6:12).' Therefore his ministers will 'be much in prayer for his Spirit' and 'much in secret converse with him.' They will be afraid to depend on their own abilities, for fear that God would then withhold his Spirit. Instead they 'should beg of God that his Spirit may accompany their administration.'[25]

Edwards has always inspired me to pray. His exhortations and example pushed me to get up earlier to seek God. It was in these times early in the morning and while running that I wrestled with problems in ministry, heartaches in defeat, conflicts with people in the church, and times of depression. It has only been these times of prayer that have kept my head up at times.

6. Recognize that Church Discipline is Necessary

Sixth, Edwards reminds ministers of the necessity of church discipline. This is one of the tasks of ministry that are unpleasant, but the avoidance of which makes things even more unpleasant. It sometimes is required when parishioners go astray in ways that would affect the public witness of the church. Edwards taught that after preaching the true gospel and the proper administration of sacraments, this is the third responsibility of the Christian minister. Usually it would mean simply a 'gentle' word of private warning or admonishment, but when there is 'gross' sin and 'they continue impenitent' after rebukes, the minister should have no reluctance to proceed to excommunication. The church should not tolerate 'visibly wicked persons,' such as unrepentant fornicators, coveters, idolaters, drunkards or extortioners, but cut them off like 'a diseased member from the body,' for three reasons: that the church may be kept pure and God's ordinances not defiled, that others may be deterred from wickedness, and that their souls may be saved. They are to be cut off from the charity of the church (no longer regarded as fellow Christians), 'brotherly society' (treated 'as an heathen man and a publican'), worship, and internal privileges (such as the sacraments). The church should behave toward them as 'our Father which is in heaven, who, though he loves many wicked men with a love of benevolence, yet he don't [sic] love them with a love of complacence' or affection. Saints are forbidden to eat with them.[26]

Such admonitions are all for the 'correction' and 'good of the person' excommunicated. It is God's way of using the devil as an instrument 'of those peculiar chastisements that their apostasy deserves.' The hope is that by this severe discipline, their 'flesh' will be destroyed and the humbled sinners will return to fellowship. In the meantime, 'the church is to have a greater concern for their welfare still than if they never had been brethren.' Saints should pray for them and care for them if they are sick or distressed. Their own family should not cut them off from family affections and obligations, nor are 'husbands and wives released from duties proper to their relations.'[27] Edwards excommunicated at least four persons from the Northampton church, one for habitual drunkenness, one for refusing to repent of slander, another for fornication and contempt for church authority, and a fourth, his cousin Elisha Hawley, for refusing to repent of fornication with Martha Root, who had sued him for paternity of her twins.[28] Today it might sound excessive to excommunicate four parishioners over twenty-one years as senior pastor at Northampton, but Edwards was actually less aggressive than some ministers in this period of New England.[29]

Church discipline is especially difficult in this culture where Christians are already thought to be intolerant. But in some cases, such as a parent's desertion of his or her family or open adultery, most even in our post-Christian society understand. I have been involved in several cases of excommunication. One was exclusion from communion after continued and unrepentant adultery. It was painful and difficult, but since it was handled in a careful and loving way by my senior colleague, we all felt we had cut out a cancer that would have killed the body. In one case, an adulteress repented and has returned to fellowship.[30]

7. You Must Be Willing to Be Unpopular

These kinds of cases require a seventh principle in ministry—willingness to be unpopular. Because ministers rely more on revelation than their own reason, Edwards warned that they might be called 'bigoted zealot[s]' who dare not exercise their own freedom of thought. But 'if you should be ridiculed by others in this day of growing error for embracing certain doctrines of revelation that are above man's comprehension, as if you were fools and put out your eyes to receive absurd doctrines by an implicit faith, care not for it, but be willing to become fools for Christ's sake, remembering that he that would be wise must become a fool.'[31]

Indeed, the faithful pastor should be willing to be disliked even by his own church. The godly minister, he taught, must be careful not to cater to his parishioners' desires. He would be a more popular preacher if he did not reprove their sins and contradict their lusts. If he preached that God would always forgive them after living a life of self-gratification, by sending up 'a few earnest cries upon a death-bed' after a life of 'drunkenness or lasciviousness or cheating and fraud,' or that God 'could not have the heart to take men and cast them into eternal burnings,' he would be much better received by many hearers. If ministers were to preach Christ only in his priestly and not kingly office 'to rule in us and over us,' or if they were sent by God to tell people how they might become prosperous and lay up for their children, or could inherit a carnal heaven like the one 'the Mahometans expect,' then they also would be far more popular.[32]

Edwards did not shrink from confrontation. Perhaps because of this determination to do what he thought was right—if not politic—he spoke surprisingly often about conflicts between pastors and their congregations, even in the years when he still enjoyed wide respect at Northampton. For example, in 1741—at the height of the Great Awakening—he warned that contention between minister and people 'is a worse calamity than a war with the Indians.' The town that suffers this 'is in a worse condition than that which is infested with cruel savages of the wilderness and cannot go about their work nor lodge in their houses without fear of their lives.' By 1750, after his own church had rejected him, he had concluded that this would not be uncommon: 'So it *very often* comes to pass in this evil world, that great differences and controversies arise between ministers and the people that are under their pastoral care.' But his stated policy was to be generous and forgiving to the 'multitudes of the common people' who were easily deceived. In March 1744, just as the Bad Book affair was heating up—a squabble over young men who taunted young women with what they learned from a book for midwives—Edwards said pastors who have endured 'ill treatment' by those who were 'misled by false teachers' should not insist on a church process of interrogation for 'every member that has behaved himself disorderly.' Instead, 'great allowances' should be made for people in the pews who err through ignorance. The apostle Paul aimed church censures against false teachers, but not against those they deceived.[33]

8. You Must be Prepared to Suffer

Because standing for principle often causes conflict, Edwards taught the eighth principle of ministry, that a good minister of the gospel needs to be prepared to suffer. Like Christ and the apostles, ministers of the gospel will suffer for the salvation of souls. True ministers will 'spend and be spent for them.' Just as Jesus was moved with compassion because the crowds were sheep without a shepherd, ministers will be moved with pity for people who walk in darkness. They will be ready to 'fill up that which is behind of the afflictions of Christ in his flesh' for the sake of saving lost souls. They should therefore imitate Christ's love for men and women: 'Many waters could not quench his love, neither could the floods drown it, for his love was stronger than death; yea, than the mighty pains and torments of such a death.'[34]

Edwards suffered much. When he described his ministry at Northampton in his *Farewell Sermon* there, it was clear these were the words of a minister who had endured much pain in ministry.

I have spent the prime of my life and strength in labors for your eternal welfare. You are my witnesses, that what strength I have had, I have not neglected in idleness, nor laid out in prosecuting worldly schemes, and managing temporal affairs, for the advancement of my outward estate, and aggrandizing myself and family; but have given myself to the work of ministry, laboring in it night and day, rising early and applying myself to this great business to which Christ appointed me. I have found the work of ministry among you to be a great work indeed, a work of exceeding care, labor and difficulty: many have been the heavy burdens that I have borne in it, which my strength has been very unequal to.[35]

But Edwards was no wimp. While preaching—and not unlike his demeanor in the years of conflict—he adopted (as Kimnach so graphically puts it) 'the steady gaze of a sheriff confronting a lynch mob.'[36] Because he felt called by God, and knew that God calls ministers to suffering, he was, as George Marsden has put it, 'willing to sail the foundering ship of his pastorate into the teeth of the storm, knowing that he and his family were likely to go down.'

Twice I have been thrown out of churches because I was orthodox on today's presenting issues. Twice I have left liberal denominations because of our stand on Scripture, sex, and marriage. Each of these times was painful—though I suffered far less than others, and particularly less than my senior pastors at two of these parishes. They were times of suffering—but also of great joy. It was largely because of Edwards that I was able to find joy and beauty amidst suffering. If for no other reason, for this I commend Edwards' eight principles for people called to the pastorate. He was able to keep his focus—during all of his times of conflict and suffering—on the beauty of God. And because of his vision of God's beauty he was able to walk in joy—while suffering all the same.

2. Faithful Ministers are Conduits of the Means of Grace

William M. Schweitzer

Introduction

We live in a day of unprecedented confusion about the nature of the ministry. Models that not so long ago would have been dismissed as bizarre innovations are now being touted as the future of the church. Young men who can barely define what it is their celebrity exemplar actually *does* let alone how one might conceivably prepare for it—how does one train to be a 'transformational architect,' anyhow?—nonetheless want to emulate them.[1] Sadly, those who go down this road forsake any assurance that the Lord will bless their ministry, for they have abandoned the certainty that comes with God's promised blessing on His own chosen means.

Even worse, however, are the effects of this confusion on the church. God alone understands exactly what His people need, and He has set in place everything that is necessary to provide it. Every part of His plan for the church is integral and essential;

nothing is extraneous or optional. Therefore, any departure from it will inevitably cause problems for the flock. When the priests in Old Testament Israel found other things to do besides teaching and administering the sacraments, the people quickly became as sheep having no shepherd (Ezekiel 34:1–6). So it will be for the poor Christian whose minister prefers to be an 'artist' or whatever trendy alternative someone comes up with next.[2]

In such a situation, the writings of Jonathan Edwards on this subject come to us like a bright light in a dark place. Edwards was under no confusion as to what faithful ministers ought to be and to do. In the ordination sermon 'Sons of Oil, Heavenly Lights,' he said, 'ministers of the gospel … are those that are improved by Christ as means and instruments of the spiritual good of his people, conveying the golden oil to the candlestick, of or communicating grace to his church.'[3] Or, as I would summarise it, ministers are *conduits of the means of grace.*

Edwards did not achieve this clarity in a vacuum. He came to it because he was already so clear on all the larger issues that controlled his understanding of the ministry. Stating explicitly what Reformed theology had previously implied, Edwards believed that God created the universe so that He might communicate His own knowledge, love and joy to elect angels and men, for His own glory. And, crucially, the way God communicates to us is through *means.* God makes use of the 'means of grace'—ordinarily, the Word of God, the sacraments and prayer—to save and perfect His people.

Knowing this, it was perfectly clear to Edwards that the job of the minister is to convey the means of grace to God's people. In turn, my purpose here is simply to relay some of the highlights of what Edwards said on this vital subject. Finally, I will close with some points of application for the church today. We begin with some relevant points in Edwards' theology.

Relevant Points of Edwards' Theology

God Communicates Himself

First of all, Edwards taught that God's objective in creation was to communicate *Himself*. Edwards outlines this grand plan in 'Miscellany' 332:

> The great and universal end of God's creating the world was to *communicate* himself. *God is a communicative being.* This communication is really only to intelligent beings: the communication of himself to their understandings is his glory, and the communication of himself with respect to their wills, the enjoying faculty, is their happiness. God created the world for the shining forth of his excellency and for the flowing forth of his happiness.[4]

Throughout all of creation and redemptive history, God is communicating Himself to elect men and angels. In the words of the Westminster Standards, He does this 'for his own glory.'

This communication is not merely 'head knowledge' but consists of God's own love and joy as well as His knowledge:

> From this view it appears another way to be a thing in itself valuable, that there should be such things as the knowledge of God's glory in other beings, and an high esteem of it, love to it, and delight and complacence in it: this appears I say in another way, viz. as these things are but the emanations of God's own knowledge, holiness and joy.[5]

It begins with knowledge because you cannot love (or believe in) someone you know nothing about. Yet the extent to which you know God is the extent to which you should love Him, because He is infinitely lovely. Anything true you learn about Him should enkindle love. And as you love God more, you will certainly enjoy the Object of your love more. This becomes an eternally upward spiral; as we grow in these things throughout eternity, we will come closer and closer—but never quite attain—to God's own condition of infinite knowledge, love and joy.

God Communicates Through The Means of Grace

So God communicates Himself to us, and the way he does this is by using *means*.[6] The Westminster Larger Catechism declares, 'The outward and ordinary means whereby Christ communicates to his church the benefits of his mediation, are all his ordinances; especially the word, sacraments, and prayer; all which are made effectual to the elect for their salvation.'[7] So, the ordinary means of grace are the Word of God, the sacraments, and prayer.[8] The order is significant. Edwards spoke of Scripture as ' ... the great and principal means of grace,' for by it the others have their basis, but the reverse is not true.[9] Scripture can stand by itself but the sacraments cannot; they must be given intelligible meaning by the Word of God. Likewise, our prayers have to be informed by the content of Scripture—and particularly God's promises—or we have no good basis to come before the throne of grace.

In addition to these three, Edwards occasionally referred to a few other things as 'means of grace.' One of these is the Sabbath. The Lord's Day, if not itself a means of grace, is certainly an ongoing appointment by which we rightly expect to receive the means of grace. I am particularly concerned to make this point here because, in our day, there are far too many evangelicals who think far too lightly of the Christian Sabbath. Listen to what Edwards says:

> As the sabbath is a day which we are especially to set apart for religious exercises, so 'tis a day wherein God especially confers his grace and blessing. As God hath commanded us to set it apart to have to do with him, so God hath set it apart for himself to have to do with us. As God has commanded us to observe the sabbath, so God observes the sabbath, too. [...] He stands ready then especially to hear prayers, to accept of religious services, to meet his people, to manifest himself to 'em on this day, to give his Holy Spirit and blessing to those that diligently and conscientiously sanctify it. That men should sanctify the sabbath, as we have observed, is according to God's institution. God, in a sense, observes his own institutions; that is, he is wont to cause them to be attended with his blessings. God's institutions are his appointed *means of grace*. He has promised his blessing with his institutions; Exodus 20:24, 'In all places where I record my name I will come unto thee, and I will bless thee.' And for the same reason may we conclude that God will meet his people and bless them, waiting upon him not only in appointed places but times and in all his appointed ways.[10]

Forget for a moment whether *we* must keep the Sabbath (although which of the other of the Ten Commandments do we question?); Edwards reminds us that *God Himself* keeps 'his own institution' by especially conferring 'his grace and blessing.'

One final 'means' to mention briefly is church discipline. Edwards said, 'And as the Word of God, so the sacraments that he has appointed, *and the discipline of his house*, he has committed to them, to be administered by them.'[11] Church discipline, which necessarily includes church government, is the appointed instrument by which the church and the ordinary means of grace committed into her hands are preserved in their life-giving integrity.

Behold the beautifully complete package: we have the appointed *means* of grace (the Word, sacraments and prayer), the appointed *place* for them (the church, as upheld by church discipline), and the appointed *time* for them (the Sabbath Day). This is God's plan for the blessing of His people. Christ meets with His people in His church on His day, there to bless them through His means of grace.

God Uses Ministers to Convey the Means of Grace

Of course we need someone to administer these chosen means. This is the work of the ordained minister. Edwards sometimes spoke of ministers as themselves being 'means of grace.'[12] Yet it becomes clear that what he meant to say was that ministers were conduits or *means of the means of grace*: '... in his wisdom and mercy, he is pleased to convey his light to men by means and instruments; and has sent forth his messengers, and appointed ministers in his church to be subordinate lights, and to shine with the communications of his light, and to reflect the beams of his glory on the souls of men.'[13]

Paradigms of the Ministry

I want now to mention some of the paradigms that Edwards uses to describe the nature of the ministry: as stewards, interpreters, looking glasses and instruments.

1. Stewards

In *Some Thoughts Concerning the Revival*, Edwards describes ministers as *steward bringing elect souls to salvation*.

These especially are the officers of Christ's kingdom, that above all other men upon earth do represent his person, into whose hands Christ has committed the sacred oracles and holy ordinances, and all his appointed means of grace, to be administered by them; they are the stewards of his household, into whose hands he has committed its provision; the immortal souls of men are committed to them as a flock of sheep are committed to the care of a shepherd, or as a master commits a treasure to the care of a servant, of which he must give an account.[14]

Similar thoughts recur in 'The Great Concern of a Watchman of Souls,' but now with some explanation regarding the ultimate purpose of this arrangement:

And now in this grand affair, and to this great purpose of an escape from eternal misery, and the obtaining everlasting glory, Christ has committed the precious souls of men to the care of ministers; that by their means they may have the benefit of his redemption, and might obtain that which he has suffered so much to procure. Christ knew that notwithstanding all that he had done to procure life for souls, they would need much care to be taken of them, and many means to be used with them, in order to their being indeed preserved from eternally perishing, and actually brought to the possession of life. And therefore he has appointed a certain order of men, whose whole business it might be to take care of immortal souls; and into their hands has committed these souls, and has betrusted them with the ordinances of his house, and the means that he has provided for their salvation; that nothing might be wanting that they need for their furniture for this for this great business; he has as it were committed to them his goods, and has given them in some respects the keys to his stores and treasury; to them are committed the oracles of God and treasure of the gospel.[15]

Consider the statement 'Christ has committed the precious souls of men to the care of ministers; that by their means they ... might obtain that which he has suffered so much to procure.' It is not merely that, apart from ministers acting on His behalf, the elect would not be brought to salvation. The even greater tragedy is that Christ would not obtain the bride for which He died.

I would also point out that '... he has appointed a certain order of men, whose *whole business* it might be to take care of immortal souls.' This is a reminder of why it is right for churches to set ministers aside from other work by paying them a suitable salary. This is no mere pragmatism—although securing the full attention of the man who is commissioned to conduct your family and friends safely to heaven sounds like a good idea—but is rather the ordinary appointment of God for the good of His church.[16]

2. Interpreters

Another of Edwards' paradigms for ministers is—like Bunyan's character in Pilgrim's Progress—that of the *interpreter*. In this, ministers are merely imitating Christ's role in eternity. As I have said elsewhere, 'Edwards believed that the saints are better off in heaven, not simply because they have a better vantage point for witnessing the ongoing affairs of God's great work of redemption but because Christ, who "has an absolutely perfect knowledge" of these events, is there to *explain* it all to them.'[17] God's self-revelation is objectively clear. Yet even for the glorified saints in heaven, our finite limitations require that someone interpret it for us. How much more so sinful people on earth, who 'don't understand God's language, and they therefore need the help and advice of ministers ... as interpreters for them.'[18] God has thus appointed ministers to serve in the crucial role of interpreting revelation for the benefit of His people.

3. Looking Glasses

2 Corinthians 3:18 was a hugely important passage for Edwards. For him, these words—'But we all, with open face beholding as in a glass the glory of the Lord, are changed into the same image from glory to glory, even as by the Spirit of the Lord'—explain the core methodology of how we are made to become like God. As photographic film is changed by the light of the exposed image until it resembles it, so we are changed into the spiritual image of Christ. But what do the words 'as in a glass' mean? What is the lens through which we see this transforming image?

Edwards takes this in two senses. The first is Christ Himself:

> We behold the glory of God as in the face of Jesus Christ, who is the brightness of God's light or glory, as it were reflected, and is the express image of the Father, the perfect image of God, as the image in a plain and clear looking glass is the express image of the person that looks in it. And that is the only way that the glory of God is seen by his church; he is seen no other way, but in this perfect and as it were reflected image. For 'no man hath seen God at any time; the only begotten Son of God, that is in the bosom of the Father, he hath declared him' [John 1:18]; he is 'the image of the invisible God' [Colossians 1:15].[19]

So Christ Himself must ultimately be the glass, for He alone is the perfect image of the invisible God.

Edwards' secondary meaning of the 'looking glass,' however, is a remarkable statement about ministers and the means of grace:

> We behold the glory of God as in a looking glass in another respect, and that is as we behold it by the intermediation of the outward means of our illumination and knowledge of God, viz. Christ's ministers, and the gospel which they preach, and his ordinances which they administer, which serve instead of a looking glass to reflect the glory of the Lord. When men read the Holy Scripture, they there may see Christ's glory, as men see images of things by looking in a glass; so we see Christ's glory in ordinances. Ministers are burning and shining lights, but then they don't shine by their own light, but only reflect the light of Christ .... By looking on those lights, they see light; they see the light of Christ reflected. 'Tis evident the Apostle is here speaking of the light of Christ's glory, as ministered and communicated by ministers of the gospel and ministers of the Spirit, which is that light and glory, as we shall show presently (so *2 Corinthians 4:2–6*). So in the words next following in the beginning of the next chapter ... he expressly speaks of the light of this glory as communicated to men by ministers this way, viz. by first shining upon them or into their hearts, and then being communicated or given from them to others, which is just as light is communicated from a reflecting glass.[20]

Thus, the secondary sense of the 'looking glass' is the minister, because this is how God shows us Christ. We are being transformed by beholding Christ in the means of grace as they are conveyed to us by faithful ministers. I am thankful for the recent portrait of Edwards that reminds us that Edwards was indeed a *man*.[21] However, the image of a man holding up a glass through which people see Christ would seem an even more accurate depiction of Edwards' self-understanding as a minister.

4. Instruments

Finally, we come to the paradigm found in the aforementioned 'Sons of Oil, Heavenly Lights' sermon. The text is Zechariah 4, where the Lord uses the image of a golden lampstand to describe Zerubbabel. Edwards applies this image to ministers as '… instruments of the spiritual good of his people, conveying the golden oil to the candlestick, of or communicating grace to his church.[22] The point is not so much that the instrument is beautiful or impressive for its own sake, but that it is doing something wonderful in conveying spiritual good to God's people.

Of course, the greatest good that could be communicated is the Holy Spirit, and Edwards thinks this is precisely what is being shown in this imagery:

> But the communication of the golden oil or divine grace to God's people is more especially what appertains to the office of ecclesiastical officers and ministers of Christ, it being the original and grand design of their office, and the work and business they are devoted to. Ministers of the gospel are said to be 'ministers of the spirit' (2 Corinthians 3:6), which is the thing signified by the golden oil.[23]

Edwards thought it obvious that oil should be a type of the Holy Spirit. And like the oil flowing through the golden tube, ministers are used as conduits of the Holy Spirit. This is because the Spirit is to be found attending the means of grace, means that were authored by and are empowered by this same Spirit.

What attribute, then, should characterise faithful ministers as instruments or conduits of grace? The answer for Edwards is that they should be—like the God they represent—*communicative*. And any communication of spiritual good involves work:

> Another thing taught us in the text is that *ministers ought to be communicative of spiritual good*. The olive branches are represented not only as constantly receiving the golden oil from the tree, but constantly communicating it to the candlestick. Not that ministers are able to bestow this precious gift of divine grace to their hearers of themselves, but they are to be diligent in the use of proper means and endeavors in order to it. They should [be], as the Apostle says, *didaktikoi*, 'apt to teach' [2 Timothy 2:24]: lovers of the souls of their hearers, earnestly desiring and laboriously seeking their spiritual good.[24]

If God is a communicative Being, surely His ministers should be communicative men. It is essential that we promote the spiritual good of our people by communicating God's Word to them.

Exhortations for Ministers Today

Allow me now to share some specific exhortations from Edwards' teaching for us today.

1. Make the Ordinary Means of Grace Your Great Business.

There are many ways for a man to spend his time. *Faithful* ministers, however, make the means of grace their great business in life. That is particularly true in terms of the ongoing study of Scripture:

> And particularly, ministers should be very conversant with the Holy Scriptures; making it very much of their business,

with the utmost diligence and strictness, to search those holy writings. For they are as it were the beams of the light of the Sun of Righteousness; they are the light by which ministers must be enlightened and the light they are to hold forth to their hearers; and they are the fire whence their hearts and the hearts of their hearers must be enkindled.[25]

Skilled craftsmen have their tools and soldiers have their weapons. If you are a minister, your tool, your weapon, is the Bible. You should learn it thoroughly. You should know how its doctrines all fit together in the coherent system of theology it teaches. And you should be able to employ it effectively through preaching, teaching and personal exhortation.

Of course we know that, however well we wield them, the means of grace remain only *means* that God must do something with. Yet this should never dissuade us employing them with all diligence and industry. In considering the role of the disciples in the miraculous provision of wine for the wedding in Cana (John 2), Edwards observes:

The servants represent gospel ministers; they have a command from Jesus' mother [i.e. from the church in her public authority, to do whatever Jesus commands], whence we may note that the way to have a plentiful effusion of the Spirit with his Word and ordinances is to be faithful in their work. They are to fill up the water pots of purification with water; that is all that they can do. They can, in the use of the ordinances of God's house and appointed means of grace and purification, 'be instant in season and out of season' [*2 Timothy 4:2*]. They can fill the water pots up to the brim. They can be abundant in preaching the word, which, as it comes only from them, is but water, a dead letter, a sapless, tasteless, spiritless thing; but this is what Christ will bless for the supply [of] his church with wine.[26]

We know that God has not put all things into our hands. We can neither turn water into wine nor sinners into saints. But the one thing He *has* put in our hands, this is certainly the thing that we should do with all of our might.

2. Don't Try to Change the Message

Edwards lived in the ascendency of Enlightenment rationalism. There is no doubt that he was tempted to blunt the sharp edges of doctrines deemed 'unreasonable' by the generality of his contemporaries. Yet Edwards resisted this temptation, and instead exhorted:

> … ministers ought not to preach those things which their own wisdom or reason suggests, but the things that are already dictated by the Spirit of God [in Scripture]. That is, they are not to preach those things that would seem right to their understandings if their understandings were left alone. But in their preaching they ought to rely on what [is] revealed and discovered ready to their hands by an understanding infinitely superior to theirs. And this revelation they are to make the rule in their preaching.[27]

This is the point that was forever being missed by the rationalists in their quest for a more 'reasonable' religion. God is the most rational Being that could possibly be imagined, and He has already spoken a comprehensive, definitive word to us. Who would dare to say, 'That is not good enough; I can do better'? Yet this is exactly what those who devise a more 'contextual' message for the times are, in effect, saying. The fact that such efforts are done in the name of evangelism or apologetics does not make them any more acceptable.

Rather, we should submit to God's Word in all humility, as stewards who are simply conveying what has been entrusted to them:

> To the person that is to be set apart to the sacred work of the gospel ministry this day: Sir, I would now humbly and earnestly recommend to you that Holy Book which God is about to commit into your hands, as containing that message which you are to deliver to this people in his name. God gives you this Word— which is his Word—to preach that, and not the dictates of your own reason. You are to preach the dictates of God's infinitely superior understanding, humbly submitting your reason as a learner and disciple to that, renouncing all confidence in your own wisdom and entirely relying on God's instructions.[28]

I can scarce imagine a more complete rebuke to the whole spirit of rationalism than this. The core of his exhortation is humility, because that is the essence of what faithful service in the ministry demands. It doesn't matter what credentials or experience we might have, we must always come as humble learners receiving from the hand of God that which we then convey to His people.

Finally, Edwards exhorts us to preach *the unadulterated, whole counsel of God*:

> Ministers should preach the gospel of Christ and not another gospel instead of it, nor should they pervert the gospel of Christ. When God sent Jonah to the Ninevites, he told him he should 'preach the preaching that he bid him' (Jonah 3:2). Ministers should not preach their own word but the word of Christ; [they] should communicate to their hearers the pure unadulterated word of God and not be as those that corrupt the word or add to it their own notions and vain imaginations, or teaching for

doctrines the traditions of men; and they should declare the whole counsel of God without adding or diminishing ...[29]

Such words should be plastered on every seminary wall. If we are going to do God's work, if we are going to fulfill our honorable task, if we are going to convey spiritual good to God's people, we must adhere to the message that God has appointed without addition or deletion.

3. Don't Try to Change the Means

We can rightly expect God to bless the means He has appointed. We cannot say that for any other means. Ministry is hard enough as it is, and there are more than enough potential sources of discouragement. Why would we want to waste our time on means we have no assurance about? Now it is true that new measures often *seem* to work, at least for a time. This effect is usually predicated upon there already being a stockpile of people who have some association with Christianity—perhaps they even grew up in the church—but are not actually believers. They know that they ought to go to church yet do not like conservative churches because, truth be told, the ordinary means of grace do little for their unregenerate hearts and minds. On the other hand, new measures will address them and their needs in ways they will appreciate.

So we have to look very closely when we are told that something 'works.' Even if there was some new measure that really *did* work, however, would we want to use it? Most would enthusiastically say yes. Edwards would say that '... ministers in their endeavors for the good of their churches and congregations should use the means of God's appointment ... '.[30] They should '... administer the ordinances of Christ as he has instituted them without mutilating or adding to them any human invention or in any respect changing them.'[31] Indeed, Edwards warns that '… we in our work use the means of God's appointment *and them only*, communicating to our hearers the unadulterated milk of the word and administering the ordinances which Christ has appointed, and *as he has appointed them.*'[32]

Why should anyone care about the means, as long as the message is getting across and people are being blessed? I think Edwards would point out that,

> The ministers of the gospel are sent of God, and all their sufficiency is of him; 2 Corinthians 4:7, 'We have this treasure in earthen vessels, that the excellency of the power may be of God, and not of us.' Their success depends entirely and absolutely on the immediate blessing and influence of God.[33]

The point is that God has arranged things so that it might be *seen* that it is all of Him. If someone were to invent a new means by which he (and anyone who imitated him) could fill any building in the world, who would get the glory for it? He would, and not God. Yet what, according to Edwards and the Reformed tradition, is the purpose of all things? To glorify God. So even if you were to accomplish such a feat, you will have succeeded only in undermining the very purpose of the universe. For this reason, 'God has chosen the foolish things of the world … that no flesh should glory in His presence' (1 Corinthians 1:27–29).

4. Don't Be a Formalist

I mean that in two senses. The first has to do with an attitude of dependence upon the supernatural agency of the Holy Spirit. We have been speaking much about the 'means of grace' but we cannot forget that they remain precisely that; only *means*. It is

God's prerogative and power to make use of them as He will. Edwards will not let us forget that:

> 'Tis of God that the redeemed do receive all their true excellency, wisdom and holiness; and that two ways, viz. as the Holy Ghost by whom these things are immediately wrought is from God, proceeds from him, and is sent by him; and also as the Holy Ghost himself is God, by whose operation and indwelling, the knowledge of God and divine things, and a holy disposition, and all grace is conferred and upheld. *And though means are made use of in conferring grace on men's souls, yet 'tis of God that we have these means of grace, and 'tis God that makes them effectual.* 'Tis of God that we have the holy Scriptures; they are the Word of God. 'Tis of God that we have ordinances, and their efficacy depends on the immediate influence of the Spirit of God.[34]

We have cautioned against using other means. But even when we employ the ordinary means of grace, we must never use them mechanically or formalistically. God is the one who makes them efficacious. This is why there is no such thing as merely 'going through the motions' in our ministry. The heart of a faithful minister is walking in utter and complete dependence upon the supernatural blessing of God through the Holy Spirit. In particular, his prayers—and the prayers of the people—must reflect that dependence. We must manifest the conviction that, if we go up there apart from God, nothing is going to happen, because God alone can make these mere means to work.

Along with that, Edwards would say that our administration of the means of grace needs to be done with appropriate *affection*. For all believers, true knowledge of God should bring right affection with it. Remaining dispassionate is not something to be proud of, but is rather something that brings upon it the condemnation of the Lord (Revelation 3:16). Ministers, as conduits of God's holistic communication, should preach with the intent of moving the affections of their hearers in a way that corresponds to the content of their message. Edwards argued against the formalists of his day and ours when he says:

> If it be so, that true religion lies much in the affections, hence we may infer, that such means are to be desired, as have much of a tendency to move the affections. Such books, and such a way of preaching the Word, and administration of ordinances, and such a way of worshiping God in prayer, and singing praises, is much to be desired, as has a tendency deeply to affect the hearts of those who attend these means. Such a kind of means, would formerly have been highly approved of and applauded by the generality of the people of the land, as the most excellent and profitable, and having the greatest tendency to promote the ends of the means of grace. But the prevailing taste seems of late strangely to be altered: that pathetical manner of praying and preaching, which would formerly have been admired and extolled, and that for this reason, because it had such a tendency to move the affections, now, in great multitudes, immediately excites disgust, and moves no other affections, than those of displeasure and contempt.[35]

We cannot forget that Charles Chauncey and the others who opposed Edwards most vehemently in his day were *formalists*. The whole idea of God acting in any direct and immediate way was utterly contrary to their instincts. As Gerald McDermott has pointed out, Deism was the root religion of the world in Edwards' day. They had a mechanical God operating as a machine, and the machine just *works*. Whether you pray fervently or not, whether you are deeply affected as you preach or not, the machine just carries on in its predetermined work. So it was that in these churches where these 'fashionable divines' (as Edwards called them) served the preaching and the administration of the sacraments was, in a word, *mechanistic*. They read their sermons, and the sermon would accomplish what a sermon was designed to do. Their concept of means was almost like the Roman Catholic idea of *ex opera operato*—by its very performance it is accomplished. Edwards denied this formalistic notion of the means of grace most emphatically. It only works because God makes it work, and they must be administered in a way—in both head and heart—that is appropriate to this reality.

5. Understand the High Privilege of Your Calling

Why is it that we are tempted to try other things besides the ordinary means of grace? I do not know anyone else's heart, but sometimes I think it is because *we do not apprehend the enormous privilege that has already been given to us as ministers*. Why are there, for instance, 'art ministers'? I suppose because some men look at the lifestyle of the artist, or at least aspects of it, and find it more appealing. Why are there celebrity or CEO pastors? Perhaps because they envy the prestige and privilege given to celebrities and businessmen. But at root, why would we ever envy anyone else's situation at all? Surely it must be because we have failed to grasp just how inherently wonderful and beautiful is the gospel ministry itself. We need to hear Edwards' exhortation:

> Consider, dear sir, how great an honor he does you whom God the Father hath made Head of the whole universe, and Lord of all things to the church; that after he has provided for the salvation of souls by his dying pains and precious blood, and the Father has committed to him all power in heaven and on

earth, that he might actually bestow eternal life on them that he died for; he should call you to be a co-worker with him, and should commit precious souls to your care, that you might be the instrument of bringing them home to him, and bringing that to pass with respect to them, for which his soul travailed in the agonies of death, and in ineffable conflicts with the dreadful wrath of God.[36]

To those who are tempted to do otherwise than the simple yet profound, weak but powerful task that has been given them to be conduits of God's means of grace, I would say this: 'consider, dear sir, how great an honor he does you.'

6. Do Not Despair

In another direction, there are some who are only too aware of the high calling of the ministry. They feel they cannot live up to the standard, and are perhaps even discouraged by the writings of Edwards because of it. The thing that I would remind you of is that *you are only a conduit.* This is good news, for the world does not rest on your shoulders. It is God's design that you should be weak, and even that you should be *known* to be weak, precisely because He wants the glory. Edwards does not merely allow for the possibility that we might be unable to do these things, *he assumes that we cannot*, at least humanly speaking. That is the point of real dependence upon the supernatural supply of the Holy Spirit, as much to carry on another day as to make the means we employ efficacious. So do not despair, but only carry on in the work, knowing that all outcomes are in the hands of God alone.

Conclusion

Faithful ministers are conduits of the means of grace. We are *mere* conduits, in that we do not get to determine what message or means

will attract people today. Even when we do everything according
to God's plan, we still do not get the credit for the results any
more than the plumbing in our house gets paid for our drinking
water. Thankfully, neither can we assume the blame when the
outcomes from our faithful ministry are not exactly what we—or
other people—would want them to be.

On the other hand, we are yet conduits *of the means of grace*,
the precious oil bringing the best of God's gifts to His beloved
children. This is a noble calling indeed. Our ambition should
never be to become something else, like a pipe contorting itself to
be a spoon and only making itself worthless in the process. Our
great ambition is to imitate our Master, to be 'communicative
beings' through whom the means of grace flow unobstructed and
uncontaminated, and all to the glory of God.

3. When the Road is Rough: Staying with what Matters Most

Roy Mellor

Introduction

' June 22nd 1750 The Reverend Jonathan Edwards was dismissed.' So stands the stark record of the First Church Northampton, MA, relating the end of one of the world's most significant Gospel ministries. Reflecting on this action, D. Martyn Lloyd-Jones commented 'Do not be surprised then, brethren, as to what may happen to you in your churches!'[1] The 230–23 male vote against Edwards was but the formal end of a long campaign to oust the troublesome Great Awakener. Outside the present-day church building in Northampton, the tourist information board hastens to add many Northampton people subsequently regretted their actions. No doubt they did. The question is, why were these actions taken in the first place?

Although there may have been various circumstantial factors involved, I want to argue that Edwards' dismissal happened primarily because he held certain convictions regarding the church and those who rightly had membership in her that virtually guaranteed this outcome from the outset. Before coming to these points, let us first take a brief look at some of the main circumstances surrounding Edwards' dismissal.

Edwards' Dismissal

There are various issues that help to explain—at least in human terms—Jonathan Edwards' fall. The Northampton people eventually referred their dispute to a council comprised of the minister and lay representative from ten other churches in the region.[2] In considering what might have moved the council to decide against Edwards, the relevant history stretches back to the Breck affair. Against the wishes of a majority of Hampshire County Association ministers, Robert Breck was ordained and installed as minister at Springfield in 1736. Breck had voiced various Arminian sentiments, and Edwards was called upon to make the case against him.[3] Years later, the Northampton people insisted on including Breck and those of like mind on the council of 1750. Edwards pointed out that,

> ... it is well known that four or five of them [ministers in the county] have heretofore had the reputation of Arminians. Some others of them are known to be strenuous opposers of the late revival of religion, for which I have been so public an advocate ... There are no less than six of them, who have either had a particular difference or controversy with me, or have in time past openly manifested some affront or disgust which they have taken.[4]

Predictably, Breck and his friends took the opportunity to repay Edwards 'in his own coin' by casting their votes against him.[5]

In terms of the congregation itself, the issue that is usually considered the most important contributing factor is Edwards' mishandling of the 'bad book affair.' This was a discipline case centred around the abuse of a midwifery manual which the scoffing ('I won't worship a whig') Timothy Root liked to call 'the Young Folk's Bible.' Confronting what we might consider eighteenth-century versions of pornography and sexual harassment on the part of various young people, Edwards publicly read out a list of names who were wanted for questioning. Unfortunately, he made no distinction between the culprits and the witnesses, causing unnecessary offense to the families of the innocent. At the time of his dismissal, Edwards would call this event the one by which he became 'so obnoxious' to the town.[6]

However, even widespread ill-will among the people requires leadership to beget action. One of the most important leaders of the anti-Edwards faction was Joseph Hawley III, an entrepreneurial character who, amongst other things, introduced knives and forks to Northampton. Hawley was a cousin of Edwards, but even more significantly he was the son of the man who brought the mid-1730s Connecticut River Valley Revival to an abrupt end by his suicide.[7] Prior to this devastating blow, this is how Edwards describes the situation in late 1734 and early 1735:

> There was scarcely a single person in the town, either young or old that was left unconcerned about the great things of the eternal world ... the work of conversion was carried out in a most astonishing manner, and increased more and more; Souls did as it were come as flocks to Jesus Christ. This work of God as it was carried on, and the number of true saints multiplied, soon made a glorious alteration in the town ... the town seemed to be full of the presence of God, it was never was so full of love, nor so full of joy; yet so full of distress as it was then.[8]

Edwards then records that in May of 1735, as the first Awakening abated, 'the Spirit of God was gradually withdrawing from us, and after this time Satan seemed to be let loose, and raged in a dreadful manner.'[9] With Joseph Hawley II's suicidal slitting of his throat, the Devil was certainly thought to have played his hand. Fourteen or so years later, it seems the third Joseph Hawley took his own turn doing the Devil's work.

Remarkably, however, Hawley later wrote to Edwards expressing remorse and asking for a frank evaluation of his conduct. Edwards replied graciously but firmly. He called on Hawley to lead the people in repentance because, as Edwards pointed out, his actions made him one of ring leaders of the conspirators whose venom knew no bounds:

> Even when I addressed myself to 'em in the language of moderation and entreaty, it was interpreted as a design to flatter people, especially the more ignorant, so to work upon their affections and so to gain a party and prevent a vote for my dismission ... [10]

In accord with Hawley's request, Edwards was forthright in attributing blame to Hawley: 'Your confident, magisterial, vehement manner had a natural and direct tendency to it.'[11] 'God's frowns' would be Hawley's lot unless he 'led' the conspirators (as he had so effectively and devastatingly led them a few years before) in 'true repentance and properly expressed and manifested.'[12] Such repentance and remorse was in fact displayed, in a way no less public than in the pages of the Boston press, and there is some hope that the two men eventually came to reconciliation.

Edwards' Convictions

Doubtless, a whole cocktail of contributory reasons for Edwards' demise in Northampton could be proposed. There were many reasons why his colleagues, congregation and even his relatives might have been poised to plunge in the knife—and indeed, they wasted little time doing so when the opportunity arose. Sadly, such a situation would hardly be unknown among faithful men serving in evangelical churches today.

However, Edwards himself did not want people to forget that he ' ... adopted and still hold the sentiments which I have publically professed ... with the fullest expectation of being driven from my ministerial office and stripped of a maintenance for my numerous family ... '[13] Edwards was under no illusions; what he knew in advance would get him fired was his *convictions*. We shall thus focus on three convictions in particular:

1. The necessity of conversion.[14]

2. The church's identity as the Bride of Christ (or the purity of the church).[15]

3. The importance of discernment.[16]

These are the issues which mattered most to Edwards, yet they are also what set him on a collision course culminating with the events of 1750.

I. The Necessity of Conversion

No doubt, many Northampton people liked the idea of communicant church membership but not the demands of true repentance and faith. Yet Edwards could never let them forget the absolute necessity of being born again. Indeed, in one of his final warnings to them, Edwards worried that the church might end up with a minister who was himself unconverted: one 'who knows nothing truly of Christ, and the way to salvation by him, nothing experimentally ... alas, how you will be exposed as sheep without a shepherd!'[17]

This is all the more interesting because of Edwards' history with George Whitefield on the unconverted ministry issue. Whitefield made a point of visiting Edwards twice during his preaching tours in 1741 and 1744. That such a powerful evangelist—Edwards himself wept under Whitefield's preaching in Northampton—could come from the compromised Church of England was likely a source of amazement to the 'last Puritan.' Unfortunately, Whitefield also had a habit of denouncing certain ministers as unregenerate. This behaviour was the source of legitimate objections against the celebrated preacher, and Edwards took it upon himself to rebuke Whitefield privately for it. Testing a 'profession' of faith was no easy matter, and writing someone off on the basis of a limited interaction or even mere reputation was a highly dubious enterprise. This demonstration of balance and caution is important for our assessment of Edwards in the Communion Controversy of 1749/50. Yet, as we see in the 'Farewell Address,' he remained deeply concerned about the dangers of an 'unconverted ministry' (albeit in more general, hypothetical terms than Whitefield's indiscrete labelling).

If remaining unconverted was a danger for ministers, it was far more so for ordinary churchgoers. Many simply did not like Christ's ultimatum: 'unless you be converted, and become as little children, you shall not enter the Kingdom of Heaven' (Matthew 18:3). For Edwards, there is no requirement more basic than this.

By this dual action of *metanoia* (repentance) and *palingenesia* (regeneration) our pride is dealt a lethal blow and God is greatly glorified. For Jonathan Edwards, the conversion of sinners is thus what matters most and he maintained a steady focus upon it.

We have already heard Edwards stress how important conversions are in the *Faithful Narrative*. Conversion to Christ is what brought a person into the real vital relationship of the Body with all of its privileges, especially the sacrament of communion. 'Conversion', wrote Edwards, is 'a great and glorious work of God's power, at once changing the heart and infusing life into the dead soul.'[18] In his *Treatise on Grace*, written in the early 1740s, Edwards defines conversion: it is 'represented as a work of creation. When God creates he does not merely establish and perfect the things which were made before, but makes wholly and entirely something new ...'[19] If there is nothing new, then says Edwards, there's nothing there! Thus it is said, 'if any man be in Christ, he is a new creature' which obviously implies that he is an exceeding diverse kind of creature from what he was before he was in Christ.'[20] A converted person is a resurrected person, a newly sighted person. Christ's call is the imparting of life and sight.

The 'new sense' is the unique term which Edwards used to describe the gift of new spiritual life in regeneration.[21] In the bestowal of the new sense, man is brought close to God and is 'the highest beauty and glory of the whole creation and is as it were the life and soul of the soul, that is given in the new creation or new birth.'[22] The new sense is exclusive to the twice born, and the regenerate life of the Christian is made possible because of it. Edwards illustrates it in the most dramatic ways possible: 'therefore the giving this new sense, with the blessed fruits and effects of it in the soul, is compared to a raising the dead, and to a new creation.'[23] The faculties of sight and sound are renewed. Without the donation of the Spirit's supernatural principles, common grace can assist but there is nothing new. The newness is a 'new holy disposition of heart', 'a foundation laid in the nature of the soul.'[24] The repeated uses of 'new sense', 'disposition' and 'infusion' point us to a minister who saw the radical internality of all this but who also saw no place for a 'visibility' or externality of Christian profession which did not exhibit a life morphed and morphing in Christ. That is the reality of conversion. But there is no triumph of subjective over objective in Edwards for the transforming cause of conversion is divine beauty: 'The sight of the beauty of divine is the first thing in the actual change made in the soul, in true conversion and is the foundation of everything else belonging to that change.'[25]

Edwards' 1733 lecture 'Divine and Supernatural Light' was surely one of Edwards' most important works.[26] Succinct and loaded with challenging content no less than vivid imagery, it was a 'game changer.' First delivered as a lecture on the cusp of the Connecticut Valley awakening of 1734–1736, it dispensed with the old 'morphology of conversion' (an approved programme of 'steps' toward conversion) and replaced it with God's sovereign prerogative to act immediately to effect conversion through the regenerative power of the Holy Spirit.[27] Edward's text was Matthew 16:17, 'Flesh and blood hath not revealed it to thee, but my father which is in heaven,' affirming the supremacy and absolute necessity of God in salvation. Supernatural regeneration brings the equipment—the 'new sense'—to perceive the saving message.

Although God uses the proclamation of the Word of God as

His ordinary means of grace, there is also a sense in which the knowledge of God in conversion is 'immediately' given. This is Edwards' version of the doctrine of illumination, in which the Holy Spirit enables people to understand the Word of God. It explains why the disciples, 'a company of poor fishermen, illiterate men and persons of low education' comprehended the truth whereas the Scribes and Pharisees generally did not. So it follows for Edwards:

> He that is spiritually enlightened truly apprehends and sees it, or has a sense of it. He don't merely rationally believe that God is glorious but he has a sense of the gloriousness of God in his heart.[28]

This is how people embrace a faith they would previously have been repulsed by. There is, averred Edwards, a huge difference between a theoretical knowledge that honey is sweet and a sensory confirmation of it in taste. 'There is a wide difference between mere speculative, rational judging anything to be excellent, and having a sense of its sweetness, and beauty.'[29] The *taste* is indispensable if you are going to be a Christian. This is also a crucial aspect of the work of sanctification in believers, as their regenerate taste leads them to gaze at the beautiful image of God in Christ and are more and more transformed into it.[30]

However, it is crucial to understand that Edwards is not just talking about 'heart knowledge' but 'the whole soul.'[31] The effects of this illuminating light and knowledge are holistic. 'It not only removes the hindrances of reason, but positively helps reason. It makes even the speculative notions the more lively. It engages the attention of the mind and causes it to have a clearer view.'[32] Edwards is the holistic theologian *par excellence*. His rejection of a head/heart dualism was complete: 'Gracious affections are not heat without light; but evermore arise from some information of the understanding, some spiritual instruction that the mind receives … '. As all the affections are thus engaged, the 'whole soul' is transformed.[33] Conversion is effected by 'This light, and this light only has its fruit in an universal holiness of life … this light, as it reaches the bottom of the heart, and changes the nature, so it will effectually dispose to an universal obedience.'[34] Not only is the whole person changed by regeneration, the change is manifested in the entirety of our conduct (a holistic effect Edwards called 'universal obedience').

Edwards pursues the point with searing logic. Because of these things, saints will be 'visible'—those who have been converted will look like they are converted. Being alive in Christ must have some observable traits, otherwise how could Christ say of the church in Sardis (Revelation 3:1) that they had a *reputation* of being alive even though they were dead?[35] Now, as this verse also makes clear, it is certainly possible for appearances to be false. The point is, however, that they *look* like the real thing. Just as counterfeit money is predicated upon there being a genuine article to imitate, so there are counterfeit Christians predicated upon there being real saints having a distinctive look.

Similarly, as the direct action of God, conversion must be *definite*. It might not always conform to a particular order or pattern. It might not be very dramatic.[36] Yet it will have definitely happened. Edwards was fond of comparing it with a resurrection. You are raised to life. You are either dead or alive. Converted or not converted. You are either saved or you are not.

Of course, all of this has real implications for church membership.

In too much of our twenty-first century church, it has become unfashionable to speak of being 'saved' as a normative description of being a Christian. It was not so in the early church, nor was it so with Edwards. Conversion meant being saved from sin by the 'washing of regeneration and renewal in the Holy Ghost' (Titus 3:5). It certainly entailed being 'added to the church' (Acts 2:47). But the addition was not before conversion. This is the basic understanding that Edwards carried with him into the communion controversy.

Yet this was certainly not the understanding that the Northampton congregation held when they administered the left boot of Christian fellowship to Jonathan Edwards on 22 June, 1750. They had been born into, and raised on, the innovations of Solomon Stoddard. How dare he tell us we have to pass his admission tests in order to take the Lord's Supper! How dare he tighten the rules that his venerable predecessor and grandfather loosened! Among other things, Edwards thus stood accused of disloyalty to the great man. Yet it was only by this move that Edwards remained loyal to a commitment he actually held in common (if more consistently) with Stoddard: the absolute necessity of conversion.[37]

2. The Church as the Bride of Christ

Turning now to the second firmly-held belief, Jonathan Edwards maintained that the church was the Bride of Christ. This was no purely notional illustration but a spiritual union having real implications for the identity and practice of the church. In his *Narrative of the Communion Controversy* written up along with *Misrepresentations Corrected* (1752), Edwards explains how this truth was being blatantly compromised in Stoddardeanism.[38] Many people were being admitted to the Church who 'made no pretense at real godliness.'[39] Edwards' conscience naturally troubled him over these contradictions. Things moved ahead when in December, 1748, a young man about to be married asked for communicant membership. In line with his resolution to tighten things up—an intention which four others affirmed that he had voiced as far back as 1746—Edwards asked this man for a profession of faith and showed him a draft example of what he would consider acceptable. After consideration, the candidate said he hoped he could so profess but would not because church rules did not require it.[40]

Edwards discussed the issue with the Church Council a few months later, in February of 1749. The Council was not in favour of any change in practice and was split as to whether Edwards should speak about it; some wanted him to be able to explain himself from the pulpit but others were against even this much. Soon thereafter, a young woman named Mary Hulbert submitted herself to doctrinal questioning by Edwards but voiced her concern at becoming the subject of contention. She agreed to publicly profess her faith if the Council agreed to it, but they did not.[41] So ignited the controversy which led to Edwards' farewell on 1 July, 1750.[42]

The 'Farewell Address' is shot through with pathos and poignancy. Edwards chose as his text 2 Corinthians 1:14, 'As also you have acknowledged us in part, that we are your rejoicing, even as you also are ours, in the day of the Lord Jesus,' thus juxtaposing the people's present and provisional judgement with God's future and final judgement on the Great Day. It concludes with a master-class on how to communicate a 'sense of an ending': 'And let us all remember, and never forget our future solemn meeting on that great day of the Lord, the day of infallible decision, and of the unalterable and infallible sentence. Amen.'[43]

A little into the 'Application,' Edwards comes to the subject we are discussing here: the true nature of the church as the Bride of Christ. On the Last Day, says Edwards,

> our late grand controversy, concerning the qualifications necessary for admission to the privileges of members, in complete standing in the visible church of Christ, will be examined and judged. Then it will appear whether … this matter be Christ's own doctrine. Then it will appear what is meant 'by the man who comes without the wedding garment' for that is the Day spoken of in Matthew 22:13.[44]

Edwards seemed in little doubt about the verdict that would be rendered.

Edwards wrote at greater length on wedding garments in his *Humble Inquiry*.[45] The communion feast is proleptic of the Wedding Feast of the Lamb. In heaven, the entry requirement will be a 'wedding garment' or Christ's righteousness: 'true piety, unfeigned faith or the righteousness of Christ which is upon everyone that believeth, is doubtless the wedding garment intended.'[46] Edwards then drew the parallel that admission to the earthly Supper should be based on the same requirement that would secure admittance into the heavenly feast. In both cases, admission is for those clothed with Christ, those who are regenerate and appear visibly to be so. Likewise, conversion did not happen *after* entrance to heaven, nor should it happen *after* admission to communion. Communion was thus not the 'converting ordinance' Stoddard tried to make it. Heaven and communion are so linked, the latter presaging the former and the means of entry the same, *you need the wedding garment to get in.*

On this point, Edwards was in self-conscious opposition to Stoddard's teaching. Stoddard had written in his *Appeal to the Learned*:

> Here [the parable of the wedding feast] is a representation of the Day of Judgement: and such persons as come for salvation without a wedding garment shall be rejected in that day. So that here nothing is being said about the Lord's Supper, all arguments from this scripture fall to the ground.[47]

So although the 'wedding garment' might be required for heaven, Stoddard argued that this parable had nothing to do with the Lord's Supper. He goes on: 'The person that had not a wedding garment was a reprobate, but everyone who partakes of the Supper without grace is not a reprobate.' Edwards replies very directly to this argument: 'I answer, all that will be found in the King's house [the church] without grace when the King comes are doubtless reprobates.'[48]

Of course, this theology had implications for baptism as well as for the Lord's Supper. But at this point, the problem went well beyond Stoddard's recent innovations in Northampton. Virtually the entire New England church had embraced the pragmatic arrangement of 1662 called the 'Half-Way Covenant.' It allowed children of parents who 'owned the Covenant' and whose lives were free from scandal yet *made no profession of personal faith*, to be baptised.[49]

The compromises inherent in this settlement bothered Edwards greatly, but not for the reasons some might suppose. It was not because Edwards was a separatist. The Northampton Church was essentially the state church of the day, and Edwards expressed no discomfort with this concept. Indeed, he was theoretically willing to serve in an even more explicitly state church situation in Scotland. Nor was it because he was an incipient Baptist. Josh Moody, writing as a Baptist minister, draws this rather tendentious conclusion: 'Edwards was only one step away from being a Baptist. His church/society separation puts him near that camp.'[50]

No, Edwards rejected the Half-Way Covenant not because it was covenantal with regard to infants but because it was halfway with regard to parents. He was a consistent, Westminster tradition paedo-baptist, and therefore held the same standard for those to be admitted to the Lord's Table as for those presenting their children for baptism.[51] Edwards actually wanted to raise both sides of this issue, but never got a chance to do so in the case of baptism simply because he lost the communion debate. He says this in a letter of 24th May, 1749 to Thomas Foxcroft:

> The greatest difficulty of all relating to my principles is here, respecting baptism. I am not sure but that my people, in length of time and with great difficulty, might be brought to yield the point for qualifications for the Lord's Supper, though that is very uncertain. But with respect to the other sacrament, there is scarce any hope of it. And this will be very likely to overthrow me, not only with regard to my usefulness in the work of the ministry here, but everywhere.[52]

He goes on to say that, in many places, ministers are strict with regard to qualifications for communion but 'not so with regard to baptism, but do admit all, on owning the covenant, not under the notion of a profession of true godliness.'[53] If indiscriminate admission to communion presented a major problem in Northampton, Edwards' opposition to the Half Way Covenant threatened to preclude Edwards' usefulness 'everywhere.'

For Edwards, the Body of Christ was not just a metaphor.[54] Being a member of that glorious body entailed union with Christ as well as access to many privileges. As Edwards repeatedly reminds us, being the bride is an exclusive relationship in which believers give themselves 'wholly' to the Bridegroom. And this is reciprocal. Christ has eyes for none other: 'The mutual joy of Christ and his church is like that of a bridegroom and bride, in that they rejoice in each other, as those that have been chosen above others, for their nearest, most intimate, and everlasting friends and companions.'[55]

Edwards saw Ephesians 5 as making explicit a type that was found throughout all of Scripture: Christ is the groom, and the church is the bride. Edwards deals beautifully with this material in a 1746 ordination sermon for Samuel Buell:[56]

> Christ has chosen his church for a peculiar nearness , as his flesh and his bone, and the high honour and dignity of espousals, above all others, ... rather than the elect angels ... he taketh not hold of angels but he taketh hold of the seed of Abraham ... He has chosen his church above the rest of mankind ... and those that are without the visible church ... and all other professing Christians ... Song of Solomon 6:9 'my dove, my undefiled is but one; she is the only one of her mother, she is the choice one of her that bare her.'[57]

Intimacy, delight and tenderness, married love; it is in fact Hephzibah and 'Beulah Land!' When you understand the full extent to which Edwards believed in the reality of the union between Christ and the Church, it becomes far easier to see why Edwards' ministry ended as it did. To maintain the Stoddardean *status quo* any longer would be an act of infidelity, of gross betrayal of Edwards' Lord.

Yet was Edwards asking for too much? Was he demanding dramatic conversion experiences or the amazing narratives of almost sinless saints? Hardly. On the contrary, it is interesting to see just how *little* he actually wanted in people's professions. His standard was that the church admit those who, 'in the eye of a reasonable judgement, are truly saints or godly persons.'[58] The 'reasonable judgement' was public rather than private, and the profession of godliness to involve repentance, faith in Christ, taking God as chief good and giving up oneself to God. That is it. As always, he rejects the need for any particular order. Consider the samples he proposes for prospective candidates:

> I hope I do find a heart to give up myself wholly to God, according to that tenor of that covenant of grace, which was sealed in my baptism: and to walk in a way of that obedience to all the commandments of God, as long as I live.

> I hope I truly find in my heart a willingness to comply with all the commandments of God, which require me to give up myself wholly to him, and to serve him with my body and my spirit. And do accordingly now promise to walk in a way of obedience to all the commandments of God as long as I live.[59]

The reasonable and altogether ordinary standard that is displayed in these sample professions would probably surprise some people. Edwards always denied that he was trying to resurrect the old Puritan practice of requiring a 'narrative of grace' or relation of one's conversion experience. As someone has pointed out, he probably would not have been pleased to learn that numerous churches and denominations have in fact resurrected that practice partially in response to the communion controversy.[60] All Edwards wanted was a simple Christian profession in the present tense.

3. The Importance of Discernment

This brings us to the third and final commitment: the importance of discernment. Having a relatively low standard for an acceptable profession of faith demands that we exercise some discernment. Edwards writes in the *Religious Affections*, 'In order to a man's being properly said to make a profession of Christianity, there must undoubtedly be a profession of all that is necessary to his being a Christian.'[61] These 'necessary' things begin with an affirmation of the objective truths of the gospel: mainly, the divine Person and atoning work of Jesus Christ. A credible profession obviously includes subjective repentance and faith in this Saviour. Yet it also includes the good works that *necessarily* accompany genuine faith. Christian living is 'the chief of all the marks of grace, the sign of signs, and evidence of evidences, that which seals and crowns all other signs.'[62] Specifically, we can look for the 'fruit of the Spirit' Paul lists in Galatians 5:22–23: 'love, joy, peace, longsuffering, gentleness, goodness, faith, meekness, temperance.'[63]

These things should be visible in the life of every believer, but the reality of them often become clear only over the passage of time. If the evidences of grace and conversion can only be observed over time, why restrict communion to those who seem to be saying the right things at that moment? And what happens when it becomes obvious that an initial positive judgment made in charity is contradicted by a patently inconsistent life? Edwards' deals with these questions in *Religious Affections*. In sum, discernment begins when a person seeks privileges but it does not end there.

Accountability should surely follow, and the church must exercise church discipline to remove those from visible membership whose lives are no longer consistent with a credible profession of faith.

Discernment involves making distinctions, and making distinctions sometimes requires exclusion. Edwards knew how to make valid distinctions; the true from the false, the counterfeit from the real, sound doctrine from the adulterated and compromised. In the course of so doing, he pointed out the distinction between believers and unbelievers. This inevitably involved exclusion (in this case, involuntary exclusion from the Lord's table), which is what the Northampton people so objected to. How ironic, then, that the people themselves made a (wrongheaded) distinction between Edwards' orthodox position and Stoddard's novelties, a distinction that resulted in the exclusion of their own minister. So when our own culture incessantly preaches 'toleration' and 'inclusion' yet proves to be among the most intolerant and excluding in history, we should not be surprised.

Discernment is needed in the church because we are not alone. Satan is real and active, and he will seek to debase all that is good with his counterfeits. We should not forget that Edwards was to become the leading expert (to this very day) in religious discernment precisely because he experienced more than his share of such things in the wake of great spiritual blessing in the 1730s. Indeed, the second book Edwards wrote on the subject of revival testifies to the need for discernment even in its title: *The **Distinguishing Marks** of a Work of the Spirit of God.*[64] Edwards clearly understood that things (and people!) were not always as they seemed. His final major work on the subject, *Religious Affections*, provides a bracing antidote to the postmodern cocktail of discernment deferral, commitment phobia, hatred of distinction and suspicion of certitude. It is, Edwards reminds us, both possible and necessary to distinguish between true and false, between truth and error.

Conclusion

Much has been said regarding the missteps that, humanly speaking, led to Edwards' dismissal from Northampton. I, however, cannot imagine a scenario in which he or any man fully committed to the convictions he held could have remained in that post indefinitely. Even had Edwards handled all the various affairs with the greatest of tact and somehow had won on the communion issue, the same convictions would soon enough have led him to pursue the practically impossible matter of the Half-Way Covenant. The result would have been the same, only at a later date.

This means that Edwards was essentially in an unwinnable scenario right from the start. Was it then all for nothing? Of course not. No man's ministry lasts forever, but everything that God does through our faithful prayer, preaching and administration of the sacraments will. Moreover, Edwards' commitment to his convictions even in the face of vicious opposition came from a more basic commitment: faithfulness to God's Word. This is the standard by which Edwards, and all ministers, must be judged. So if in the providence of God you are serving in a similar situation of difficult opposition, be encouraged to stay with what matters most.

I conclude with one final distinction. Edwards articulated it best in one of his greatest post-revival sermons: 'True Grace, Distinguished from the Work of Devils' (1752). 'True Grace' points to the highest of all distinctions, that between beautiful holiness and grotesque profanity, between what is of God and what is of the Devil.[65] Therefore, good evidences of grace:

> differ in their foundation, or in that belonging to them, which is most fundamental in them, and the foundation of all the rest, which pertains to them, viz. an apprehension, or sense of the supreme holy beauty or comeliness of divine things as they are in themselves, or in their own nature.[66]

This 'supreme holy beauty' *is* the distinguishing mark of God. It thus cannot be imitated by the Devil—"Tis God alone can bestow it.'[67]

Edwards' distinctive message concludes, as does this chapter, with a magnificent peroration:

> 'Tis the dawning of the light of glory. 'Tis the day-star risen in the heart, this a sure fore-runner of the sun's rising ... 'Tis something from Heaven ... it tends to heaven. And those that have it ... shall certainly arrive in heaven at last, where this heavenly spark shall be increased and perfected, and the souls of the saints, all be transformed into a bright and pure flame, and they shall shine forth as the sun, in the kingdom of their Father. Amen.[68]

4. Jonathan Edwards: Pastor-Apologist

Jeffrey C. Waddington

Introduction

By all accounts, Jonathan Edwards was brilliant. There is little doubt that he was America's greatest theologian. It is also true that Edwards figures among the nation's greatest philosophers, and some think that his great promise as a scientist was sadly under-realized.[1] Yet by choice and by conviction, he was a pastor.[2] Edwards' forays in these other disciplines were done in the interest of apologetics, a task which he considered to be a necessary part of the minister's job. As such, these pursuits were no diversion from Edwards' ministerial calling but aspects of it. In this chapter, we therefore consider Edwards as pastor-apologist.

Many will already know that Edwards was heavily involved in apologetics, making contributions in that area which would outstrip most 'professional' apologists.[3] Yet, as we have just said, Edwards was no professional apologist but a gospel minister. Beyond his concern for the prosperity of the Church generally, he had very real pastoral concerns regarding the caustic effects of false philosophies and doctrines on his own flock. Edwards did not think of himself as being exceptional in doing this work, but was convinced that *all* ministers were called 'to defend the faith once for all delivered to the saints' (Jude 3). It is therefore appropriate that we should take him as an example of how Christian ministers may go about defending the faith today. Let us consider some of the ways in which Edwards served as pastor-apologist in print and in the pulpit: in his defense of the first Great Awakening, in his defense of key Reformed distinctives, and in his defense of some basic issues of the faith.

Apologist for the Great Awakening

Edwards' writings in defense of the Awakenings are sometimes treated as if they had little to do with his larger apologetic endeavors, but this is mistaken.[4] The faith that Edwards defended was not a generic Christianity but the experimental Calvinism of his Puritan forbearers, a religion in which the possibility of God acting supernaturally to bring about sudden progress is inherent. Edwards thus brought the same searing intellectual powers to bear on the defense of the work of God in the revivals as he did for his most abstract philosophical treatises. We will consider Edwards' own development in assessing and defending the awakening before concentrating on Edwards' discussion of the 'new sense.'[5]

Jonathan Edwards' own assessment of the Awakening matured over time. With each successive publication on the subject, his evaluation becomes more sophisticated. Edwards' first report of the Awakening in the *Faithful Narrative* (1737) is almost uniformly positive. As time passed, however, not only did the voice of anti-awakening 'Old Light' critics grow but Edwards himself had to face up to certain complexities. The reality of some of the professions of faith that had been made during the awakening in Northampton were beginning to look rather suspect. Moreover, Edwards was concerned about the pseudo-supernatural phenomena that some other pro-revival men were tolerating or even promoting. Such concerns are manifested in Edwards' intermediate work, *The Distinguishing Marks* (1742) which is directed as much towards the movement's uncritical supporters as towards its critics. In a nutshell, Edwards calls for wisdom and self-assessment. The presence of unusual phenomena, often associated with the awakening, neither proved nor disproved that the Holy Spirit was active in the awakening. Likewise, the presence of spurious professions does not disallow the genuine conversions any more than Satan's chaff among Christ's wheat (Matthew 13:24ff).

The most mature form of Edwards' critically appreciative evaluation is found in *Religious Affections* (1746).[6] Here we find Edwards as a mature physician of souls, offering a balanced consideration of the marks of true religion. Edwards first considers a number of elements that neither affirm nor disconfirm that one is the subject of true religious affections. He then offers a detailed consideration of twelve signs that evidence true religious affections. The twelfth sign is practice. How do you know if you possess true religious affections? Simple; you know because you actually live the Christian life.[7] In the language of the Westminster Standards, '... good works, done in obedience to God's commandments, are the fruits and evidences of a true and lively faith: and by them believers ... strengthen their assurance' (*Westminster Confession of Faith*, CF 16:2).

But what is the *source* of this distinctive Christian practice?

Edwards believed that it arose from the 'new sense' or 'spiritual understanding,' which are essentially synonymous with regeneration and sanctification. The new sense or 'sense of the heart' was the result of the work of the Holy Spirit in the life of the individual believer. As Edwards was clear to point out, the new sense involved no new doctrine, but a new love or appreciation for the doctrines already taught from Scripture. To put it another way, the new sense involved seeing what had been true all along—the loveliness of Christ, for example—but had not been appreciated because of the effects of sin.

How does this discussion pertain to apologetics? Much in every way. Apologists often focus narrowly on convincing people of rational propositions about God. Jonathan Edwards pointed out that one could possess a great deal of 'speculative' knowledge about God—even the Triune God of the Bible—without actually being a believer. What distinguished Christian from non-Christian was, among other things, *love* for the Divine Subject of all that speculative knowledge. Here is Edwards:

> There is a distinction to be made between a mere notional understanding, wherein the mind only beholds things in the exercise of a speculative faculty; and the sense of the heart, wherein the mind don't only speculate and behold, but relishes and feels. That sort of knowledge, by which a man has a sensible perception of the amiableness of and loathsomeness, or of sweetness and nauseousness is not just the same sort of knowledge with that, by which he knows what a triangle is, and what a square is. The one is mere speculative knowledge, the other sensible knowledge, in which more than the mere intellect is concerned; the heart is the proper subject of it, or the soul as a being that not only beholds, but has inclination, and is pleased or displeased. And

yet there is the nature of instruction in it; as he that has perceived the sweet taste of honey, knows more about it, than he who has only looked upon it and felt of it.[8]

Edwards thinks that it is entirely possible to have speculative knowledge without it making a shred of difference in one's life. It is only the Holy Spirit working in the heart and mind of man that transforms speculative knowledge into spiritual knowledge.

On the other hand, Edwards the pastor-apologist would be quick to point out that genuine faith must also be an *informed* faith:

Such is the nature of man that nothing can come at the heart but through the door of the understanding: and there can be no spiritual knowledge of that which there is not first a rational knowledge. It is impossible that anyone should see truth or excellency of any doctrine of the gospel, who knows not what that doctrine is. A man cannot see the excellency and love of Christ in doing such and such things for sinners, unless his understanding be first informed how those things were done. He cannot have a taste of the sweetness and divine excellency of such and such things contained in divinity, unless he first have a notion that there are such and such things.[9]

Saving faith in Christ requires knowledge about who Christ is and what he has done for sinners. The Holy Spirit uses that speculative knowledge in the bringing of an individual to faith in Christ. When we recognize that the 'new sense' is simply another way of talking about regeneration or effectual calling, we realize that the new sense arises from the Holy Spirit *enlightening* the fallen sinful mind about Jesus Christ and *renewing* the fallen sinful will so that a sinner embraces the Christ offered in the gospel by faith.

Apologetics, as with preaching the gospel in a worship service or witnessing on a street corner, depends upon the active working of the Holy Spirit. Apart from Him, the only thing that will happen is information transfer. While that is not necessarily a bad thing, at best it yields only people having a 'historical faith.'[10] The application for us is that we must do our work as pastor-apologists in prayerful dependence upon the Spirit rather than arrogant dependence upon 'sure-fire' arguments. Moreover, since unbelievers do not yet have the new sense imparted by the Holy Spirit, it is rather obvious that they cannot rightly assess the evidence available to them. Therefore, it makes absolutely no sense for the Christian to pretend to think like an unbeliever as he or she presents evidence for the Christian faith or attempts to answer criticisms of the faith.[11]

Finally, it should be clear that Edwards did not disassociate apologetics from the rest of his ministry. Apologetics was *one element* of his work *as* a Christian minister. This does not mean that he could not distinguish between his preaching and his more specialized apologetic work. It simply means that his apologetic endeavors must be held together with his other efforts as part and parcel of his overall ministry. That ministry included defending the unusual work of the Holy Spirit in the midst of the awakening as well as some much-needed clarification of the roles of knowledge and affection in salvation.

Apologist for the Reformed Faith

Having considered the revival background of Edwards' apologetics and some of the issues that went along with it, we look now at the Northampton pastor's efforts to defend some of the main distinctives of the Reformed faith. In particular, a robust doctrine of original sin, a 'compatibilist' understanding of freedom of the will, and an Augustinian view of God's chief end in the creating the world.

Original Sin

Throughout the history of the Church, one of the least popular doctrines is the Pauline doctrine of original sin. This was as true in Edwards' day as it is in our own. In an attempt to craft a theology more amenable to the 'reasonable' spirit of the age, English Presbyterian John Taylor taught that Adam and Eve were created in a neutral condition. He thought that the fall was replicated in the rest of the race by way of imitation: that death was not a form of divine judgment but a gracious limit on the fallout of sin.[12] As a defender of the Reformed faith, Edwards was compelled to take issue with him. This he did in his landmark treatise *Original Sin*.

Edwards first reasserted the foundation for the Reformed position, which is that Adam and Eve were created perfectly righteous and holy:

> In a moral agent, subject to moral obligations, it is the same thing, to be perfectly *innocent*, as to be perfectly *righteous*. It must be the same, because there can no more be any *medium* between sin and righteousness, or between being right and being wrong, in a moral sense, than there can be a medium between straight and crooked, in a natural sense … therefore he was immediately under a rule of right action: he was obliged as soon as he existed, to act right.[13]

Against Taylor, Edwards argued that Adam and Eve were fully integrated creatures right up until their fall (Ecclesiastes 7:29). Adam and Eve both knew and loved God. They understood precisely how they ought to relate to Him. Their faculties were in full strength and in perfect harmony (that is, their thoughts and affections were not at odds with each other as they would be subsequent to the fall). The soul of man, with regard to quickness and clearness of its faculties, was then like an angelic being—as a flame of fire. The natural image of God that consisted in reason and understanding was then complete.

Edwards pointed to man's excellent endowments in his unfallen condition. His mind shone with the perfect spiritual image of God, being without any defect in its holiness and righteousness, or any spot or wrinkle to mar its spiritual beauty. God had put his own beauty upon it; it shone with the communication of his glory. As a result, man enjoyed uninterrupted spiritual peace and joy. His mind was full of spiritual light and peace as the atmosphere in a cool and calm day.[14]

For our purposes here, it should be noted that, in basic terms, Adam and Eve possessed by nature what would be regained in the new sense (Ephesians 4:24; Colossians 3:10). Our first parents were created with their intellect and will fully functioning in a cooperative fashion. This, of course, would be lost in the fall—the fallen intellect and will would be infected by sin and fall out of sync with each other.

Edwards will argue further that a universal propensity to sin (that men sin everywhere and at all times) requires a universal inclination to sin:

A common and steady effect shews, that there is somewhere a preponderation, a prevailing exposedness or liableness in the state of things, to what steadily comes to pass. The natural dictate of reason shews, that where there is an effect, there is a cause, and a cause sufficient for the effect; because if it were not sufficient, it would not be effectual: and that therefore, where there is a stated prevalence in the cause; a steady effect argues a steady cause.[15]

Whereas Taylor had argued that sin is prevalent merely because of imitation, Edwards argued that Adam's progeny have a tainted *nature* that made sin inevitable and universal.

How can we understand the link between Adam and the rest of us? The Reformed tradition begins with the federal headship of Adam. That is, Adam was not just the father of the human race biologically but was constituted by God to be the federal head of the race spiritually. Adam thus acted as a representative of the whole human race. Edwards affirmed all this, but he offered a somewhat unique explanation of how Adam was our federal head in terms of his understanding of personal identity. In contradistinction to John Locke's theory of mental continuity, Edwards thought that our identity as individuals is constituted and upheld by God.[16] Just as God upholds an individual through time and space as one specific person, so He constitutes Adam and the rest of the human race as something like a single entity in terms of federal headship.

Finally, Edwards rejected Taylor's notion that death is somehow to be regarded a blessing rather than a curse. Death, for Edwards, is a judicial sentence passed on fallen humanity because of the one act of Adam (Romans 5:12–21). Death is not a hedge of protection that God provides to limit the effects of the fall but a fearful punishment.

Throughout *Original Sin*, Edwards seeks to defend a Reformed understanding of Adam's fall and the estate of sin and misery that resulted from it. This is not to say that his articulation was a mere repetition of previous formulations; there are some unique and indeed, debatable, aspects to it.[17] The point is that Edwards sought to defeat a false doctrine he knew would undermine the faith and wreak havoc in the lives of Christians who came to be influenced by it. As a pastor of Christ's blood-bought flock, Edwards felt keenly his obligation to protect those under his care.

Freedom of the Will

Freedom of the Will is justly considered among the best of Edwards' compositions. As we consider it here, we are mindful that he wrote it with an apologetic purpose—to challenge the rising influence of Arminian ideas in New England.[18] Edwards' basic strategy in the book was to expose the incoherence of the libertarian notion of 'free will' and then offer in its place an account of the will that was fully compatible with orthodox theology no less than with reason.

The explanation that Edwards articulates is a form of *compatibilism*. That is, a proper notion of free will is fully compatible with divine sovereignty. The foundation of Edwards' argument here is his firm belief in the unitary operations of the human soul. God made man as an integrated creature having both intellect and will, and both these faculties have been equally (albeit differently) degraded by the effects of sin. What is the relationship of these faculties to one another? Although one might get the idea that he is teaching the primacy of the will, it is more accurate to say that Edwards holds a primacy of *orientation*. One is either bent in on oneself or one is oriented toward the glorious Triune God. This primacy of orientation figures heavily into Edwards' consideration of the freedom the will.

The false notion that Edwards is particularly responding to is the idea that the will exists in a state of perfect equilibrium, inclined neither one way nor another. Somehow, it moves out from this state of perfect equilibrium without any internal or external motivation whatsoever. The Arminians invested great importance to this strange concept of free will, such that they thought only decisions made on this basis could legitimately be held accountable. Edwards points out that such a notion is logically incoherent, impossible, and if that were not enough, amoral. Everything apart from God Himself has a cause, and Edwards demonstrates that to say that the human will acts without motivation is equivalent to saying we have here an effect without a cause. Even if such a thing were possible, it certainly would not result in morally valuable decisions. It is precisely because a good man out of his good character and love to God chooses to do good that this decision is accounted morally good. A perfectly indifferent act of the will would be perfectly amoral.

In this place of this libertarian free will, Edwards offers what might be called the 'liberty of spontaneity.' The will is not like some small person that resides inside a man and tells him what to do. The will is nothing more or less than the man or woman *choosing* this or that action, and there are always reasons—whether good or bad—why people choose as they do. Our actions are motivated by what attracts or repulses an individual, and we know from Scripture that the will is determined by the orientation of an individual either in sin or in godliness.

In all this, we must keep in mind that Edwards wrote as a pastor. The ideas in *Freedom of the Will*, together with works such as *Original Sin* no less than *Religious Affections*, actually have massive implications for everyday concerns ranging from preaching to pastoral counseling. We should, for instance, place before our people the whole spectrum of inducements to Christ and Christ-likeness in as convincing and affecting a manner as we can. Yet we understand that only God can change the basic orientation of the heart in supernatural regeneration.

Beyond these very real pastoral implications, the single most important reason Edwards took up the pen against Arminianism was to defend God's honour. As arcane as the arguments in *Freedom of the Will* might at first appear, there is a simple yet profound theological concern that lies behind them: Arminianism destroys the glory of God. God is sovereign in redemption and man contributes precisely nothing apart from his sin, and to claim otherwise would undermine God's very purpose in the glorious work of redemption.

The End for Which God Created the World

This larger point is the subject of one of Edwards' final complete works, *The End For Which God Created the World*. His thesis is rather simple: God created the world to communicate Himself or, in other words, to manifest His glory.[19] Again, one might be tempted to think this is an abstract and impractical subject, but Edwards knew that there is scarcely anything better for a Christian than to be shown the character of God together with the reason for his own existence. In keeping with the basic two-part structure shown in several of his major works, the first part is rational argument for his thesis and the second is a biblical demonstration of it from Scripture.[20]

Edwards first has to defend his thesis from an objection that is likely to be raised in our day no less than his: is God not prideful to seek His own glorify? This problem—as with many other similar objections—involves a wrongheaded transfer of our situation to that of God. When a human being seeks to increase his own glory we rightly judge him arrogant. This is because, at the most basic level, we are creatures of the dust created precisely to give glory to our Creator. Moreover, as fallen people, there is no proper glory to manifest. All that we are in ourselves as fallen creatures is sinful, and our mistaken attempts at self-glorification inevitably demonstrate this. Humility is thus a cardinal Christian virtue, one exemplified by Christ Himself throughout His state of humiliation (Philippians 2). God's situation, however, is categorically different. As the Creator, it would be wrong not for Him to receive all glory. Likewise, God is the most perfect being in existence, and His glory is nothing more than the fullness of this truth being disseminated. Of course, God does not *need* to manifest his glory externally, yet it is hardly unbecoming that He chooses to do so.

Edwards spends some time explaining the differences between 'ultimate' and 'chief' ends and how they relate to one another. This is groundwork for his argument that God receives his ultimate purpose of self-glorification by intelligent beings (angels and men) carrying out their 'chief end' in re-emanating glory back to Him. At this point, Edwards echoes the first question of the Westminster Shorter Catechism: 'What is the chief end of man? Man's chief end is to glorify God and to enjoy Him forever' (WSC 1). Since we are most happy when we do what we are designed to do, it is not only for God's glory alone but also for our own joy and happiness that we glorify Him. Once again, this is of enormous pastoral importance. Purposelessness is among the worst plagues of our time. For our people to understand their actual *raison d'être* and to actively pursue it by expanding the glory of God in every facet of life is an inestimable blessing. Edwards himself certainly exemplified this in his life's work as a minister and pastor-apologist.[21]

Pastor-Apologist Conversant with the Intellectual Universe

Given the nature of our vocation, it would be all too easy for us to be held captive to the immediate concerns of our congregation and family. Yet Edwards would remind us that the pastor is called by God to be the resident theologian and apologist for his people. This means he must be familiar with not only the practical challenges facing the people today, but also with the trends that will impinge upon the thinking, practices, and spirituality of the people of the church tomorrow. Indeed, every Christian is called to resist the world's pressure to squeeze us into its mold (Romans 12:1–2) and to take captive all our thoughts for Christ (2 Corinthians 10:5); it is difficult to see how the pastor could help his people do these things if he does not keep himself abreast of the intellectual and cultural world around him.

Of course, this requires proactive, disciplined study, but this is no wasted effort. In the larger picture, Edwards reminds us that the human mind was created precisely for the purpose of worshiping and glorifying God, and this is enabled by our ongoing intellectual exercise:

> Our business should doubtless much consist in employing those faculties, by which we are distinguished from the beasts, about those things which are the main end of those faculties. The reason why we have faculties superior to those of the brute given us, is, that we are indeed designed for a superior employment. That which the Creator intended should be our main employment, is something above what he intended the beasts for, and hath

therefore given us superior powers. Therefore, without doubt, it should be a considerable part of our business to improve those superior faculties. But the faculty by which we are chiefly distinguished from the brutes, is the faculty of understanding. It follows then, that we should make it our chief business to improve this faculty ... therefore it must be a great part of man's principal business, to improve his understanding by acquiring knowledge.[22]

Because we have a higher purpose than the beasts, we have been given higher intellectual faculties. It therefore ought to be our 'chief business' to 'improve' our understanding by 'acquiring knowledge.' If this is the case with the people, how much more so the minister.

Despite his rather backwoods physical location, Edwards was fully conversant with the intellectual universe of his day. He kept up with the latest trends in science, history, geography, philosophy, politics, biblical studies and theology. [23] He was in continual correspondence with friends overseas who frequently filled book requests for him and would recommend books and journals for him to read. In so doing, Edwards was not pursuing harmless diversions from an uninteresting pastoral charge but was actively fulfilling his understanding of the ministry. We say 'actively' because he was not blithely imbibing the intellectual currents of the day but was engaged in ongoing intellectual combat for the glory of God and the protection of his flock.

To get a sense of some of the ways Edwards interacted with the intellectual currents of his day, we will consider two examples of his work: 'Miscellany' 837 and 'Notes on Scripture' 416.

'Miscellany' 837 and the 'Scandal of Particularity'

Those who have read recent scholarship about Jonathan Edwards will know that he was greatly concerned about Enlightenment thought and with its religious offspring, Deism.[24] One of the Deist's main weapons was the 'scandal of particularity,' in which the fact that only some people have access to the Bible is turned as an objection against Christianity.[25] They argued that whatever was necessary to know about God must be available universally, for it would surely be unfair of God to restrict his saving activity to Israel and the limited geographic confines of eighteenth century Christianity. How could God hold people accountable for knowing what they could not know? Saving knowledge must therefore be found in nature and reason, and the Bible could add to it nothing essential.

Edwards responded with a comprehensive case for the necessity of special revelation. Nature might have theoretically been sufficient for Adam in his unfallen perfection, but even then, God saw fit to provide verbal instructions. In any case, there is no question that nature could never be sufficient for fallen sinners in need of redemption by Christ. Moreover, to whatever extent that we might know true things about God in nature, we simply do not know them in their all-important relationship to Christ:

> The whole of Christian divinity depends on divine revelation; for though there are many truths concerning God and our duty to him that are evident by the light of nature, yet no one truth is taught by the light of nature in that manner in which it is necessary for us to know it. For the knowledge of no truth in divinity is of any significance to us any otherwise that it, some way or other, belongs to the gospel scheme, or has relation to Christ the Mediator. It signifies nothing for us to know anything of any

one of God's perfections, unless we know them as manifested in Christ; and so it signifies nothings to us to know any part of our duty, unless it will [bear] some relation to Christ .... And therefore we stand in the greatest necessity of a divine revelation.[26]

Saving religion thus involved another 'scandal of particularity' which the Deists failed to reckon with: the irreducible particularity of Christ. Apart from Him, there can be no saving knowledge (Acts 4:12).

'Notes on Scripture' 416 and the integrity of Scripture

As part of this picture, early higher criticism sought to chip away at the Bible's trustworthiness and authority by deconstructing its integrity. Among many other places, Edwards responded in his *'Notes of Scripture'* notebook, entry 416.[27] Here, the larger issue is the Mosaic authorship of the Pentateuch, and the specific objection being addressed is the argument that the original 'law of Moses' would never have included all the historical material that we find in the finished Pentateuch:

'Tis the more likely that the history of the Pentateuch should be a part of that which was called the law of Moses, because it is observable that the words, law, doctrine, statute, ordinance, etc., as they were used of old, did not only intend precepts, but also promises, and threatenings, and prophecies, and monuments, and histories, or whatever was revealed, promulgated, and established, to direct men in or enforce their duty to God ... And 'tis probable that when we read of the great things of God's law (Hosea 8:12), and the wondrous things of God's law, that thereby is not only intended precepts and sanctions, but the great and wondrous works of God recorded in the law. 'Tis evident that the history is as much of an enforcement of the precepts (and is so made use of), as the threatenings, promises, and prophecies; and why then should it not be included in the name of the law as well as they? There is something of history, or a declaration of the great acts or works of God, in that [which] is by way of eminency called the 'law,' viz. the Decalogue, in that there is a declaration of the two greatest works that the history in the Pentateuch gives an account of, viz. the creation of the world and the redemption out of Egypt out of the house of bondage.[28]

The law and the unfolding of the narrative of redemption in the Torah reveal that the law and the historical narrative were not separate elements that were added together at a later point, but were integral to one another. In other places, Edwards would point out that the later Old Testament bears a uniform witness to the integrity of the Pentateuch no less than Jesus upholds the Mosaic authorship of it in the New Testament. This was all part of Edwards' comprehensive demonstration of why we can believe with confidence that Moses wrote the first books of the Bible.[29]

Pastor-Apologist in the Pulpit

Jonathan Edwards is remembered today as an outstanding evangelical preacher. What is probably less known is the extent to which he addressed apologetic issues from the pulpit. Edwards would frequently deal with issues ranging from Latitudinarianism to Atheism even in his routine sermons. One example of Edwards' apologetic preaching would be the sermon 'Light in a Dark World, A Dark Heart.'[30] Edwards is concerned about the rise of Deism in the American colonies—a fear that was, incidentally, fully justified—and is refuting the notion that mankind had sufficient information in nature to worship and serve God aright:

> They [Deists] reject the Bible and all revealed religion, and hold
> that the Bible is a mere human book and Christ, a cheat; [that]
> God never gave any revelation of his mind any other wise than
> by the light of nature. This of late has made amazing progress
> in our nation. Deism has been growing in our nation for some
> time, till at length it has grown fashionable, [so that a] great part
> of the nation are become deists. [The] Bible is derided, Christ
> openly blasphemed, and all doctrines and miracles ridiculed in
> public houses and open streets. And 'tis surprising to see what
> darkness and confusion they have run into, having set up their
> own reason as a sufficient guide. 'Tis strange to see where their
> boasted light has led them. Some of 'em hold one thing, and
> others another, about another world and future state; and some
> deny any, but hold that men die like brutes.[31]

It is all very well claiming that we have the 'light of nature' and
do not need Scripture, but where did this vaunted reason lead the
Deists? Only into further darkness and confusion, as has always
been the case among those bereft of the true light. Whatever shred
of truth was to be found among such people was not a result of
their 'reason' but was the unacknowledged residual effect of prior
exposure to special revelation.[32]

Edwards thus integrated apologetic concerns into his preaching.
Primarily, he was doing this as a preventative measure, knowing
that these things would eventually reach his rural congregation. Yet
he often spoke as if he expected there to be representatives of these
groups already seated there, and in some sense, there were. Given
his peerless understanding of the depths of human depravity in
intellectual no less than moral terms, Edwards was only reasonable
to suspect that some of these false ideas had probably crossed
the minds of his hearers. As a zealous evangelist of the lost and

compassionate pastor of the tempted, Edwards was compelled to say something in defense of the saving truth of God's Word. Of course, he understood that the apologetic encounter did not end with mere information transfer, but demanded the supernatural working of the Holy Spirit in enlightening the mind and renewing the will.

Conclusion: Lessons From Jonathan Edwards, Pastor-Apologist

While there is no man that should be imitated in every regard, the contemporary church could choose a lot worse example to follow than Jonathan Edwards. Here are some lessons that today's pastor-apologists can learn from him:

1. Stay current

A minister is the resident apologist for the congregation he serves. As such, he must understand the basic contours of the intellectual environment enough to respond to the challenges it poses to the Christian faith. Even if we are not quite as assiduous as Edwards, we should at least remain as current as a physician catching up on the latest developments in medicine.

2. Warn the flock

2 Peter 2:1 tells us clearly that 'there will be false teachers among you, who will secretly bring in destructive heresies.' It *will* happen, and faithful shepherd must perpetually be on the look-out for them to appear among the voices seeking to influence the church. When he sees something coming, he should warn his flock with all the earnestness of Jonathan Edwards.

3. Strengthen believers

The minister must be conscious of the ongoing need to help individual members to withstand the opposition of an unbelieving world. On a daily basis, ordinary believers will be confronted with an array of challenges to biblical Christianity, whether explicit or implicit. If you don't think that, you need to spend more time with your people! It is our job as ministers to confirm and strengthen them in the truth, and help them find good answers to the troubling questions they will face.

4. Don't sell out the faith trying to defend it

The minister must do all of these things in ways that are fully consistent with orthodox truth. We are called to defend the whole of the Christian faith, not concede the difficult parts in order to gain a hearing. Jonathan Edwards was as concerned to defend distinctive Reformed doctrines such as original sin and divine sovereignty as he was to uphold the existence of God. Yet even Edwards let his apologetic motivations get the better of him in a couple of cases.[33] We must keep in mind the inescapable fact that the cross is foolishness to the world (1 Corinthians 1:18), and so we cannot expect to win every argument while remaining faithful. Similarly, if we feign thinking like an atheist in order to win someone to Christ, we will quickly find ourselves in a bind when we speak with greater consistency. Edwards defended the faith as a Calvinist Christian, and so should we.

5. Jonathan Edwards: Missionary to the Indians

Jon D. Payne

On a wintry Lord's Day in January 1751, in the frontier village of Stockbridge, Massachusetts, Jonathan Edwards preached one of his first sermons as a prospective missionary to the Mohawk and Mohican Indians. His text was Acts 11:12–13 in which Peter recalls his divine instruction to go to Cornelius, the man who would soon become the first non-Jewish or 'heathen' convert to Christianity.[1] Edwards made a connection between the biblical narrative and the situation unfolding before him, not only for his Native American Indian hearers but also for himself. The recently dismissed Northampton preacher had embraced a new role in God's great work of redemption: missionary to the Indians.

Edwards began his sermon with a brief description of the history and nature of biblical missions.[2] He informed the Indians that, during Christ's public ministry he 'chose twelve men ... that he might teach ... instruct ... and fit [them] to be ministers to preach the gospel.' After Christ's resurrection and ascension, and in response to the Great Commission (Matthew 28:18–20), the twelve disciples 'went all over the world, and a great many turned to the true God and to the Christian religion …'.[3] Peter preached the gospel to Cornelius's household and 'they all gladly received the word and it filled [them] full of joy to hear [the good news] concerning Jesus Christ, the Saviour of men.' The disciples then 'preached the gospel to others in all parts of the world, so that … a great many nations turned Christian … who before were heathen.' In what may have the most dramatic moment in the sermon, Edwards declared to the Indians, 'Now I am come to preach the true religion to you and to your children, as Peter did to Cornelius and his family, that you and all your children may be saved.'[4]

Edwards would go on to serve as a missionary pastor to the Mohawk and Mohican Indians in Stockbridge for almost seven years (1751–1758), a fact that might come as a surprise to some readers. His work as a preacher, pastor, theologian, philosopher and seminary president all tend to be better known. Indeed, his service among the Indians is sometimes viewed almost as if it were an accident. If anything, we might think of the Princeton presidency as somewhat 'accidental' and his missionary calling—albeit occasioned by an involuntary departure from his Northampton pulpit—was actually in the fullest continuity with his longstanding convictions regarding the church's duty to evangelize the Native Americans.[5]

Edwards' mission to the Indians also serves as a helpful corrective to some misguided trends in thinking about missions that seem to be gaining ground in our day. Apart from a few details that we might not recommend, Edwards provides us with a refreshingly clear example of the church carrying out her mandate to make disciples of all nations through the ordinary means of grace.[6] My purpose in the following pages, therefore, is threefold: first, to provide some historical context for Edwards' call to the mission field; second, to furnish an overview of Edwards' approach to Christian mission; and third, to consider what today's church might learn from Edwards' understanding and application of the Great Commission.

Historical Context: From Northampton to Stockbridge

George Marsden remarks that the 'scene of America's greatest theologian and colonial America's most powerful thinker being run out of [Northampton] and forced into exile in a frontier village has intrigued observers ever since.'[7] It is indeed a fascinating situation. How could Edwards' own congregation, after such a long and notable ministry, turn against him? We consider this question as we set the scene for Edwards' move to the mission field.

Edwards was pastor of the Northampton Church from 1729–1750. The remarkable spiritual Awakenings were as well known in Edwards' day as they are in our own. Moreover, the congregation could not have been ignorant of Edwards' notoriety as a writer.[8] All of this came to a premature end and the question is, why? In recent times, the 'Bad Book' episode, in which Edwards handled some aspects of a discipline case indelicately, has grown in importance as if it were the *real* reason behind his departure. John Gerstner liked to emphasize the (mostly unregenerate) congregation's desire to escape from Edwards' unrelenting sermons. While not dismissing such factors entirely, I think we need to focus on the issue that Edwards himself, the Northampton congregation, and the members

of the Hampshire Association that had the final say on the dismissal
would all have identified as the actual reason: Edwards' change of
mind regarding qualifications for the Lord's Supper.⁹

Edwards was never completely at ease with his predecessor
Solomon Stoddard's view of the Supper as a 'converting ordinance,'
in which anyone is admitted so long as they meet the standard of
'orthodoxy, moral sincerity, and lack of scandal.'¹⁰ Edwards—along
with the entire orthodox tradition before and after—believed that
to receive the Supper rightly one must also at least claim to believe
that which the Lord's Supper signifies and seals: the gospel of
Jesus Christ. Finding he could not continue to support Stoddard's
unbiblical innovation, Edwards began requiring communicants to
make some testimony of experiential faith in the Lord.

Edwards rightly believed that the Lord's Supper was for the
regenerate, and the unconverted—or at least those who made no
pretense of being believers—should be prevented from coming to
the Table. In a letter to the Reverend John Erskine of Scotland,
dated May 20, 1749, Edwards writes:

> I have nothing very comfortable to inform of concerning the
> present state of religion in this place. A very great difficulty has
> arisen between me and my people, relating to qualifications
> for communion at the Lord's table. My honored grandfather
> [Solomon] Stoddard, my predecessor in the ministry over
> this church, strenuously maintained the Lord's Supper to be a
> converting ordinance; and urged all to come who were not of
> scandalous life, though they knew themselves to be unconverted.
> I formerly conformed to this practice, but I have had dared no
> longer to proceed in the former way: which has occasioned great
> uneasiness among my people, and has filled all the country with

noise; which has obliged me to write something on the subject, which is now in the press.[11]

The 'very great difficulty' that emerged in Edwards' congregation over conflicting views on the Lord's Supper grew progressively worse until finally, in June 1750, 207 of 230 male members voted to remove Edwards from his pastorate.[12] Shortly thereafter, on Lord's Day July 1, the prominent New England minister preached a farewell sermon to his flock of twenty-two years.

It was a painful time for the Edwards family. Four days later, in another letter to John Erskine, Edwards referenced the 'multitude of distracting troubles and hurries' amidst his 'extraordinary circumstances ... [and how he is] as it were thrown upon the wide ocean of the world, and know not what will become of me and my numerous and chargeable family; nor have I any particular door in view, that I depend upon to be opened for my future serviceableness.'[13] Edwards expressed understandable concern that 'most places in New England that want a minister would not be forward to invite one with so chargeable a family, nor one so far advanced in years, being forty-six the fifth day of last October.'[14] Notwithstanding his difficult circumstances, Edwards wrote that his future and family were 'in the hands of God, and I bless him. I am not anxious concerning his disposal of us. I hope I shall not distrust him, nor be unwilling to submit to his will.'[15]

The following year Edwards was not without several new opportunities for pastoral ministry. Possibilities included pastorates in Connecticut, Northampton (a faction of his former congregation wanted him to plant a new church), Virginia, and Scotland.[16] However, God called Edwards to Stockbridge to serve as a missionary to the Indians and as pastor to the small congregation of English colonists there.[17] On July 1, 1751, the day that Edwards arrived in Stockbridge to commence his new call as a missionary. He wrote to his friend the Reverend Thomas Gillespie and asked to be remembered 'at the throne of grace, with regard to all my trials, and with regard to my new circumstances, and the important service I have undertaken in this place.'[18]

Edwards On Mission

Jonathan Edwards possessed a keen interest in Christian mission from his earliest days as a gospel minister. A commitment to mission is recognizable in his letters, sermons, and personal involvements.[19] In a series of sermons preached in 1739, which were published posthumously in 1774 in Scotland under the title 'A History of the Work of Redemption,' the Northampton minister carefully explains the providential unfolding of God's saving purposes from the fall of mankind to the end of the world. In this work Edwards confidently and optimistically refers time and again to the 'success' of the 'propagation of the gospel' (or missions) since the ascension of Christ, in spite of the constant barrage of Satanic persecution. Satan and the kingdoms of this world seek to undermine and destroy God's redemptive purposes, but God's sovereign plan cannot be thwarted. This is seen most clearly in the death, resurrection, and ascension of Christ:

> Satan before had exalted his throne very high in this world, even to the very stars of heaven, reigning in great glory in his heathen Roman empire; but never before had he such a downfall as he had soon after Christ's ascension. He had, we may suppose, been very lately triumphing in a supposed victory, having brought about the death of Christ, which he doubtless gloried in as the greatest feat that ever he did; and probably imagined he had totally defeated God's design by him. But he was quickly made

sensible, that he had only been ruining his own kingdom, when he saw it tumbling so fast so soon after, as a consequence of the death of Christ. For Christ, having ascended, and received the Holy Spirit, poured it forth abundantly for the conversion of thousands and millions of souls.[20]

According to Edwards, therefore, the success of the propagation of the gospel in the conversion of 'millions of souls' should be of no surprise, since it is 'agreeable to what Christ and his apostles foretold'—that Christ will build his church and the gates of hell will not prevail against it (Matthew 16:18).

Christian missions for the famed New England pastor is the 'principal moving force in the history of redemption,' that which God uses to triumph over evil, gather and perfect his elect, magnify his triune glory, and restore all things.[21] Clearly, missions has a central place in Edwards' theology. While we could not say that *missions drove his theology*—and the relationship between these two things is being misplaced all too frequently in our day—it is absolutely true that *his theology drove missions*.

In addition to his understanding of the Bible's teaching on the nature, role, and aim of the missionary task, Edwards' relationship with David Brainerd (1714–1747) should not be underestimated as helping to shape Edwards' view of missions.[22] Brainerd, who was himself a pioneer missionary to the Native American Indians, made a deep impression on Edwards as he spent the final months of his life in Edwards' Northampton home in 1747. One would assume that during Brainerd's season of illness the two ministers would have discussed at length the subject of Christian missions, particularly as it related to his gospel labors among the Indians.

After Brainerd died of tuberculosis, Edwards was compelled to temporarily set aside his labor on *Freedom of the Will* and produce what would become his most notable publication: an edited version of Brainerd's diary entitled *The Life and Diary of the Rev. David Brainerd*. Not only was this book meant to encourage readers to emulate Brainerd's godly piety, it also had the stated intention to cultivate a sincere zeal for Christian mission—to 'encourage God's people to earnest prayers and endeavors for the advancement and enlargement of the kingdom of Christ in the world.'[23] Edwards, profoundly impacted by Brainerd's zeal for Christian mission among the Indians, remarked during his funeral sermon:

> But a little before his death, he said to me, as I came into the room, 'My thoughts have been employed on the old dear theme, the prosperity of God's church on earth. As I waked out of sleep (said he) I was led to cry for the pouring out of God's Spirit for the advancement of Christ's kingdom, which the dear Redeemer died and suffered so much for.'[24]

According to Edwards, Brainerd served as 'an excellent example' of a 'missionary who sought the prosperity of Zion with all his might.' His gospel work with the Native Americans inspired Christians to 'pray for the conversion of the Indians on this continent, and to exert themselves in the use of proper means for its accomplishment.' With theocentric optimism Edwards hoped that 'God's extensive work of grace among the Indians was 'but a forerunner of something yet much more glorious and extensive of that kind.' Moreover, he hoped that it would motivate Christians to 'honor the Lord with their substance, by contributing, as they are able, to promote the spreading of the gospel among [the Indians].'[25]

Edwards' hopes for *The Life and Diary of David Brainerd*

were more than realized. The book proved to be one of the most influential volumes on Christian missions in the last 250 years. It has deeply impacted untold numbers of missionaries, including notables such as William Carey, Henry Martyn, Adoniram Judson, and Jim Elliot.

It is evident, then, that Edwards was a pastor-theologian with a heart for Christian mission. God's mission to magnify his glory and accomplish his sovereign decree by applying Christ's redemptive work to the elect in every nation through the ministry of the church shaped his theological system and ignited his heart. Therefore, it should not surprise us that the famed New England preacher passed up the comforts of a town pastorate for the hardships of missionary life on the edge of the wilderness. Edwards was devoted to making 'disciples of all nations.'

Lessons for Today

It is hard to compare Edwards' mid-eighteenth century colonial situation to our own. The world was a very different place back then. Life was much simpler, and myriad approaches to missions and church planting—missional, seeker-friendly, emergent, incarnational, satellite—that we have to deal with today simply did not exist. Yet the most important context remains ever the same: the nature of the human problem, the mission of the church, and the unlimited power of the Holy Spirit. Therefore, we find in Edwards' theology and practice of missions important and timeless biblical principles that apply to every generation and cultural setting, certainly including our own.

Devoted to Gospel Proclamation

Christ's mandate for making disciples through the proclamation of the whole counsel of God was Edwards' first priority in mission. The divinely ordained message, means, and aim of the gospel were never minimized in order to accommodate the unique characteristics of Mohican culture. Edwards was sensitive to his context without attempting to 'contextualize' the message he communicated.[26] His confidence was not grounded in his understanding of or identification with Indian culture—dress, music, language, or art. Rather, his confidence was in the bold and faithful proclamation of the Word of God, that which God promised to bless for the salvation of the elect (c.f. Romans 10:14–17; 1 Corinthians 1:18–2:5; 1 Peter 1:23–2:3).

Edwards catechized his children in the Westminster Shorter Catechism, and surely approved of its teaching that the 'Spirit of God maketh the reading, but especially the preaching, of the Word, an effectual means of convincing and converting sinners, and of building them up in holiness and comfort, through faith, unto salvation' (Q.89).[27] The efficacious nature of Gospel preaching was just as true for the American Indians as it was for the British colonists. And it is just as true for our hearers today. God, in His divine wisdom, has chosen the 'foolishness of preaching' to save His elect (1 Corinthians 1:18–25; 1 Peter 1:23–25; Ezekiel 37:1–14).

Notwithstanding his commitment to unashamed biblical preaching, Edwards was far from being insensitive to his surroundings. In fact, he took pains to make the ministry of God's Word accessible to the Indians as well as to facilitate the provision of their basic temporal needs. In this, Edwards' preaching to the Indians becomes for us a stellar example of accommodation without compromise.

At the most fundamental level, Edwards demonstrated his approach simply by composing over 200 original sermons for the Indians rather than simply preach old Northampton sermons. In so doing, Edwards' showed the attention to his audience that any faithful preacher will have: 'It is clear from the extant manuscripts that Edwards worked hard to adapt his rhetoric to the limited capacity of his hearers.'[28] A fellow missionary familiar with Edwards' preaching ministry to the Indians wrote in a letter that, 'to the Indians he was a plain and practical preacher; upon no occasion did he display any metaphysical knowledge in the pulpit. His sentences were concise and full of meaning; and his delivery, grave and natural.'[29] While tailoring his sermons to better accommodate the Indians through his highly valued interpreter, John Wauwaumpequunnaunt, Edwards clearly retained his deep and abiding commitment to the bold proclamation of the whole counsel of God.[30] The intellectual level, language, and illustrations may have changed, but the deep theological content and searching spiritual message did not.

One example of this is found in Edwards' early sermon to the Indians entitled, 'Heaven's Dragnet.' Interestingly, this sermon was essentially an abstract of a series on the Parable of the Net (Matthew 13:47–50) that he preached to his Northampton congregation in the summer of 1746.[31] It is possible that Edwards' chose to preach on this particular passage early in his ministry at Stockbridge in 'an attempt to engage the hunter-gatherer culture of the Indians.'[32] However, the main thrust of the message was precisely the same as it was in Northampton: the sobering truth that every person, rich or poor, white or brown, is either a member of the kingdom of heaven or a member of the kingdom of hell.

According to Edwards, 'the people of Christ are separated from the rest of the world to be a peculiar people to him, to be Christ's part, as the net cast into the sea separates the fish that are in it from all the rest in the sea that they may belong to the fisherman and be his part of the fish of the sea, while the rest are let alone and are not meddled with.'[33] On the last day, when Christ returns, the wicked will be 'severed from among the just, [and] shall be cast into a furnace of fire. After the day of judgment, not only will the souls of men be punished; but their bodies, which shall be raised from the dead, shall be thrown into eternal fire.'[34] However, for Christians, 'the country they are to live in forever with Christ, their king, is heaven.'[35] In light of this truth, the New England preacher exhorts his Indian hearers to 'take heed to yourselves that you ben't at last found some of the bad fish that be cast away. See to it that your hearts are right with God.'[36] If Edwards selected this particular biblical imagery to connect with the situation of his hearers he betrayed not the slightest interest in trying to leverage a 'gospel narrative' that was already to be found in the pagan culture. He simply preached the text and skillfully applied it to his hearers, all without downplaying or ignoring the doctrine of eternal hell.

In preparation for the Lord's Supper in August of 1751, Edwards preached a brief sermon to the Indians from Psalm 1:3, 'He is like a tree planted by streams of water that yields its fruit in its season, and its leaf does not wither.' Having been raised near the banks of the Connecticut River, this rich imagery was meaningful to Edwards and his Indian congregation alike. He explained to the Mohicans that 'Christ is to the heart of a true saint like a river to the roots of a tree that is planted by it.' Then, in a profoundly pastoral and lucid manner, Edwards outlines the way in which Christ is a river of life to His redeemed people. Through his faithful interpreter,

Edwards provides five simple but profoundly meaningful points to prepare the congregation for communion:

1. As the waters of a river run easily and freely, so the love of Christ. [He] freely came into the world. [He] laid down his life and endured those dreadful sufferings. His blood was freely shed: blood flowed as freely from his wounds as water from a spring.

2. Christ is like a river in the great plenty and abundance of his love and grace. The love of Christ is great, [and he has] done great things from love. The good things that are the fruits of his love are infinitely great. The happiness that he gives [is] worth more than all the silver and gold in the world.

3. Waters of a river don't fail: [it] flows constantly, day and night … little brooks dry up in a very dry time, but the waters of a great river continue running, continually and from one age to another, and are never dry. So Christ never [leaves] his saints that love him and trust in him: the love of Christ never [ceases].

4. A tree planted [by a river] is never [dry]: so Christ is never [exhausted]. The soul [of a saint] is joined to Christ and they are made one. As the water enters into the roots [of the tree], so Christ enters the heart and soul of a godly man and dwells there.

5. Water refreshes; so [Christ] refreshes and satisfies [the heart], and makes us rejoice. Water gives life and keeps it alive; so [Christ enlivens the heart and] makes it grow: makes it grow beautiful and fruitful.[37]

Edwards' missionary preaching, therefore, took on 'a renewed simplicity' in both form and substance.[38] He took into account his cultural context and accommodated the limited capacity of his hearers, all without diminishing or setting aside the message of Scripture or the divinely appointed method of its delivery. The Word and sacraments, God's means of grace, were central in Edwards' ministry at Stockbridge. If only this were true of all modern church planters and missionaries today, when 'proper sensitivity to diverse cultural contexts is sometimes turned into an ideology that leads to distortions of or distractions from the gospel.'[39]

In an effort to reach the lost, many churches expend a significant portion of their energy, time, wit, and resources on attempting to understand and incorporate the world's cultural fads and trends into their worship and programs, rather than seeking to be faithful in the ordinary ways that God has promised to gather and perfect His elect. Whether in first-century Ephesus, eighteenth-century Stockbridge, or the twenty-first century Charleston, the ordinary means of Word, sacraments, and prayer are God's ordained tools for making disciples and building his church (Matthew 28:18–20; 16:18; Acts 2:42; 1 Corinthians1:18–2:5; 4:1; 2 Timothy 4:2–5). Of course, it was not in the instruments themselves that Edwards placed His confidence, but in the power of God in and through them. Unless the Lord builds the house—even with His ordained tools—we labour in vain.

In the *History of the Work of Redemption*, Edwards comments on the impressive and unlikely propagation of the gospel in the early church considering the 'powerful opposition' of the Roman government. What cause could possibly explain the spread of the gospel in such hostile conditions? According to Edwards, the

'Roman Empire had subdued many mighty and potent kingdoms; they subdued the Grecian monarchy, though it made the utmost resistance: and yet they could not conquer the Church which was in their hands.' Edwards continues:

No other sufficient cause can possibly be assigned for this propagation of the gospel, but only God's own power. It was not the outward strength of the instruments which were employed in it. At first, the gospel was preached only by a few fishermen, who were without power and worldly interest to support them. It was not their craft and policy that produced this wonderful effect; for they were poor illiterate men. It was not the agreeableness of the story they had to tell to the notions and principles of mankind. This was no pleasant fable: a crucified God and Saviour was to the Jews a stumbling-block, and to the Greeks foolishness. It was not the agreeableness of their doctrines to the dispositions of men: for nothing is more contrary to the corruptions of men than the pure doctrines of the gospel. This effect therefore can have proceeded from no other cause than the power and agency of God: and if the power of God was thus exercised to cause the gospel to prevail, then the gospel is his word; for surely God does not use his almighty power to promote a mere imposture and delusion.[40]

Stirring words for the church today; we would do well to heed them.

The simple fact is that the mission of the Church and the means of it being accomplished have not changed since Christ instituted them (Matthew 28:18–20; Acts 2:42) nor will they until He returns. Unlike some today who are choosing cultural relevance over biblical fidelity, Edwards was firmly committed to that which God promised would be efficacious in the lives of His people (Isaiah 55:10–11). David Wells is right when he states:

> The biblical Word is self-authenticating under the power of the Holy Spirit. This Word of God is the means by which God accomplishes his saving work in his people, and this is a work that no evangelist and no preacher can do. This is why the dearth of serious, sustained biblical preaching in the Church today is a serious matter. When the Church loses the Word of God it loses the very means by which God does his work. In its absence, therefore, a script is being written, however unwittingly, for the Church's undoing, not in one cataclysmic moment, but in a slow, inexorable slide made up of piece by tiny piece of daily dereliction.[41]

Edwards' commitment to the means of grace, while serving as a missionary on the frontier, is a tremendous encouragement to missionaries and church planters everywhere. While he certainly made accommodation for the Indians' capacity and situation in his preaching, he never negotiated the centrality of the Word nor compromised the content of its message. He believed God's sure promise that the gospel, preached from all of Scripture, is the power of God unto salvation for all people.

Devoted to the Indians

As mentioned above, Edwards was thoroughly attentive to the significant and ongoing temporal needs of the Indians. Though committed to the means of grace and serious discipleship, his head was not in the theological clouds. On the contrary, Edwards was personally involved with meeting many of the practical needs at the Stockbridge Mission. His letters bear out the fact that he fought for his Indian congregation on numerous affairs. He served as the Indians' advocate with the British governing authorities in Boston regarding such matters as land allocation, education, and daily provisions. Rooy expounds:

> Edwards carried responsibilities for the boarding school for Indian boys; he made regular reports to commissioners for Indian affairs and the London Society for the Propagation of the Gospel (from whom much of his salary came) and sought their approval for their actions. Other facets of his work involved discriminating between English commercial and religious interests, administering funds, and unraveling duplications of work by rival missionaries.[42]

It is wrong, therefore, to conclude that the Stockbridge missionary 'had little interest in the Indians except as souls to be saved.'[43] No, Edwards was a shepherd who loved his sheep. The British authorities were not always easy to work with or quick to respond to requests. However, it is said of his years at Stockbridge that he 'not only contended with some formidable adversaries over practical matters but often prevailed.'[44]

The proper education of the Indian children at Stockbridge was of utmost importance to Edwards. To be sure, Edwards was a man of his time, and he desired to make civilized, literate, and loyal English subjects of the Indians. These aims are easily recognizable in a letter to Sir William Pepperrell on November 28, 1751:

> I cannot but think it might be a pretty easy thing, if proper measures were taken, to teach children to spell well, and girls as well as boys. I should think it may be worth the while, on various accounts, to teach them to write, and also to teach them a little of arithmetic, some of the first and plainest rules. Or, if it be judged that it is needless to teach all the children all these things, some difference might be made in children of different

genius, and children of the best genius might be taught more things than others. And all would serve, the more speedily and effectually, to change the taste of Indians, and to bring them off from their barbarism and brutality, to a relish for those things, which belong to civilization and refinement.[45]

In the same letter, however, Edwards makes it abundantly clear that the 'main design of the whole Indian establishment' is to promote the salvation of the children.' In order to make disciples of the Indian children he recommends that:

> beside their attending public worship on the Sabbath, and the daily worship of the family, and catechizing in the school, and frequent counsels and warnings given to them, when all together, by their teachers; each child should, from time to time, be dealt with singly, particular care should be taken to teach and direct each child, concerning the duties of secret prayer, and the duty pressed and enforced on every one.[46]

As we can see, Edwards was more than just an aloof English missionary who traversed between study and pulpit with little concern for the temporal needs of the Indians. Edwards referred to the Indians as "my people', and noted happily that they 'steadfastly adhere to me despite the concerted efforts of the Williams family— his own relatives—to alienate them from him.'[47] Murray adds that 'indifference to their physical needs, as well as injustice in dealing with their grievances, incurred his anger. Possibly he got closer to [the Indians] then to those in Northampton.'[48] Therefore, Edwards was devoted to the Indians— chiefly as a herald of the gospel, but also as an under-shepherd keeping watch over the congregation's conspicuous temporal needs.

The Greatest Need

The pattern that we see in Edwards' ministry to the Stockbridge Indians is an example for missionary-pastors today. Firstly, supreme attention is given to the ministry of the Word. Edwards' confidence does not reside in his own abilities or innovative outreach techniques, but in the life-giving Word of God. Making disciples through the regular preaching and teaching of 'all that Christ commanded' was an unmistakable priority (Matthew 28:18–20; Acts 20:27). The Stockbridge Indians' greatest need was deliverance from Satan, sin, and eternal damnation. As with Christ and the apostles, Edwards understood his and the church's primary calling and purpose to be the proclamation of the Gospel which is the 'power of God unto salvation for everyone who believes' (Romans 1:16–17).

Secondly, Edwards' approach to missions was informed and fuelled chiefly by biblical theology, and not by cultural or pragmatic considerations. His first question was not, 'What does the culture require?' but rather, 'What does the Bible say?' Edwards believed that man is essentially the same in every age, a depraved and rebellious sinner, and thus has the same essential need, God's grace and forgiveness through faith in Jesus Christ. Whether one is preaching to first century Greeks or eighteenth century American Indians, the root problem and ultimate need are the same.

In his *History of the Work of Redemption*, Edwards eloquently elucidates the grand narrative of God's unfolding plan of redemption, a sovereign and gracious plan to apply the accomplished work of Christ to the elect in every age and every nation. While circumstances change the message and means of the gospel do not:

The work of redemption is carried on in all ages, from the fall of man to the end of the world. The work of God in converting souls, opening blind eyes, unstopping deaf ears, raising dead souls to life, and rescuing the miserable captives out of the hands of Satan, was begun soon after the fall of man, had been carried on in the world ever since to this day, and will be to the end of the world. God has always had such a church in the world. Though oftentimes it has been reduced to a very narrow compass, and to low circumstances; yet it has never wholly failed.[49]

The destruction of Satan's kingdom 'will not be accomplished at once,' however, 'as by some great miracle, like the resurrection of the dead.' No, Edwards clearly states that 'this work will be accomplished by means, by the preaching of the gospel, and the use of the ordinary means of grace, and so shall gradually be brought to pass.'[50]

This gradual, yet powerful, influence of the ordinary means of grace in the establishing and strengthening of churches is what we witness in the early church (Acts 14:21–23; 15:41; 16:5). It is also what will serve to build Christ's Church in every age and in every place. The ministry of God's Spirit and Word are trans-temporal and transcultural, efficacious to save, gather, and perfect in every age and culture those whom the Father set his love and affection upon before the foundation of the world (Ephesians 1:4). Therefore, the strategy of churches and missions agencies to reach the nations by sending and supporting Christian artists, musicians, baristas, and athletes to redeem culture and *do life* with the community for the sake of the gospel may be well-intentioned, but it is foreign to Scripture and the Great Commission (Matthew 28:18–20). In our zeal to be relevant to our culture and identify with unbelievers we too often exchange God's strategy for our own. Well-meaning

Christians who head to the mission field to carry out their sundry vocations (often at a high price to the church) may fulfill the Great Commandment (love your neighbor), but not, by definition, the Great Commission (preach, baptize, make disciples, and teach all that Christ commanded).[51] The Church must renew its commitment to identify, call, and support qualified, trained, gifted, and ordained men to plant churches at home and abroad.[52]

Few remember Jonathan Edwards for his role as a Christian missionary-pastor to the Stockbridge Indians in colonial Massachusetts. This is regrettable, especially in a day of unprecedented confusion regarding missions. Edwards' theological and practical legacy should be a powerful encouragement to the church to re-examine her priorities, methods, and strategies in mission. May his example yet call us to recover the solid, biblical foundations for Christian missions, to the glory of the Triune God.

6. The Influence of Jonathan Edwards on the Church in Britain

John J. Murray

Jonathan Edwards was without doubt the greatest American theologian, and his enduring imprint on the church and nation there are well known. Next to his native land, however, no other country benefited more from Edwards than Great Britain. Due to the crucial role Edwards' writings played in movements ranging from the 18th century revivals to the 20th century recovery of the Reformed faith, one might argue that his influence here was even more decisive. In this essay, I shall describe the main elements of Edwards' influence in the United Kingdom over the past three centuries before offering some brief assessments.

The 18th Century

1. The revival of 1734–35 and the publication of the Faithful Narrative

The start of the influence of Edwards must be traced back to the revival at Northampton in New England in 1734–35. Such a revival was so unknown at that time that news of it did not meet with immediate affirmation even in other parts of New England. Benjamin Coleman, one of Boston's senior ministers, wrote to Edwards to find out more. Edwards replied in a comparatively brief letter on May 30, 1735. Coleman was impressed enough to pass on part of Edwards' reply in a letter to the two English Nonconformist leaders, John Guyse and Isaac Watts, with whom he regularly corresponded. When Watts shared this with his London congregation, there was an immediate request to have this in print and with more details. Dr Guyse wrote to Coleman accordingly, and the request was passed on to Edwards indirectly. This resulted in a much fuller letter, dated 6 November 1736, from Edwards to Coleman in which in eight large and tightly packed sheets he elaborated upon his earlier report.

Coleman reduced the letter to eighteen pages and included it as an appendix to another work, *The Duty and Interest of a People, among whom Religion has been Planted*, written by Edwards' uncle the Rev. William Williams of Hatfield.[1] Coleman had it on the streets in Boston and off to his correspondents in London by mid-December, 1736. In two separate letters in early 1737, Watts implored Coleman to publish the whole of it—'we have not heard anything like it since the Reformation, nor perhaps since the days of the apostles'—and pledged five pound to its American subscription.[2] By mid-October the entire text was at the London printers, edited, with a fourteen-page preface by Guyse and Watts, and a title of their own devising: '*A Faithful Narrative of the Surprising Work of God in the Conversion of Many Hundred Souls in Northampton and the Neighbouring Towns and Villages of New-Hampshire in New-England*' (London, 1737).

Following publication in London, it was printed in Edinburgh and sold there and in Glasgow. This marked the beginning of Edwards' relationship with a group of Presbyterian ministers in Scotland. Within a year the *Faithful Narrative* was in its second edition.[3] Edwards, however, had some complaints with the British edition. Common to authors of every age, he found some well-intentioned editorial emendations had resulted in errors, for example 'Hampshire' for 'New Hampshire' in the title. And, although he could understand why some material might be unsuitable for a British readership, he found the Guyse and Watts preface entirely too detached. What were they implying? Not surprisingly, the first American issue of the *Faithful Narrative* appeared in 1738 without the Guyse and Watts preface. It had, instead, an unqualified recommendation by four Boston ministers as well as a letter to Coleman signed by six Hampshire ministers—first among them the venerable William Williams—attesting to the events described in the account.[4]

In evaluating this situation we should recognise that Guyse and Watts were elder statesmen of English nonconformity, and were thus staking their reputations on the testimony of an unknown young pastor in New England. Having not witnessed these events themselves, they felt compelled to write a reserved preface and to delete some material that, true or not, seemed odd enough to potentially endanger the credibility of the whole. The chief reason for Guyse's and Watts' caution was that the age in when conversions like the ones described by Edwards were common had long since passed. The prevailing religious mood of the day was one of deadness and formalism. Guyse and Watts mourned this situation, and firmly believed that only a God-given revival could change things. This was, of course, why they were willing to promote the publication of Edwards' letter notwithstanding the risk: 'May a plentiful effusion of the blessed Spirit also descend on the British Isles, and all their American plantations, to renew the face of religion there!'[5]

Was their hope realized? Iain Murray offers this assessment: 'Edwards' *Faithful Narrative* was possibly the most significant book to precede the great evangelical awakening on both sides of the Atlantic. Between 1737 and 1739 it went through three editions and twenty printings. In Britain it gained the attention of the younger generation of men whose voices were soon to startle both the church and nation.'[6] As we shall see, I think we can say that Watts and Guyse were fully vindicated in their decision to secure a hearing for Jonathan Edwards in Great Britain.

2. The Effect of the Faithful Narrative in Scotland

The effect of Edwards' *Faithful Narrative* is seen most directly in the movement associated with the Cambuslang revival of 1742. In brief, William McCulloch (1691–1771) was inducted to the Church of Scotland parish of Cambuslang in 1731 and laboured without much fruit for ten years. When the reports of the revival in New England began to reach him, he made it 'his practice to take some of them (the reports) into the pulpit during worship and to read to his congregation the latest news from overseas.' In the autumn of 1741 one of his congregation reflected: 'hearing a minister (meaning McCulloch) on a fast day, after sermon, read some papers relating to the success of the Gospel abroad; I was greatly affected at the thought that so many were getting good, and I was getting none.' It was at this time that an appeal was made for the publication of a weekly paper.[7]

The appeal must have been successful, for in December 1741 the first religious periodical ever to be published in Scotland appeared. Under the editorship of William McCulloch, *The Weekly History* or 'An Account of the Most Remarkable Particulars relating to the present progress of the Gospel, By the encouragement of the Rev Mr Whitefield, Glasgow' was thus begun. Each eight-page issue contained a compilation of reports, letters, poems and selections from devotional writers. At first it was largely dependent upon material from a similar journal in London *The Weekly History* that had begun earlier in 1741. That situation changed radically, however, when the revival came to Cambuslang itself in February 1742. From there, the work spread rapidly throughout the land and provided more than enough Scottish material for McCulloch's *Weekly History*. The paper ran for exactly fifty two issues before McCulloch discontinued it.

The point for us here is that the Cambuslang revival came to a people who had been given a desire for revival and, most importantly, *the impetus to pray for it*. Thanks in large part to Edwards' crucial early efforts, they had been reading about events elsewhere and were praying earnestly that such things might be done among them. God then used the means of their prayers—and we can never forget that prayer is a means of grace—to grant their request agreeable to His will.

3. The Correspondence of Scottish ministers with Edwards

Although Edwards' *Faithful Narrative* had been reprinted in Scotland in 1737, it was only in 1742 that his reputation as a theologian was established in the country. In that year John M'Laurin of Glasgow and James Robe of Kilsyth, two of the leading evangelical preachers of the Church of Scotland, established correspondence with Edwards. In 1743 this correspondence was extended to William McCulloch of Cambuslang, John Erskine of Edinburgh, John Willison of Dundee and Thomas Gillespie of Carnoch. Although the initiative for the Edwards-Scotland connection came from the Scottish side, Edwards looked on the prospect of corresponding with these Scots ministers as a gift and a privilege. By 1743 he had already received sufficient reports about the Scottish revivals for him to have gained a sense of the spiritual orientation and theological calibre of the men wanting to write to him and he felt genuinely honoured. In 1745 he wrote: 'I esteem my correspondents with you and my other correspondents in Scotland a great honour and privilege and hope that it may be improved for God's glory and my profit.'[8]

Edwards laid out a comprehensive defence of the revivals in a series of works—*The Distinguishing Marks of a Work of the Spirit of God* (1742), *Some Thoughts Concerning the Present Revival of Religion* (1743) and later *Religious Affections* (1746). In addition to pointing out the many precedents for revival in Scripture and church history, one of Edwards' main contributions was to delineate the difference between genuine and counterfeit spiritual experience. Believing these works represented the best presentation of experimental religion available, Edwards' Scottish correspondents freely appropriated them to defend the revivals against their detractors and to safely shepherd the subjects of the revivals.

Of all Edwards' correspondents in Scotland, the most influential would prove to be John Erskine. Edwards had made a deep impression on Erskine through his *Discourses on Various Important Subjects* (1738), and in particular, 'Justification by Faith Alone.'

Erskine published some of his own sermons in 1745 under the title *The People of God Considered as all Righteous*, in which he was at pains to indicate his great debt to Edwards.

Throughout the remaining years of his life, Erskine would spend time, money and much energy promoting Edwards' work. Almost from the moment he began corresponding with Edwards, Erskine sought to enhance, encourage and stimulate the growth and impact of Edwards' writing and publishing ministry. This is nowhere more evident in the flow of books, pamphlets and sermons Erskine sent to Northampton; it is calculated that his contribution could have amounted to a third of Edwards' library. He also contributed a steady supply of information to Edwards regarding the religion, learning and morals on the Continent. When Edwards was dismissed from Northampton, Erskine and the other Scottish correspondents were key sources of support. Money was collected for Edwards and his family, and Erskine even offered him employment in the Church of Scotland.

Erskine also sought to actively promote his works among his fellow Scots. With the aid of M'Laurin, he procured Scottish subscriptions for eighty-eight copies of the first edition of Edwards' *Freedom of the Will*, published in Boston in 1754. Following Edwards' death, Erskine—with the co-operation of the Rev Dr Jonathan Edwards, Jr.—became editor of some of the unpublished manuscripts. The result was the publication in Edinburgh, in 1774, of the series of sermons that Edwards had preached at Northampton in 1739 entitled by Erskine, *A History of the Work of Redemption*. There followed in 1793, *Miscellaneous Observation on Important Theological Subjects* and in 1796, *Remarks on Important Theological*

Controversies, publications which further cemented Edwards' theological legacy in Scotland.

4. The Concert for Prayer

One of the most far-reaching effects of the revivals in Scotland was surely the 'Concert for Prayer.' Edwards explains the origin of this movement thus:

> In October, AD 1744 a number of ministers in Scotland, taking into consideration the state of God's church and of the world of mankind, judged that the providence of God, at such a day, did loudly call such as were concerned for the welfare of Zion, to united extraordinary applications to the God of all grace, suitably acknowledging him as the fountain of all spiritual benefits and blessings of his church, and earnestly praying to him that he would appear in his glory, and favour Zion, and manifest his compassion to the world of mankind, by an abundant effusion of his Holy Spirit on all the churches, and the whole habitable earth, to revive true religion in all parts of Christendom ... and fill the whole earth with his glory.[9]

Among the sponsors were McCulloch, Robe and M'Laurin. John Gillies said of M'Laurin: 'He was the chief contriver and promoter of the concert of prayer.'[10]

The concert of prayer was at first promoted only by personal letters. The next year, they published an account in the *Christian Monthly History for 1745*, No 1. These men pledged themselves to try to persuade others to join with them in this work and to consider the best means of bringing it forward.[11] In 1747 several of the Scottish ministers had subscribed to a printed *Memorial* that invited still more people to unite in prayer. Five hundred copies were sent to New England, and one fell into the hands of Jonathan Edwards. In 1747 Edwards preached a series of sermons in its favour. He then prepared a work for publication entitled, *An Humble Attempt to Promote Explicit Agreement and Visible Union of God's People for the Revival of Religion and Advancement of Christ's Kingdom on Earth, Pursuant to Scripture Promise and Prophecies, Concerning the Last Time* which appeared in print in January 1748. In it, Edwards argued in favour of the Scottish proposal to formalize and extend the Concert of Prayer, involving international agreements to regularly scheduled extraordinary prayers for awakenings, either in societies or privately, on Saturday evenings or Sabbath mornings and on quarterly days of prayer.[12] Much could be said about the effects of this work, but it is at least possible that the Concert of Prayer laid the foundation for the great progress of the gospel in this country in the decades that followed, not to mention the modern missionary movement.

5. The Effect of the Faithful Narrative in England

Edwards' *Faithful Narrative* also had a profound influence in England. We shall consider this influence among each of the three main denominations: the Methodists, the Church of England and the Reformed Baptists.[13]

a. Methodism

The publication of the *Faithful Narrative* in 1737 came at a crucial moment for Methodism. It appeared right around the time of John Wesley's Aldersgate experience and Charles Wesley's 'Pentecostal joy' in 1738, at a point when Methodism was in its infancy. John Wesley's *Journal* for October 9, 1738 contains this entry: 'I set out for Oxford. In walking I read the truly surprising narrative of the conversions lately wrought in and about the town of Northampton, in New England. Surely "this is the Lord's doing and it is marvellous in our eyes.""[14]

Convinced of the importance of Edwards' *Faithful Narrative*, John Wesley produced an abridgement of it that would be among his most popular works. His attraction to Edwards, however, went beyond this one work; he also reprinted *The Distinguishing Marks* (1744), *Some Thoughts Concerning the Present Revival* (1745), *The Life of Brainerd* (1768) and *The Treatise on Religious Affections* (1773). These did much to popularize a certain version of Edwards for a large number of English evangelicals. Wesley's first two abridgments of Edwards were produced as cheap, pocket-sized unbound paperbacks that sold for eight pence. This succeeded in getting Edwards out to the people, yet the figure they served to popularise was one carefully shorn of his Calvinism. Wesley describes Edwards tellingly as one who 'connects together and confirms' all the worst historical examples of Stoicism and Calvinism. In short, Edwards was a fatalist. In the preface to his edition of the *Religious Affections* Wesley summarises his attitude toward the American colonial: 'Out of this dangerous heap, wherein much wholesome food is mixt with much deadly poison, I have selected many remarks and admonitions which may be of great use to the children of God.'[15]

However opposed he was to Edwards' theology, Wesley was yet an admirer of his spirituality, zeal and defence of revivals. He was therefore quite willing to make use of the revival writings, but only after he had purged them of the anti-Arminian message that their author thought was God's point in bringing revival at all.[16] Edwards was thus pressed, violently and ironically, into the service of Wesley's evangelical Arminianism. John Ryland, Sr. pronounced Wesley's version of *The Life of David Brainerd* 'this most partial and mutilated abridgement ... '. Yet even so, there were things about Edwards that Wesley could not, and would not, efface: 'Let every preacher read carefully over *The Life of David Brainerd*,' said Wesley, 'Let us be followers of him as he was of Christ in absolute self-devotion.' For over one hundred years, Wesley's version of Edwards continued to exert a steady influence upon English Methodists.

b. The Church of England

The three men who exerted the greatest influence in shaping evangelicalism within the Church of England in the second half of the eighteenth century all had a high regard for Edwards. They were John Newton (1725–1807), Thomas Scott (1747–1821) and Joseph Milner (1744–1797). Newton, who was a mentor to Scott, claimed in 1762 'Edwards was my favourite author.' In 1778 he gave him 'the laurel for divinity in this century.' When people wrote to Newton on theological problems, he sometimes referred them to one of Edwards' works for an answer. In later life, Newton would modify his view regarding one of them, Edwards' *Freedom of the Will:* 'If I understand it I think it rather establishes fatalism and necessity than Calvinism in the sober sense.'[17] Thomas Scott, however, was more of a theologian and embraced even this aspect of Edwards. Newton once introduced Scott to a group of local Baptists as 'the man who he hoped would prove the Jonathan Edwards of Old England.' Scott claimed an early acquaintance with Edwards, Brainerd and the New England divines. He acknowledged that these writers had instilled in him a concern for the unevangelised several years before there were any organised missionary societies.

c. The Particular Baptists

Perhaps the most significant influence of Edwards was on the Particular Baptists in England. It was Edwards' *Freedom of the Will* that delivered them from hyper-Calvinism and his *Life of Brainerd* and *An Humble Attempt* that gave impetus to the missionary movement.

In order for Edwards to exert this influence, however, his works needed to be made available. Yet there was a time when his manuscripts languished for lack of will to edit and publish them, if not lack of interest generally. It was not until seven years after Edwards' death that his disciple Samuel Hopkins (1721–1830) managed to get his biography *Life and Character of Edwards*, together with eighteen of Edwards' sermons, printed in Boston. The *Two Dissertations* followed shortly afterwards. Hopkins was disappointed with the response and gave up the idea of preparing any more manuscripts for the press.

Unbeknownst to Hopkins, however, some leading Baptists in England were more than pleased with his labours. John Collett Ryland and his son John Ryland Jr. cherished their copy of the first volume of the *Life and Character*. The flyleaf is inscribed 'John Ryland jun 1773—his Book and an inestimable one it is. The Life of the greatest, wisest humblest & holyest of uninspired Men! And 18 of his sermons. If ever I lend it I desire the utmost Care must betaken of it.' Then below this, in another hand, his father wrote: 'J R j having bo't a new one for himself for 2/6d, re-turned this to his Father October 1786 J Ryland sen.'[18] Another ministerial father and son duo, the Reynolds, also shared a heavily-annotated copy of Edward's *Life of Brainerd*.

This access to Edwards' thought would prove critical, for these men were among a number of pastors from the Northamptonshire and the Midlands region who were pre-occupied with the theological and practical implications of high Calvinism. How could it possibly be the duty of the unconverted to believe if they had not the power to do so? In practical terms this meant that many preachers felt restrained in the appeal they could make to a mixed congregation to repent and believe. John Ryland, Sr. represented the view that we should not offer the Gospel indiscriminately from the pulpit, but should only declare a general warrant or provision of salvation in the work of Christ. These men, and the Reformed Baptist movement with them, were thus in grave danger of falling into the *cul-de-sac* of hyper-Calvinism.

In the 1760s and 1770s, however, the younger John Ryland, John Sutcliffe and Andrew Fuller were reading Edwards for themselves and began to see the true implications of his theology. The effects of this exercise are seen in remarks made at Sutcliffe's funeral:

> I cannot say when he became first acquainted with the writings of President Edwards, and other New England divines, but he drank deeply into them ... The consequence was that while he increased in his attachment to the Calvinistic doctrines of human depravity, and of salvation by sovereign and efficacious grace, he rejected as unscriptural, the high, or rather hyper, Calvinistic notions of the Gospel, which went to set aside the obligations of sinners to every thing spiritually good, and the obligations of the Gospel being addressed to them.

The book that had the greatest impact on their thinking was, of course, Edwards' *Freedom of the Will* (1754). To Ryland Jr., Edwards' distinction between moral and natural inability was absolutely crucial. The sinner could be freely invited to respond to the gospel because they were under no natural inability to comply with its terms. It was precisely this argument that unhinged the hyper Calvinism of Ryland Sr. and his circle. Fuller, having wrestled with *The Freedom of the Will*, published *The Gospel Worthy of All Acceptation* in which he demonstrated that there was no contradiction between God's sovereignty in election and the universal obligation on all who hear the Gospel to believe in Christ.

Jonathan Edwards' beneficial influence on eighteenth century Baptists in Britain is almost incapable of exaggeration. Through his narrative of revival no less than his theological writings Edwards provided the foundation for an evangelical Calvinism which stood as a robust alternative to the Wesleyan movement. He produced theological keys which unlocked the closed doors of hyper Calvinism, with no concessions to Arminianism or Antinomianism. He fired the English Particular Baptist imagination with his own involvement with revival and his description of the remarkable missionary endeavours of David Brainerd among the American Indians. What English Baptist yearned for, as their Association letters testify so often, Edwards articulated and exemplified—an evangelical Calvinism that could reach out into all the world with the Gospel of Christ.

Edwards' influence did not end there, however. In 1784, Sutcliff, Ryland and Fuller received a parcel of books from Dr John Erskine of Edinburgh. In the parcel was Jonathan Edward's *Humble Attempt*. That same year, the annual meeting of the Ministers Association at Nottingham passed a resolution organising a 'Concert of Prayer'. The Association agreed to set apart an hour of the evening of the first Monday in every month for social prayer for the success of the Gospel. Fuller's sermon preached on the first occasion of meeting was printed and to it was added, *Persuasives to a General Union in Extraordinary Prayer for the Revival and extent of real Religion.*

John Sutcliff decided to fan the growing interest by reprinting Edward's *Humble Attempt* in 1789.

Beyond the impetus for prayer, Edwards played a decisive role in the incident that is often seen as the beginning of the modern missionary movement. William Carey was present at a ministers' meeting in Northampton in 1786. Towards evening when the public services were over and some were sitting for discussion, John Ryland Sr. invited one of the younger men to propose a subject for discussion. Carey suggested the following motion: 'Whether the command given to the apostles to teach all nations was not obligatory on all succeeding ministers to the end of the world, seeing that the accompanying promise was of equal extent.' The old Mr Ryland's sharp reply reflected the hyper-Calvinist thinking that would have snuffed out foreign missions entirely: 'Young man, sit down, sit down, you are a miserable enthusiast … When God pleases to convert the heathen, He will do it without your aid or mine … certainly nothing can be done before another Pentecost.'[19] Carey, bolstered as he was by Edwards' evangelical Calvinist theology and missionary zeal, was undeterred. In 1792 Carey published *An Enquiry into the Obligations of Christians to use means for the Conversions of the Heathen* and in the same year he preached his memorable sermon from Isaiah 54.2–3, its theme being, 'Expect great things from God; attempt great things for God.' And so began the modern history of foreign missions.

It was Edwards' principles in *Freedom of the Will* that helped to liberate English Calvinism and to make a dynamic theology of mission possible for Calvinists. The greater number of the English-speaking missionaries whose service began in the last decade of the eighteenth century and the first three decades of the nineteenth century had their background in that liberated Calvinism. A good representative of Edwards' indirect influence on missionary work was David Bogue, a Scot who influenced a whole generation of missionaries. Bogue was using Edwards in his teaching, but a generation of LMS missionaries remembered Bogue rather than Edwards.

The Concert of Prayer also had an influence on the state of the churches at the end of the eighteenth century. The Particular Baptists were joined by the Congregationalists and by the Calvinistic and Wesleyan Methodists in Wales. One of first places for revival to break out was in Bala in North Wales at the end of 1791 under the ministry of Thomas Charles (1755–1814). This was followed by extensive outbreaks in Cornwall from 1799.[20]

In the 19th Century

Interest in Edwards' writings waned in the latter part of the 18th century, but made a remarkable recovery in the early part of the 19th century. This recovery would provide the foundation for Edwards' influence in Victorian Britain.

1. The Resurgence in Edwards' Writings

In his *Jonathan Edwards: A New Biography,* the Rev Iain Murray gives us an insight into the influence of Edwards at the beginning of the 19th Century. He writes:

> In Britain the early nineteenth-century resurgence of Edwards' publications not only matched that of North America but far exceeded it. Even John Erskine who died in 1803 could scarcely have anticipated the flood of Edwards' material to appear in British bookshops in the next forty years. An eight volume edition of his *Collected Works* was published at Leeds, Yorkshire

1806–11, soon to be improved in a London edition of 1817, with two supplementary volumes of posthumous material added at Edinburgh in 1847. Undeterred by this edition already in print, another British publisher, rightly foreseeing the problems of the permanent marketing of such a large set succeeded in packing more content than in the original eight volumes into a two-volume edition of the Edwards' *Works* which came out in 1834. This edition was to go through ten printings by 1865 and is the one which remains in print today. Perhaps the most remarkable thing about this boom in the publication of Edwards' material is the fact that despite the availability of his collected *Works* printings and reprintings of his individual books multiplied simultaneously.[21]

Publishing decisions tend to be business decisions, and the multiplicity of collected editions and simultaneous individual volumes point to the fixture that Edwards had become in 1820s and 1830s Britain. By that time, the general Christian public had become his readers.

2. The Resurgence in Scotland

John Erskine, the great promoter of Edwards' writings in Scotland, died in 1803. In that same year Thomas Chalmers, who was destined to be his successor as leader of the evangelicals in the Church of Scotland, was inducted to Kilmany, Fife. Chalmers was educated at St Andrews University where the Professor of Divinity, although not aligned with the evangelicals, acknowledged a heavy debt to Edwards. Although Chalmers was thus taught to respect Edwards, it was only after his subsequent conversion around 1810 or 1811 that he became a disciple of the New England divine. After exercising a fruitful ministry in Glasgow, he became a Professor of Divinity and instilled the worth of Edwards into his students. He said 'My theology is that of Jonathan Edwards,' and 'There is no European Divine to whom I make such frequent appeals in my classrooms as I do to Edwards.'[22]

Chalmers' influence on his students is best seen in Robert Murray M'Cheyne. M'Cheyne records in his Diary for 22 June, 1832 the simple note: 'Bought Edwards' Works.' Three days later: 'Then after reading a little of Edwards' works: Oh that heart and understanding may grow together, like brother and sister, leaning on one another.' On 27 June he writes: 'Life of Brainerd. Most wonderful man! ... I cannot express what I think when I think of thee. Tonight more set upon missionary enterprise than ever', and a day later: 'Oh for Brainerd's humility and sin-loathing dispositions.'[23] Again, 'How feeble does my spark of Christianity appear beside such a sun! But even his was a borrowed light, and the same source is still open to enlighten me.' The brothers Andrew and Horatius Bonar were also avid readers of Edwards, and in 1880, the aged Andrew visited Northampton and was 'much stirred up' by the memories it evoked.

In the 20th Century

In the first half of the 20th century, Edwards was remembered mainly as a philosopher and eminent eighteenth-century thinker. Very few voices were to be heard in defence of Edwards as a theologian for the contemporary church of that day; the prevailing opinion was that his dogma virtually prohibited any further usefulness for his writings. All that would change, however, with the recovery of the Reformed faith that came later in the 20th Century. Edwards' writings were themselves one of the chief instruments used by God to bring about this movement, primarily through the receptive hands of A. W. Pink and D. M. Lloyd-Jones, and later, through the Banner of Truth Trust.

1. A. W. Pink

The very first dawning of a change in the course of the century can be traced back to the writings of A. W. Pink (1886–1952). Soon after moving to the United States in 1910, he became aware of some of the writings of Jonathan Edwards. In the summer of 1918, he was attempting to read through all four volumes of Edwards' *Works* (1881 edition) and in a 1936 letter he mentions that 'they were very searching and they were much blest to me almost 25 years ago. His *Religious Affections* is one of his best.'[24] It is no coincidence that Pink wrote his best selling title, *The Sovereignty of God*, in that same year of 1918. From that time until now, this book has been used to bring untold numbers of students and ministers to a belief in the doctrines of grace. Pink also used extracts from Edwards in his influential *Studies in the Scriptures*, and recommended him to readers who were asking for guidance on which authors to study.

2. D. M. Lloyd-Jones

Even more significant for the 20th Century revival of the Reformed faith, however, was Edwards' influence on Dr D. M. Lloyd-Jones. This influence, however, initially came via Pink. 'The Doctor' began to read Pink's *Studies in the Scriptures* in 1942. Giving advice to young Paul Tucker, he said: 'Don't waste time reading Barth and Brunner. You will get nothing from them to aid your preaching. Read Pink.'[25] Then there was that experience that the Doctor had under an attack of Satan in 1949. He recalls that 'when his eye caught just a word in a sermon of Pink's which lay open beside his bed—the word was "glory" and instantly, like a blaze of light' he felt the very glory of God surrounded him.[26]

After this very significant yet indirect contact through Pink, Dr Lloyd-Jones came to read Edwards for himself in 1927. Lloyd-Jones had read Arthur Cushman McGiffert's *Protestant Thought Before Kant* (1911), in which McGiffert writes 'his [Edwards'] practical interest throughout was to humble man and to convince him of his total depravity and absolute bondage to sin, and so startle out of his easy indifference and complacent self-confidence.' These words alerted Dr Lloyd-Jones to the existence of the *Works of Edwards*. In 1927 while waiting for a train connection in Cardiff he called at John Evans bookshop and relates what happened: 'There, down on my knees in my overcoat in a corner of the shop, I found the two volume 1834 edition of Edwards which I bought for five shillings. I devoured these volumes and literally just read and read them. It is certainly true they helped me more than anything else.'[27] Later he said: 'I was like the man in our Lord's parable who found a pearl of great price. Their influence upon me I cannot put into words.'

In 1942, Lloyd-Jones gave an address to the Crusader Union when he exhorted his audience: 'I would commend to you a very thorough study of that great American divine, Jonathan Edwards. It was a great revelation to me to discover that a man who preached in the way he did could be honoured of God as he was, and could have such great results in his ministry.'[28] Many years later at the Westminster Conference in 1976, Lloyd-Jones confessed that evaluating Edwards was 'one of the most difficult tasks I have ever attempted.' He found the theme almost impossible. 'I am afraid', he told his listeners, 'and I say it with much regret, that I have to put him ahead even of Daniel Rowland and George Whitefield. Indeed I am tempted, perhaps foolishly, to compare the Puritans to the Alps, Luther and Calvin to the Himalayas and Jonathan

Edwards to Everest! He has always seemed to me to be the man most like the apostle Paul.'[29]

Edwards was for Dr Lloyd-Jones 'pre-eminently the theologian of Revival, the theologian of experience, or as some have put it "the theologian of the heart."' Indeed he could say that 'no man knew more of the workings of the human, regenerate and unregenerate than Jonathan Edwards.' Later he insisted: 'If you want to know anything about true revival, Edwards is the man to consult. His knowledge of the human heart, and the psychology of human nature, is quite incomparable.'[30]

3. Iain H. Murray and the Banner of Truth

A further move towards the recovery of the writings of Edwards came through Iain Murray at the time he was a student at Durham University. He was given a copy of the two-volume British edition of *The Works of Jonathan Edwards* (then a rarity in the second hand market) from the daughter of a retired Methodist minister, Rev James Shiphardson, in Durham City. Iain later wrote in his biography of Jonathan Edwards published in 1986, 'they remain treasured.'[31] When the Banner of Truth Trust commenced its publishing work in 1957, with Lloyd-Jones' Westminster Chapel as it initial 'warehouse', three volumes of the *Select Works of Jonathan Edwards* were among its first publications. In 1974, the Banner of Truth Trust reprinted the 1834 'rare' two volume set of the *Works of Jonathan Edwards* and a new generation was introduced to his writings. In the first ten years of the Trust, between eight and nine thousand sets were sold.

In 1957, the same year that the Trust was formed, but entirely independent of each other, Yale University Press issued the first of twenty-six volumes of a new critical edition of Edwards' Works. This project would span the next half-century and would prompt an almost unprecedented flood of scholarly interest in Edwards.

Assessment

In conclusion, here are six summary assessments of Edwards' influence for us to consider in our own day.

1. We see the impact that one God-centred life and ministry can have on the increase of the kingdom of God across nations and through centuries. It was the 'blood-earnestness,' as Chalmers called it, of Edwards' life that made it count for so much over three centuries and in many lands.

2. Had Edwards had not occupied the role of the foremost theologian in the Christianity which was revived in the 18th century, the British Church might have been estranged from the faith of the Reformers and Puritans. Wesley's Methodism threatened to do just that, but Edwards played a major role in conserving Reformed orthodoxy. This is because, in his own day, Edwards sought not to innovate but mainly to reassert the theology of Owen, Turretin, Van Maastrict and the Westminster Divines in the face of 'fashionable divinity.'

3. Edwards recognised that what was needed in his day was preaching, revival and missionary endeavour. It was a day for prayer and action, for seizing the opportunities offered by the new horizons of an expanding world. His God-entranced world view was encouraged by what he heard from England and Scotland. His *Humble Attempt* was instrumental in furthering revival and giving impetus to the missionary movement. His Post-millennial view gave hope and expectation to the Church. He wrote the following to one of his Scottish correspondents:

> I should have more hope for the union, fervency and unfailing
> constancy of the prayers of God's people, with respect to the
> religious affairs of the present day, than anything else; more than
> from the preaching and writing of the ablest and best friends
> to the work of God's Spirit.[32]

4. Edwards' influence was, paradoxically, that of a man *who
did not seek influence* but rather put faithfulness to God
before every other consideration. During the 'Communion
controversy' in Northampton, Solomon Williams made a
case for retaining the *status quo* over qualifications for taking
communion based on expediency. He warned that Edwards'
views would lead to a small, uninfluential church. Edwards
replied that it was lack of holiness, not lack of numbers, which
hindered the advance of the church. He was content to leave
influence and results entirely to God. He knew that 'success'
is not to be judged in the short-term. The Christian's business
is to honour God, and in His own time God will honour His
truth and those who are faithful to it.[33]

5. Edwards' *Life of David Brainerd* did much to prompt
prayer and action and missionary endeavour in Britain and
worldwide. Brainerd came into Edwards' life unplanned, yet
in the providence of God it would prove to be among the
most momentous of meetings. After Brainerd's death Edwards
undertook the preparation of his journal for printing as a
labour of love. He wanted Brainerd to be read as an example
of a real Christian, showing what the power of godliness and
'vital religion' truly is. In an Appendix he said: 'There is much
in the preceding account to excite and encourage God's people
to earnest prayers and endeavours for the advancement and
enlargement of the kingdom of Christ in the world.' The

missionaries who testify to Edwards' influence include Francis Ashbury, Thomas Coke, William Carey, Henry Martyn, Robert Morrison, Samuel Mills, Frederick Schwartz, David Livingstone and Jim Elliot.

6. As faith in the historic, Protestant Christianity revived, so did an appreciation of the doctrinal and spiritual values which Edwards represented. The propensity of Edwards' *Works* to regain attention and to re-assert their message is shown from a study of history. More than once, his writings have been judged obsolete, only to re-appear with renewed power and significance. The discovery of Edwards' writings has produced significant turning points in the development of men of God who, in turn, have made an impact on their own generation for good.

The Means of Grace

7. Edwards on the Divinity, Necessity and Power of the Word of God in the World

Douglas Sweeney

Introduction

Edwards believed deep in his bones that the Bible was divine. For that reason, he was convinced it was only those with 'the mind of Christ' (1 Corinthians 2:16) who could truly understand the scope and teaching of Scripture. It was the Holy Spirit of God who inspired the 'pen-men' who wrote the Bible in the first place, it is the Holy Spirit who unites believers to the eternal Word of God, and it is the Spirit who can alone enable Christians to plumb 'the deep things of God' (1 Corinthians 2:10) through supernatural illumination.

Edwards was well aware that this concept was no longer in vogue among the intellectual elite. There were many in his day who were teaching that the Bible should be treated like 'any other book,' the text shorn of any assumption of divinity and the exegete standing in no need of divine assistance. Edwards read such writers—men whom he could only assume were 'natural' or unregenerate men (1 Corinthians 2:14)—avidly, not merely to stay current on 'corrupt' thought but actually to consult them on their insights into holy writ. Edwards could use them despite the fact that he, as with orthodox Christians since the time of the apostles, was convinced that they were fundamentally wrong about the nature of the Bible.

In what follows, I present the fruit of Edwards' thought and preaching on the character of Scripture based on years of careful gleaning through the whole of Edwards' corpus. Inasmuch as Edwards never actually published anything on the subject, let alone a full-scale treatise on it, I have had to organize his thoughts on Scripture for him loosely. I ask for your indulgence as I air what Edwards said in a rather non-traditional way (for a more systematic treatment on the subject of revelation, I would commend Bill Schweitzer's *God is a Communicative Being*).[1] But to those who listen as I limn for you what Edwards said of the nature of the Bible and the qualities requisite to interpreting it well, I can promise edification. I will focus on Edwards' conviction that the Bible is from God, and therefore, that the Spirit-filled believer has a cognitive advantage when it comes to understanding Scripture. I conclude with some practical exhortation.

'The Emanation of His Glory'

Edwards often spoke of Scripture as the very 'Word of God,' an 'Emanation of his Glory.' Not surprisingly (considering his thoroughgoing trinitarianism) he also wrote of Scripture as the precious 'word of Christ,' or 'the epistle of Christ that he has written to us.' The Bible bears 'the voice of God' to us by virtue of the Spirit. It evokes in us 'a strange and unaccountable kind of enchantment.' God caters to our weakness when He speaks to us in Scripture. He condescends to finitude, accommodating ignorance—but *speaks* nonetheless, for His glory and our good. Thus the Bible is 'a perfect rule' and 'guide to true happiness.' It functions, when appropriated in faith and earnest practice, as an essential 'word of life,' a 'sweet, ... life-giving word.'[2]

Edwards view of biblical inspiration might strike some today as being especially high, yet it was commonplace among the Christians of his day. He taught that God 'indited' the Scriptures (i.e. proclaimed, pronounced, or composed them) through the Bible's human authors and thus 'dictated' to ministers the things they are to preach.[3] He followed Mastricht's reading of 2 Timothy 3:16 ('All scripture is given by inspiration of God,' etc.), which articulated a traditional Protestant view.[4] He quoted Owen on the manner in which the canon was inspired (in a note on the pattern of the Temple given to David):

> The Spirit of God acted and guided the prophets 'as to the very organs of their bodies, whereby they expressed the revelation which they had received by inspiration from him. They spake as they were acted by the Holy Ghost [2 Peter 1:21] .... So when David had received the pattern of the temple, and the manner of the whole worship of God therein by the Spirit, he says, 'All this the Lord made me understand in writing by his hand upon me, even all the work of this pattern' [1 Chronicles 28:19]. The Spirit of God not only revealed it unto him, but so guided him in writing of it down, as that he might understand the mind of God out of what himself had written; or he gave it him so plainly and evidently, as if every particular had been expressed in writing by the finger of God.[5]

Many other Reformed writers had a similar view of the matter.

All allowed that God inspired different genres differently, using multiple human authors in a variety of settings with a diversity of pedigrees, temperaments, and styles.

In the words of William Ames, written in a text used by Edwards while at Yale,

> divine inspiration was present among those [biblical] writers in different ways. Some things were altogether unknown to the writer in advance, as appears in the history of past creation, or in the foretelling of things to come. But some things were previously known to the writer, as appears in the history of Christ written by the apostles. Some things were known by a natural knowledge and some by a supernatural. In those things that were hidden and unknown, divine inspiration was at work by itself. In those things which were known, or where the knowledge was obtained by ordinary means, there was added the writers' devout zeal so that (God assisting them) they might not err in writing.[6]

These Reformed theologians rarely verged on a passive view of Scriptural dictation, as if God had dropped the Bible from the blue on golden plates. But neither did they focus on the personal contributions of the Bible's human authors to the degree that most late-modern biblical scholars would. In the main they taught, in Edwards' words, that God chose His penmen, gave them ears to hear Him speaking and 'extraordinary gifts' for relaying His Word to others, and revealed in and through them 'an infallible rule of faith and works and manners to the church,' a 'sure rule which if we follow we cannot err.'[7]

'The Gospel ... Don't Go Abroad a Begging for Its Evidence'

As one would assume given his lofty view of biblical inspiration, Edwards sided with thinkers like Calvin who said that Scripture is self-authenticated (αὐτόπιστον), full of inherent proof of its divine source and power. He affirmed the famed defense of the Puritans' 'plaine translation' of the Psalter in the Massachusetts *Bay Psalm Book* (1640): 'Gods Altar needs not our pollishings.' He said as much himself scores of times throughout his life. For as he put the matter briefly in his book, *Religious Affections* (1746), 'The gospel of the blessed God don't go abroad a begging for its evidence, so much as some think; it has its highest and most proper evidence in itself.'[8]

He attributed the faith of true believers in the Word to what he called 'intrinsic signatures of divinity' within it. 'They see that excellency and ... image of God in the Word,' he attested, 'that constrains the mind to assent to it and embrace it as true and divine.' Or morphing sensory metaphors, the Lord's people 'hear God speak' amid the pages of the Bible. They recognize His voice. To them, 'he speaks like a God. His speech is ... excellent, holy, wise, awful and gracious,' Edwards claimed. He compared this recognition of the voice of God in Scripture to the glimpse that Peter got of Jesus' glory in the gospels on the Mount of Transfiguration. 'Peter, when he saw this, his mind was strongly carried to believe, and he was sure that Christ was a divine and holy person without sitting down to reason about it; he was convinced and assured at once irresistibly, and was as it were intuitively certain.' Likewise, saints sense the presence and glory of God within His Word. It is a 'lamp' that shines a heavenly light of glory round about them. Or as Jeremiah prophesied so many years ago (Jeremiah 23:29), it is a 'fire' and a 'hammer' that 'dissolves the Rocky Hearts of the chil[dren] of men.'⁹

In keeping with tradition, Edwards touted both 'external' and 'internal' proofs of the Bible's credibility. 'God is not wont to speak to men,' he told his flock, without providing us 'sufficient means to know' that He is speaking. 'He has given the world great evidence that [Scripture] ... is his word. [Both] external [and] internal' evidence abounds. There are 'all the kinds of evidence' for Scripture, he averred, 'it is possible a revelation should have: there are all kinds of internal evidences from the majesty, holiness, sublimity, harmony, etc.; and there are all kinds of external evidences, prophecy and miracles' confirmed outside the canon. Nevertheless, he deemed the Bible's inner testimony to be the decisive factor for most people. Scripture is for everyone, he taught, and the laity have little time to trudge through the evidence that lies beyond its bounds. Most are simply 'not capable of any certain or effectual conviction of the divine authority of the Scriptures, by such arguments as learned men make use of,' he advised. Common people need the Spirit's help discerning the Word of God—and this is part of what He grants to those who turn to Him in faith. 'The child of God doth ... see and feel the truth of divine things,' he said. The saints 'can feel such a power and kind of omnipotency in Christianity, and taste such a sweetness, and see such wisdom, such an excellent harmony in the gospel, as carry their own light with them, and powerfully do enforce and conquer the assent and necessitates their minds to receive it as proceeding from God, and as the certain truth.'¹⁰

Whether or not we taste this sweetness, see this wisdom and believe, Edwards taught that Holy Scripture always wins its way in the world, ever glorifies the Lord by vindicating truth and justice. 'God's word always comes as [a] conqueror,' he claimed: 'those ... not conquered by conversion shall be conquered by destruction and the execution of its threatenings.' He cautioned congregations in this manner time and again, threatening everyone who listened with the power of the Word—and giving enemies a reason to call him obstinate and proud. While still in his late-twenties he forewarned his wary flock, 'When God sends his messengers to preach his word, his word shall not be in vain .... God will obtain his end, let men treat his word how they will.' Three years later he reminded them, if Scripture 'don't profit [you] it shall hurt. It will be either food or poison. It shall not return ... void.' Shortly after George Whitefield swept through town the first time (October 1740), bringing the Great Awakening with him, Edwards tried to get his people to 'improve' or benefit from they heard. 'The word of God will take hold of all that hear it,' he assured them, whether in 'one way or another .... Every part of the message that God sends shall be effectual.' To 'the elect,' Word and Spirit yield 'eternal salvation, [to] reprobates, everlasting condemnation.'[11]

'They Tremble at God's Word'

Thus, 'truly religious persons,' those who appreciate the power and authority of Scripture, often 'tremble at God's word' [Isaiah 66:2,5]. They find it 'piercing, awful, and tremendous,' Edwards noted, and their hearts melt before it. 'The word in its powerful efficacy,' in mortifying sin and converting people to Christ, 'does ...cut the soul asunder.' So at Psalm 29:3 ('the God of glory thundereth'), Edwards wrote in the 'Blank Bible': 'Lightning and thunder is a very lively image of the word of God .... 'Tis exceeding quick, and exceeding piercing, and powerful to break in pieces, and scorch, and dissolve, and is full of majesty.' As he put this to his congregation in 1749,

the 'Hammer of the Law subdues the Heart with … Compulsion.
[B]ut the fire of the Gospel sweetly subdues …. [It] kindles that
Holy Flame in the soul that never shall go out.'[12]

'Trembling at the Word' could stem either from fear or from
sweet delight in the things of God. And while the former cause
prevailed among the anxious and oppressed, the latter shot
adrenaline through the saints. Edwards explained, revelation 'is a
sweet sort of knowledge' to the Christian. 'He loves to view and
behold the things of … God; they are to him the most pleasing
and beautiful objects in the world. He can never satisfy his eyes
with looking on them, because he beholds them as certain truths
and as things of all the most excellent.' Scripture is sublime to him.
He cannot get his fill. Because, as Edwards preached at Yale at
the apex of the Awakening, when God is at work in the world He
effects esteem for the Word. In an effort to help students identify
the work of God amid the fervor of revival and distinguish it from
Satan's counterfeit spirituality, Edwards encouraged listeners to
ground spiritual passion on the contents of the Bible: 'That spirit
that operates in such a manner, as to cause in men a greater regard
to the Holy Scriptures, and establishes them more in their truth
and divinity, is certainly the Spirit of God,' he assured them.[13]

In Edwards' estimation, Preachers should do all they can to
arouse such godly tremors in the saints. Indeed, 'the impressing
divine things on the hearts and affections of men' is one of the
main reasons God ordained the preaching of the Word. 'And
therefore,' Edwards reasoned, 'it don't answer [that] aim … merely
for men to have good commentaries … and other good books of
divinity.' While these may provide 'a good doctrinal or speculative
understanding' of the Bible, 'yet they have not an equal tendency

to impress [it] on men's hearts and affections.' Edwards granted that recalling 'what was heard in a sermon is oftentimes very profitable,' but claimed that 'for the most part, remembrance is from an impression the words made on the heart,' and that 'memory profits' people insofar 'as it renews and increases that impression.' Thus ministers should not shy away from poignant preaching. It is better for their people than the reading of good books. And it conveys a better feeling for the great things of God 'than a moderate, dull, indifferent way of speaking.'

An appearance of

> ... affection and earnestness in the manner of delivery, if it be very great indeed, yet if it be agreeable to the nature of the subject, and ben't beyond a proportion to its importance and worthiness of affection, and there be no appearance of its being feigned or forced, has so much the greater tendency to beget true ideas or apprehensions in the minds of the hearers, of the subject spoken of, and so to enlighten the understanding .... I should think myself in the way of my duty to raise the affections of my hearers as high as possibly I can, provided that they are affected with nothing but truth, and with affections that are not disagreeable to the nature of what they are affected with.

Mere cognition is deficient when it comes to holy writ. Until the Word descends deep into the heart of the believer, bearing the passion fruit of love, it will not be understood. 'Was there ever an age wherein strength and penetration of reason, extent of learning, exactness of distinction, correctness of style, and clearness of expression, did so abound?,' Edwards queried his enlightened, modern readers. 'And yet was there ever an age wherein there has been so little sense of the evil of sin, so little love to God, heavenly-mindedness, and holiness of life, among the professors of the true religion? Our people don't so much need to have their heads stored, as to have their hearts touched,' he concluded famously, 'and they stand in the greatest need of that sort of preaching that has the greatest tendency to do this.'[14]

Edwards testified frequently that Word and Spirit do in fact enthrall the twice born. 'Persons after their conversion often speak of things of religion as seeming new to them,' he noted in his *Faithful Narrative* (1737). 'It seems to them they never heard preaching before; that the Bible is a new book: they find there new chapters, new psalms, new histories, because they see them in a new light.' He alleged, furthermore, that 'all true Christians' have a 'conviction of the ... the things of the gospel.' And he offered several examples in his writings on revival and regenerate spirituality. His own zeal for Scripture blossomed after his conversion. His congregation felt a yearning for the Bible as revival blazed in 1735: 'While God was so remarkably present amongst us by his Spirit, there was no book so delighted in as the Bible,' Edwards wrote. He recounted to a clergy friend in Boston, Benjamin Colman, during the same season of grace, 'Their esteem of the holy Scriptures is exceedingly increased .... There have been some instances of persons that by only an accidental sight of the Bible, have been as much moved ... as a lover by the sight of his sweetheart.' Further, his encomium to David Brainerd's passion for the Bible stood for decades as a standard of Edwardsean biblicism. Five days before he died, Brainerd lay in bed in Edwards' house, girding himself for glory. 'In the evening, as one came into the room with a Bible in her hand, he expressed himself thus; "Oh, that dear book! that lovely book! I shall soon see it opened! The mysteries that are in it, and the mysteries of God's Providence, will be all unfolded!"'[15]

'Had It Not Been for Revelation'

Edwards taught that sacred Scripture is essential to our flourishing, even in public life. He accentuated the need for both reason and revelation, for knowing both 'what reason and Scripture declare' on relevant matters. He thought the 'doctrines of Christianity' themselves 'most rational, exceeding congruous to ... natural reason.'[16] Moreover, he affirmed the Catholic dictum that to understand the world and its relationship to God we need the 'book of nature' as well as the 'book of Scripture.' However, he prioritized the Bible over other sources of knowledge as the authoritative interpretive guide. As he argued in *Distinguishing Marks of a Work of the Spirit of God* (1741), 'all that is visible to the eye is unintelligible and vain, without the Word of God to instruct and guide the mind.' And as he preached in a sermon on this theme a few years earlier,

> We make a distinction between the things that we know by reason, and things we know by revelation. But alas we scarce know what we say: we know not what we should have known ... had it not been for revelation .... Many of the principles of morality and religion that we have always been brought up in the knowledge of, appear so rational that we are ready to think we could have found 'em out by our own natural reason .... [But] all the learning, yea, all the common civility that there is in the world, seems to be either directly or indirectly from revelation, whether men are sensible of it or no .... Everything that is good and useful in this fallen world, is from supernatural help.[17]

This became a central theme in his response to English deists. In opposition to their call for a religion of nature and reason, Edwards insisted on the need of supernatural revelation—even for the maintenance of a healthy civic virtue.

We have already seen that Edwards firmly believed that God has spoken in the Bible. It is 'unreasonable,' in fact, he said, 'to suppose that ... there should be a God, an intelligent voluntary being, that has so much concern with [us], and with whom we have infinitely more concern than with any other being, and yet that he should never speak.' Further, if God has really divulged Himself in writing in the Bible, we should honor holy Scripture as 'the fountain whence all knowledge in divinity must be derived.'[18] We should also grant it pride of place in secular conversation on the world and our place within it—topics treated by the deists and other non-traditional thinkers under 'natural religion.' Edwards argued in his 'Miscellanies' in 1728, 'were it not for divine revelation, I am persuaded that there is no one doctrine of that which we call natural religion [but] would, notwithstanding all philosophy and learning, forever be involved in darkness, doubts, endless disputes and dreadful confusion.' He repeated this conviction in his notes on the 'Importance of Doctrines & of Mysteries in Religion.' Many moderns 'deceive themselves thro' the Ambiguity or Equivocal use of the word REASON,' he wrote. 'They argue as tho we must make our Reason the highest Rule to Judge of all things[,] even the doctrines of Revelation.' But 'this way of Rejecting every thing but what we can first see to be agreeable to our Reason Tends by degrees to bring every Thing relating not only to revealed Religion but even natural Religion into doubt[,] to make all appear with Dim Evidence like a shadow or the Ideas of a Dream till they are all neglected as worthy of no Regard.' He also preached about this notion to the people of Northampton in a sermon later printed on the history of redemption. Our reason tells us much about the work of God in the world, he said, but 'nothing else ... informs us what [the] scheme and design of God in his works is but only the holy Scriptures.'[19]

Supernatural revelation and the spiritual light it offered were, for Edwards, essential for clarifying the nature of reality. It was not that the world could not be known without the Bible, or that Scripture was a textbook in history or natural science. Rather, for Edwards, Word and Spirit shone a light on worldly wisdom, rendering knowledge more real, sure, even beautiful than before. In a remarkable notebook entry dating from 1729, he depicted this so vividly that I quote him here at length:

> A mind not spiritually enlightened [by means of the Bible and God's Spirit] beholds spiritual things faintly, like fainting, fading shadows that make no lively impression on his mind, like a man that beholds the trees and things abroad in the night: the ideas ben't strong and lively, and [are] very faint; and therefore he has but a little notion of the beauty of the face of the earth. But when the light comes to shine upon them, then the ideas appear with strength and distinctness; and he has that sense of the beauty of the trees and fields given him in a moment, which he would not have obtained by going about amongst them in the dark in a long time. A man that sets himself to reason without divine light is like a man that goes into the dark into a garden full of the most beautiful plants, and most artfully ordered, and compares things together by going from one thing to another, to feel of them and to measure the distances; but he that sees by divine light is like a man that views the garden when the sun shines upon it. There is ... a light cast upon the ideas of spiritual things in the mind of the believer, which makes them appear clear and real, which before were but faint, obscure representations.[20]

Edwards said as much in churches dozens of times throughout his life, heralding special revelation and the clarity it yielded as a brilliant, heavenly light, which illuminated for saints a world more vivid, polydimensional, and brimming with vitality than anything they had ever known before. He told his people revelation works 'in the hearts of those' who 'truly entertain it' like 'a light that shines in a dark place.' The 'spiritual understanding' it provided, furthermore, was 'like a gleam of light that breaks in upon the soul through a gloomy darkness. Of all the similitudes,' in fact, employed in Scripture 'to describe to us this spiritual understanding, light is that which doth most fully represent it and is oftenest used.'[21]

Edwards drafted scores of pages on this 'supernatural light,' as well as its role in the production of a 'spiritual understanding,' stating that spiritual light from Scripture constitutes a greater blessing 'than any other privilege that ever God bestowed.' Readers who receive this light and keep it 'bring forth Christ' in their hearts; Christ is truly 'formed in them'; they are bonded through the Word with the living Word of God; and this union is 'more blessed' than 'to have Christ' within one's 'arms, or at the breast, as the virgin Mary had.' Spiritual knowledge even grants what Edwards spoke of in a sermon as 'an earnest' or 'the dawnings' of the beatific vision. It enables the people of God to share in the very life of God (2 Peter 1:4). For the assistance in the souls of those who have this special blessing 'is not only from the Spirit, but it also partakes of the nature of that Spirit.'[22]

'Spiritual Understanding ... Denied to the Unregenerate'

The best posture for disciples who would understand the Bible, argued Edwards, was 'to sit at Jesus' feet.' That is to say, they should 'go to him whose Word it is and beg of him to teach,' for 'he has reserved to himself this work of enlightening the mind with spiritual knowledge, and there is no other can do it; there is none teaches like God.' With Mary of Bethany in the gospels, the sister of Lazarus and Martha—who took 'a pound of ointment of spikenard, very costly, and anointed the feet of Jesus, and wiped his feet with her hair' (John 12:3)—they should be careful not to distract themselves with '[trouble] about many things.' Rather, as Jesus said to Martha, only 'one thing is needful: and Mary hath chosen that good part' (Luke 10:41–42), for she had clung to Christ and hung on His every word. Similarly, we should cling to every word that comes from the mouth of God, for 'the word of God is the great means of our eternal good …. 'tis the most necessary means, and without which our souls must famish.' It is like 'MILK,' Edwards mused, flowing 'from the breasts of the church.' It is like 'rain' for which God's people have 'a great and earnest thirsting.'23

Those who avoid this humble posture never really understand the true spirit of the Bible. Unconverted, proud people miss the Spirit's main points. As Edwards cautioned in a talk on Jeremiah 8:8 ('the pen of the scribes is in vain'), 'The Bible is all in vain to Them That continue in sin.' Or as he said when treating passages like 1 Corinthians 2 and the parable of the sower, 'There is a spiritual understanding of divine things, which all natural and unregenerate men are destitute of.'

Natural men and hypocrites may boast of an extensive understanding, and may have natural abilities in a much greater strength than a godly man, and may abound in acquired knowledge, and may be able to reason with great strength about the holy Scriptures and the doctrines of religion; but yet he [*sic*] does not, nor can he, understand the Word of God …. Ungodly men are so far from understanding the Word of God, that those things that are the main things of revelation, the principal things of the gospel

and what are the very quintessence and end of all, are what they
have no notion at all of and which the godly only apprehend; as
particularly, such things as these: the glory of God, the excellency
and fullness of Jesus Christ, the nature of holiness, the reason and
foundation of duty. These things are the very main things of the
Scripture. They are the greatest doctrines of God's Word, and they
are the very end of revelation and its life and soul; and yet they are
such as natural men have no idea or apprehension of.

Edwards granted that God lavished 'common grace' and
'illuminations' on the unconverted scholar. But He gave the Holy
Spirit to the godly reader of Scripture and thus tendered her a
cognitive advantage. A regenerate person 'sees things in a new
appearance, in quite another view, than ever he saw before: ... he
sees the wonderfulness of God's designs and a harmony in all his
ways, a harmony, excellency and wondrousness in his Word: he
sees these things by an eye of faith, and by a new light that was
never before let into his mind.' Further, 'spiritual knowledge' grows
by the 'practice of virtue and holiness,' a practice not pursued by
those too proud to serve the Lord. 'For we cannot have the idea [of
anything in the mind, whether physical or spiritual] without the
adapted disposition of mind, and the more suitable the disposition
the more clear and intense the idea; but the more we practice, the
more is the disposition increased.'[24]

Others had said as much before, though not always with the same
psychological apparatus. Such epistemological claims date from
the age of the ancient church and had been echoed in Edwards'
favorite, early modern Protestant sources. Even the Westminster
divines confessed 'the inward illumination of the Spirit of God
to be necessary for the saving understanding of such things as are

revealed in the Word.'[25] Yet after the rise of higher criticism—and especially in light of Spinoza's opposition to the notion that the Spirit gave believers needed help interpreting Scripture—Edwards felt a burden to proclaim this doctrine boldly and he did so with greater specificity than most. 'The believer' has 'such a sight and such a knowledge of things that, ever since [conversion], he [has become] another man,' Edwards preached. 'The knowledge that he has is so substantial, so inward, and so affecting, that it has quite transformed the soul and ... changed his ... innermost principles.' Twenty years later he repeated this assertion in his opus on the *Affections*: 'a spiritual taste of soul, mightily helps the soul, in its reasonings on the Word of God, and in judging of the true meaning of its rules; as it removes the prejudices of a depraved appetite, and naturally leads the thoughts in the right channel, casts a light on the Word of God, and causes the true meaning, most naturally to come to mind.'[26]

Edwards gleaned from Locke's *Essay Concerning Human Understanding* (7th ed., 1716) to explain this cognitive change—or at least he made use of idealist understandings of the way we come to know things and combined them with the language of sensationalist psychology. (He was neither a strict empiricist nor a thoroughgoing rationalist and, though he read the *Essay*, he did not usually cite it when developing this theme.) As he argued in the *Affections*, 'the passing of a right judgment on things, depends on an having a right apprehension or idea of things' in the mind; and, regrettably, unconverted sinners lack a 'sense' of divine things. He expanded on this notion in his 'Miscellanies' notebooks: 'sinners must be destitute even of the ideas of many spiritual and heavenly things and of divine excellencies, because they don't experience them. It's impossible for them so much as to have the idea of faith, trust in

God, holy resignation, divine love, Christian charity; because their mind is not possessed of those things.' Edwards believed that this was 'why the things of the gospel seem ... so tasteless and insipid to the natural man. They are a parcel of words to which they in their own minds have no correspondent ideas; 'tis like a strange language or a dead letter, that is, sounds and letters without any signification.' And he preached about this doctrine using Locke's famed description of direct and reflex knowledge:

. There is a direct knowledge, and there is a reflex knowledge. The direct knowledge is the knowledge the Christian hath of divine things, without himself, of the truth and excellency of the things of the gospel. The reflex knowledge is that which he obtains by reflecting and looking inward upon his own heart, and seeing the operations and actings of that, and the workings of the Spirit of God therein. By this reflection, the Christian obtains to know what regeneration is; and what are those actings of the Spirit of God which are so frequently spoken of in Scripture; and the whole applicatory part of religion, which is one half of divinity, and which every natural man is ignorant of.

Word and Spirit leave no mark upon the unconverted mind. The 'natural man' may attain extensive knowledge of the Bible—its ancient Near Eastern backgrounds, its writers and their languages— but not the spiritual data it describes.[27]

Even the saints, though, must work to understand the Bible rightly. Their regenerate disposition rarely obviates the need for careful study of the canon. 'We must be much in reading the Scriptures,' Edwards urged his people often, 'if we would get spiritual ... knowledge.' We 'must be pretty well versed in the Scripture[s], before [we] can see their scope and drift, their connection, harmony and agreement,' he explained. 'A notional knowledge of divine things, must go before a spiritual.' For intimacy with God comes from time spent in reading the Bible, meditation, and prayer, not just superficial spiritual trysts or rapturous affairs. As Edwards liked to say to businesspeople in his parish, God 'gives us the gold' in providing us with Scripture but bequeaths it 'in a mine that we might dig for it and get it in a way of our own industry.' This deepens our desire for it and draws us near to Him. If biblical treasure were 'thrown plentifully before every man's face, and everyone could have it without any labor or industry, it would not be prized as it now is.'[28]

Conclusion

Edwards prized the Bible more than anything else in the world, for it put him in touch with God more reliably and constantly than anything in the world. Intimate knowledge and love of God loomed on Edwards' mental horizon as a pearl of great price, the holy grail of exegesis. He attended to the Word of God to get to know his Maker and to imitate his Lord, sharing fellowship with God by the help of the Holy Spirit—and enabling those to whom he spoke and wrote to do the same.

Do we share Edwards' love for, attention to, and confidence in the power of the Word? Does it ever make us *tremble*? Or have we grown so concerned about the sin of 'bibliolatry' that questions such as this appear naïve and superstitious? Edwards could have learned a lot about the history of the Bible and its ancient Near Eastern contexts from late modern successors. He committed errors in his biblical exegesis, some of which were attributable to early modern Protestant prejudices. But we can learn from him about the speech, strength, and signatures of God in holy Scripture, which could lead, by the Spirit, to the breaking down of our own cultural biases.

Naturalistic tendencies surround Western Christians in the early twenty-first century. They pervade our churches and schools, yielding spiritual complacency and outright unbelief. Edwards faced these problems too. He spent his life serving a state church in the age of Christendom and felt a burden to combat the plague of nominal Christianity. He demonstrates the potential of laboring to instill a vivid sense, an urgent impression, of God's activity in the worlds of those entrusted to our care. In fact, the reason we read him today is that he bolsters our belief in—and raises our affections through—the reality of God and God's activity in our midst. So, as ministers in mostly non- or post-Christian cultures, we would do well to follow his lead in working creatively to stem the tide of unbelief and apathy, encouraging instead a robust biblical supernaturalism. God is calling us now, as He called Edwards long ago, to deepen the faith of those around us in the reality, the centrality, the beauty and practicality of the things of God in Scripture.

Lord, help us in this crucial task. Help us by your Spirit to taste and see that You are good, and to share this spiritual sense more effectively with others. We pray these things for Jesus' sake. Amen.

8. Jonathan Edwards and the Bible: Christ, the Scope of Scripture

Stephen R. C. Nichols

> ... Christ and his redemption are the great subject of the whole Bible .... The whole book, both Old Testament and New, is filled up with the gospel, only with this difference, that the Old Testament contains the gospel under a veil, but the New contains it unveiled, so that we may see the glory of the Lord with 'open face.'[1]

Introduction

Arising from Scripture itself, a basic principle in Reformed and Puritan thought is that Christ is the scope of all of Scripture, the *scopus Scripturae*. This does not mean that the Scriptures speak *only* of Christ, but it does mean that, like the bullseye of a target, He is at the centre of everything they do speak of. In Richard Muller's apt summary of the Reformed understanding, the 'center of Scripture ... is the redemptive significance of Christ at the very heart of God's saving revelation.'[2] John Owen (1616–83), for example, insists that when reading the Scriptures the essential principle must be remembered that 'the revelation and doctrine of the person of Christ and his office, is the foundation whereon all other instructions of the prophets and apostles for the edification of the church are built, and whereinto they are resolved ....'3 A more familiar expression of this principle found in the advice of English Puritan divine, Isaac Ambrose (1604–64): 'Keep still Jesus Christ in your eye, in the perusal of the Scriptures, as the end, scope and substance thereof: what are the whole Scriptures, but as it were the spiritual swaddling clothes of the holy child Jesus?'4

Jonathan Edwards is heir to this Reformed and Puritan tradition. Employing what might be termed a 'whole-Bible hermeneutic' he interprets Scripture, discovering Christ to be the true scope and sense of the whole Bible. Again, this does not mean that the Bible speaks of Christ and of nothing else, but that Christ is the very heart and centre of everything it does speak of. When Edwards was invited by the trustees of the College of New Jersey in 1757 to become the college's next President, he included in his response outlines for two major works he was engaged upon: 'A History of the Work of Redemption' and 'A Harmony of the Old and New Testament.' His description of the 'Harmony' reveals much of Edwards' understanding of Christ as the scope of Scripture. The work would be divided into three parts:

> The first [part] considering the prophecies of the Messiah, his redemption and kingdom; the evidences of their references to the Messiah, etc. comparing them all one with another, demonstrating their agreement and true scope and sense; also considering all the various particulars wherein these prophecies have their exact fulfillment [sic]; showing the universal, precise, and admirable correspondence between predictions and events. The second part: considering the types of the Old Testament, showing the evidence of their being intended as representations of the great

things of the gospel of Christ: and the agreement of the type with the antitype. The third and great part, considering the harmony of the Old and New Testament, as to doctrine and precept.

Edwards notes that the work will cover 'a very great part of the holy Scripture' and was intended to lead the mind to 'a view of the true spirit, design, life and soul of the Scriptures, as well as to their proper use and improvement.'⁵

In this chapter, I will follow Edwards' three-fold structure, looking in turn at what he says on the Christological scope of prophecy, the issue of typology and 'doctrine and precept' (faith and practice). I will conclude with an estimation of Edwards' value to us today.

I. Prophecy

First, as Edwards outlines in the letter to the college trustees, the biblical prophets are united in their witness to the coming Messiah, his redemption and Kingdom. From the *protevangelion* pronounced in Genesis 3:15, all the prophets spoke of Christ and His work of redemption. He is the true scope and sense of their words. In Him, the prophecies find their exact fulfilment and only in Him do they 'harmonize', to draw on one of Edwards' favourite categories.

Edwards' reading reveals a familiarity with the trans-Atlantic debate concerning Jesus' Messiahship and the fulfilment of Old Testament prophecies. In *The Reasonableness of Christianity*, John Locke had reduced Christian confession to that of Jesus as the Messiah, whose coming was foretold in Hebrew prophecies and whose mission was authenticated by miracles.⁶ His friend and disciple, the Deist Anthony Collins (1676–1729) made the fulfilment of prophecies the sole criterion for judging the truth of the Christian religion, and entitled chapter six of his *A Discourse of the Grounds and Reasons of the Christian Religion*, 'VI. That if those proofs [to Jesus' Messiahship] are valid, Christianity is invincibly establish'd on its true foundation.'7 But, Collins warned,

> ... if the proofs for [C]hristianity from the Old Testament be not valid; if the arguments founded on those books be not conclusive; and the prophecies cited from thence be not fulfill'd; then has Christianity no just foundation: for the foundation on which Jesus and his apostles built it is then invalid and false.

Collins then argued that the Apostles had taken prophecies from the Jewish Scriptures and interpreted them not in the literal sense in which they were intended, but in a 'secondary, or typical, or mystical, or allegorical, or enigmatical sense' to demonstrate their fulfilment and thereby establish the Messianic identity of Jesus of Nazareth.8

Collins' conclusion was devastating:

> [T]he prophecies cited from the Old Testament by the authors of the New, do so plainly relate, in their obvious and primary sense, to other matters than those which they are produc'd to prove; that to pretend they prove, is, to give up the cause of Christianity to the Jews and other enemies thereof; who can so easily show, in so many undoubted instances, the Old and New Testaments to have no manner of connection in that respect, but to be in an irreconcilable state.9

Edwards nowhere engages with Collins directly, though his 'Harmony of the Old and New Testament' likely has in view Collins' criticisms in its apologetic goal: to show the Bible is coherent only when its scope is taken to be that of Christ, his redemption and kingdom. Edwards shares Collins' convictions that interpretation must operate according to a ruled use of language and take notice of the intention of the human author, but his own commitment to the divine authorship of Scripture means that he cannot finally endorse the univocity Collins demands of the biblical text. Figurative language (metaphor) and figurative history (types) are not additional senses in the way Collins had claimed. Instead they are part of the divinely intended literal sense and combine to speak ultimately of the Messiah.

Edwards concedes that the New Testament writers sometimes applied Old Testament texts in ways not envisaged by their human authors, or 'penmen.' A single text might have more than one referent. Edwards writes,

[T]he Scripture often includes various distinct things in its sense. It is becoming of him who is infinite in understanding and has everything in full and perfect view at once, and when he speaks, sees all things that have any manner of agreement with his words, and know how to adapt his words to many things, and so to speak infinitely more comprehensively than others, and to speak so as naturally to point forth many things: I say, it becomes such a One, when he speaks, to speak so as [to] include a manifold instruction in his speech. That expression in the Old Testament, 'Out of Egypt have I called my son' [Hosea 11:1], has respect to two distinct things, as is manifest beyond all contradiction, and many other phrases in the Old Testament applied in the New.[10]

God sometimes said more through the prophets' words than they themselves understood; only in the course of redemption

history would the fullness of their meaning as prophetic types of
the Messiah become clear. In this way prophecy may sometimes be
said to have had a double reference: first to a Messianic type, and
then to its antitype in Christ. Yet because they are both intended
by the divine Author, these are both rightly to be considered the
'literal sense' of Scripture.

Men who were united in their opposition to Collins—many of
whom Edwards read—differed over how to address this matter
of double-reference prophecies. William Whiston (1667–1752)
rejected the notion of types altogether.[11] Dissenting minister Samuel
Chandler (1693–1766) believed that, while some prophecies might
have a double fulfilment, in the majority of cases the prophecy
could be divided so that part might be said to concern an immediate
fulfilment, while part referred to a more distant event.[12] Anglican
theologian and philosopher Samuel Clarke (1675–1729) defended
the notion of prophetic types when he noted that the same words
might have reference to 'some near event' but also to 'the great
events which providence had in view.'[13] Arthur Ashley Sykes
(ca. 1684–1756) found the notion of types absurd and would
only countenance them when the prophet made it clear he was
employing the device.[14] In contrast to Whiston and Sykes, Edwards
was enthusiastically in favour of types as a unifying feature of
redemption history witnessed in Old and New Testaments. At times
he notes, like Samuel Chandler, that a prophecy may be dissected
in such a way that it is seen to respect two events: one immediate,
the other more distant. At other times, like Clarke, he endorses the
notion of prophesied types. Regardless, Edwards was steadfastly
committed to upholding prophecy's ultimate reference to Christ.

The question of the degree to which the prophets understood

the full range of referents of their own messages is one with which Edwards seems to have wrestled throughout his life.[15] Occasionally he suggests the prophets were well aware of the typical character of the referent they intended; they knew their messages had both an immediate referent and an ultimate Messianic one. Consequently, the prophets may have spoken of the ultimate referent (the antitype) in terms of the more immediate referent (the type), or moved seamlessly from one to the other.[16] At other times, however, he notes that the prophets themselves did not always have the Messiah in view, their chief concern being only a more immediate referent.[17] Therefore, against Collins, Edwards asserts that in reading the prophets 'we need not seek an interpretation which it would be natural for the prophets themselves to understand by it, for the Holy Ghost spoke in what words he pleased to, and meant what he pleased, without revealing his meaning to the prophets.'[18] With Collins, Edwards agreed that the language itself must be interpreted in a reasonable way and that the author's intent must be respected. Yet crucially, the author whose intent we should respect is primarily the *divine* one: the Holy Spirit. Edwards denies that the typical and antitypical fulfilment of a prophecy comprise two distinct senses of the prophecy, in the way that Collins employed the term to describe literal and figural readings of the same text. Although Edwards uses the terms 'literal sense' and 'figural sense,' he uses them in a different way from Collins, to refer to two stages of historical fulfilment. Thus there is one literal sense—the intention of the divine author—which may embrace more than one historical referent. Yet the scope of the prophets is always Christ.

We turn now to the second of Edwards' Messianic components, typology.

2. Typology

The history of the typological exegesis of the Bible is well-documented. In the early church, there was a hermeneutical parting of the ways between Antioch and Alexandria in the distinction between *typology* (defined broadly as events linked on a linear historical plane) and *allegory* (events that serve as mere symbols of higher spiritual truths). From Origen the Alexandrian school developed through Augustine, Ambrose and John of Cassian into what became known as the *quadriga*, the four-fold sense of Scripture employed by medieval exegetes. If the literal sense of a biblical text did not yield the Christian virtues of faith, hope and love, the interpreter departed from the literal sense and sought these in the text's other senses: its allegorical sense (which taught things to be believed), its tropological sense (which taught things to be loved or done) and its anagogical sense (which taught things to be hoped for).

Though not entirely free from their medieval heritage the Reformers were marked by their concern for the grammatical historical literal sense of the biblical text. In their hands typology again came to the fore, linking Old and New Testaments into one meta-narrative focussed on Christ. And yet there was already in Edwards' immediate heritage something of an 'imagistic consciousness', distinct from, though informed by, Scripture's typology. Cotton Mather's (1663–1728) *Magnalia Christi Americana*, the ecclesiastical history of New England, expressed the parallel between the New England experiment and the great biblical drama of Old Testament Israel. Similarly, Mather's *Agricola* echoed English Puritan John Flavel's *Husbandry Spiritualized* as a litany of nature's illustrations of spiritual truths.[19]

Examination of Edwards' catalogues of reading reveals that of the many Puritan manuals of biblical typology his favourite was *The Figures or Types of the Old Testament* by Samuel Mather (1626–71), Cotton's uncle.[20] Mather defined a type as 'some outward or sensible thing ordained of God under the Old Testament, to represent and hold forth something of Christ in the New'. Consequently, interpreters 'must not indulge their own fancies as Popish writers use to do, with their allegorical senses as they call them; except we have some Scripture ground for it. It is not safe to make anything a type merely upon our own fancies and imagination.'[21] In answer to the question, 'How can we tell what is a type ordained by the Lord?' Mather declared, 'There answer is we cannot safely judge of this but by Scripture.' There must either be express warrant in Scripture for the type-antitype relationship, or there must be a sufficient weight of evidence from various parts of Scripture to suggest a typical relationship was intended, even if not explicitly specified.[22]

Guided by the larger contours of his thinking—particularly by philosophical idealism and the notion that reality is communicative—typology underwent a transformation in Edwards' hands. Space does not permit discussion of Edwards' metaphysics here, but to him the whole of creation 'imaged' its divinely-communicated spiritual substance, in some sense more real than the images themselves, and in which the images found their consummation.[23] Material creation comprised a language of types designed by God for his self-communication to his saints. Biblical types were but one example of this universal imaging system. The difference between Edwards' typology and that of his heritage is illustrated by comparison once again with Samuel Mather.

Mather notes that, 'Before the Gospel there were no Gospel types .... There were some things extant before that were made types afterward; but they had not that *schesis*, that habitude and relation to Christ and the Gospel, 'til there was a Gospel or promise of life by Christ, that blessed Seed.'[24] In other words, God imbued aspects of creation with typological significance only *after* the fall, at the announcement of the *protevangelion* in Genesis 3:15. In contrast, Edwards affirms that 'things even before the fall were types of things pertaining to the gospel redemption.'[25] To Edwards, creation has always shadowed forth spiritual truths, their spiritual substance and consummation. Creation is the vehicle of God's self-communication and the means to his self-glorification. As such the biblical history expressed in the Old Testament 'type' and New Testament 'antitype' testified to a larger scheme of imaging that comprised all of reality. No longer simply a tool that links Old and New Testaments in a limited and explicit relationship of temporal Christological prefiguring and fulfilment, typology is for Edwards 'a certain sort of language in which God in wont to speak to us,' found not only throughout the Bible but writ large in nature and history.[26]

To Edwards, the Bible functions like the grammar book for this universal typological language. To limit one's use of the language to its explicit expressions in the Bible—as Samuel Mather had urged—would be merely to rehearse the exercises in the grammar book without ever attempting to use the language as it was intended. 'God han't expressly explained all the types of Scriptures, but has done so much as is sufficient to teach us the language.'[27] Indeed, to Edwards, Scripture's very silence speaks loudly its expectation that its readers become competent interpreters of types. He notes the fact that the writer to the Hebrews does not explain the Temple's theology fully:

> That many more particulars in the form of the sanctuary and its various parts, vessels and utensils, than are explained is evident by Hebrews 9:5, 'And over it the cherubims of glory shadowing the mercy seat; of which we cannot now speak particularly,' plainly intimating there [are] many particulars in those things representing heavenly things which he now thought it not expedient to explain.[28]

Would the writer to the Hebrews not want us to explore what he had left silent? Edwards found it inconceivable that he would not.

Edwards' departure from the tradition represented by Samuel Mather has left him open to the charge of allegory.[29] Stephen Stein accuses him of poetic 'flights of exegetical fancy' and of exercising his 'exegetical imagination without limit.'[30] It is true that Edwards does exercise a freedom in his typological exegesis that his tradition did not know, but as with prophecy, Edwards assumes that the spiritual substance of the type is part of the divine author's intention in his communication. To interpret a type is not therefore to read into it a secondary sense distinct from its literal sense (as was the case in the medieval *quadriga*). The typological reading is part of the literal historical sense intended by the divine author. Furthermore, Edwards' interpretation of types is not only invited by Scripture, but closely constrained by it. Those critical of his interpretation of types have arguably underestimated his careful attention to the grammatical historical considerations of the text and his reliance on the analogies of faith and Scripture.[31]

To limit one's typological exegesis to the explicit correspondences between the Testaments as in Mather's approach was wrong for a further reason, according to Edwards. It would mean that the Old Testament saints were prevented from searching out the meaning of the overwhelming majority of types that were presented to them. Edwards frequently affirms that there is epistemic progress through redemption history, such that the later a saint lived in redemption history the greater his or her understanding of the gospel.[32] Nevertheless, he also assumes that the innumerable types presented to the Old Testament saints were means of grace that instructed them in the gospel of Christ. He writes:

> If we may use our own understanding and invention not at all in interpreting types, and must not conclude anything at all to be types but what is expressly said to be and explained in Scripture, then the church under the Old [Testament], when the types were given, were secluded from ever using their understanding to search into the meaning of the types given to 'em; for God did, when he gave 'em, give no interpretation.[33]

The Old Testament saints were instructed in the faith, being presented with the gospel under innumerable shadows and types even though many of these shadows and types were neither explicitly identified as such nor interpreted to them.

To Edwards the Old Testament in every detail shadows forth its 'more excellent' end and spiritual substance. '[A]lmost everything that was said or done, that we have recorded in Scripture from Adam to Christ, was typical of gospel things. Persons were typical persons; their actions were typical actions … their land was typical land; God's providences toward them were typical providences; their worship was typical worship … and indeed the world was a typical world.'[34] When Edwards turns his universal typology to the question of the relationship of Old and New Testaments it delivers a Christological relationship manifest, not as it was for Samuel Mather only at finite specific points, but at every moment.

3. Doctrine

To Edwards, Christ is the object of faith and the centre of the life of faith of the church in every age. Prophecies and types combine to preach Christ, but history itself is the history of God's redemption of the elect in Christ. Central to understanding this history is God's covenant of grace.

The Covenants in a History of Redemption

The doctrine of the covenant was fundamental to Reformed and Puritan theology and, Perry Miller's objections notwithstanding, it was fundamental to Edwards' theology also.[35] To Edwards the covenants provided a basic framework of redemption history focussed on Christ, undergirding the Christological scope of Scripture.[36]

Briefly, an eternal *covenant of redemption* between the Divine Persons preceded all of God's dealings with man. At creation, God entered into a *covenant of works* with Adam, in which God promised salvation to humanity on the condition of perfect obedience. Following Adam's disobedience and Fall, God graciously entered into another covenant with him, one that did not depend upon the works of man. This *covenant of grace* was, in the words of the 'great Turretine' (Francis Turretin), 'a gratuitous pact entered into in Christ between God offended and man offending, in which God promises remission of sins and salvation to man gratuitously on account of Christ, man however, relying upon the same grace promises faith and obedience.'[37] This covenant of grace was conceived as running through both Old and New Testaments. Though its substance remained constant throughout its temporal expressions, its administration differed. During the infancy of the church the grace was veiled, the covenant being administered through promises, prophecies, sacrifices and other types. As the *Westminster Confession* declared, these were all 'foresignifying Christ to come: which were, for that time, sufficient and efficacious, through the operation of the Spirit, to instruct and build up the elect in faith in the promised Messiah.'[38] The work of the incarnate Son however, fulfilled all the signs and shadows, rendering them obsolete. Thus according to the *Westminster Confession*, when considering Old and New Testaments 'there are not ... two covenants of grace, differing in substance, but one and the same, under various dispensations.'[39]

The gracious covenants instituted by the Father at successive points in redemption history were temporal expressions of the eternal covenant of redemption, and Edwards follows the Reformed tradition in maintaining the substantial continuity of these covenants through redemption history. He argues that the covenant of grace established in the New Testament is not substantially different from that which God entered into with Israel, any more than 'that the covenant that God entered into with Israel at Mt. Sinai was specifically diverse from that which he entered into on the plains of Moab, because that is spoken of as another covenant (Deuteronomy 29:1).'[40] Edwards makes eight points of comparison between the dispensations under Moses and Christ:

1. The *substance* of salvation is the same: sinners are by nature objects of divine wrath, but the elect in both dispensations are called, justified, adopted and sanctified.

2. The *medium* of salvation is the same: in both dispensations, God's people are saved by the same Mediator's suffering and satisfaction of divine justice.

3. The Divine Person who *applies* redemption is the same: the Holy Spirit.

4. The *method* of bestowing salvation is the same: justification by faith alone.

5. The external *means* of applying the benefits of salvation are the same: the ordinary means of grace, principally, the Word of God.

6. The previous five characteristics are represented under each dispensation, though the nature of this revelation differs.

7. These same things are not only 'in some sort exhibited or represented' to the later church, but were 'in some degree made known and revealed' to the church at the time.

8. With the revelation comes the promise of fulfilment and right to enjoyment of those things revealed.[41]

Edwards yet acknowledges that the covenant of grace is *administered differently* throughout redemption history. Comparing the dispensations under Moses and Christ, Edwards comments: '… the same exercises of faith were then required as are now, but there was a difference, answerable to the difference of the revelation in which the Mediator and his salvation is exhibited.'[42] Among the outward expressions in which the life of faith of the Old Testament church differed from that of the New Testament one Edwards identifies,

...the degree and manner of weanedness from the world, self-denial, spirituality of worship, heavenly-mindedness, love to men, the degree and manner of our loving them, forgiveness of injuries, love to enemies, love to the wicked, love to all mankind, etc. According to the more particular and full revelation of the grounds of these duties, and the new obligations laid upon us to them, evangelical duties, with their grounds, were not so fully revealed, so particularly prescribed, nor so much insisted on.[43]

The plainness of God's revelation was dependent on the administration of the covenant. Under Moses the gospel was exhibited under a veil. In the New Testament that veil was removed and the gospel realities displayed plainly. There is therefore an increasing clarity of gospel revelation through redemption history. The title Edwards chooses for his second 'great work' is not incidental: 'The Harmony of the Old and New Testament'—note the singular 'Testament'—expresses both continuity in substance as well as discontinuity in administration of the single covenant of grace. Nevertheless, as Edwards demonstrates the deep interrelatedness of Scripture using his tools of expanded typology and the Spirit-given 'new sense of the heart,' he inevitably emphasises the essential continuity between Old and New Testament expressions of the covenant. This emphasis on the covenant's substantial similarly is epitomised by Edwards' understanding of the object and content of faith of the saints in Old and New Testaments.

The Object and Content of Faith

According to Edwards the Old Testament saints heard the gospel of Christ through means of grace that were appropriate to their dispensation, which in their case meant (Messianic) prophecies and types. Edwards writes that, under the guidance of the Holy Spirit, the Old Testament elect were 'much enlightened by the plain prophecies which they had of Christ.'[44] Additionally, they had Messianic types to lead them to faith in Christ. For example, Edwards writes concerning the sacrificial system: '[B]y this ceremonial law, the gospel was preached to them [the Israelites] ... Those sacrifices were to point forth Christ and to lead them to trust in him, to prepare the church for the reception and entertainment of him when he came.'[45] Thus Edwards stands squarely in a Reformed and Puritan tradition in seeing Christ as the object of saving faith in both Old and New Testaments. In contrast to recent scholarship that suggests he believed possession of an unrealized 'disposition' was sufficient to salvation, the eighteenth-century Reformed Puritan is explicit that the elect knew and 'closed with Christ' in a manner fitting to their dispensation.[46]

It is true that Edwards sometimes speaks of the saints having only 'implicit faith' in Christ. However, this concept has nothing whatsoever to do with someone lacking the possibility of knowing the Saviour. Edwards' idea of 'implicit faith' is the temporary situation when those who have heard the gospel believe but are not immediately conscious of the Second Person of the Godhead as the specific object of their faith. This phenomenon happens in every age. In the *Faithful Narrative* (1735), Edwards recounts it happening in his own day among the recently-awakened in Northampton:

> It must needs be confessed that Christ is not always distinctly and explicitly thought of in the first sensible act of grace (though most commonly he is); but sometimes he is the object of the mind only implicitly. Thus sometimes when persons have seemed evidently to be stripped of all their own righteousness, and to have stood self-condemned as guilty of death, they have been comforted with a joyful and satisfying view, that the mercy and

grace of God is sufficient for them; that their sins, though never so great, shall be no hindrance to their being accepted; that there is mercy enough in God for the whole world, and the like, when they give no account of any particular or distinct thought of Christ; but yet when the account they give is duly weighed, and they are a little interrogated about it, it appears that the revelation of the mercy of God in the Gospel is the ground of this their encouragement and hope; and that it is indeed the mercy of God through Christ that is discovered to them, and that 'tis depended on in him, and not in any wise moved by anything in them.[47]

Thus, 'implicit faith' does not refer to a *permanent* situation regarding the *objective* grounds of salvation but is only a *temporary* stage in the *subjective* awareness of some saints, and this is an occasional feature of each dispensation and of every era. As attention to his wider corpus reveals, Edwards is unequivocal that the Old Testament saints consciously closed with Christ for their justification, just as the saints did in Edwards' day.

Edwards is also explicit that the appearances of the LORD in the Old Testament were appearances of the Son of God, the Divine Mediator:

[W]hen ... we read in the sacred history what God did from time to time towards his church and people, and what he said to them, and how he revealed himself to them, we are to understand it especially of the second person of the Trinity. When we read after this of God's appearing time after time in some visible form or outward symbol of his presence, we are ordinarily if not universally to understand it of the second person of the Trinity, which may be argued from John 1:18 .... [and] Colossians 1:15, intimating that though God the Father be invisible, yet Christ is his image or symbol by which he is seen.[48]

Thus whenever God appeared in the Old Testament, the saints had opportunity to see Christ.

Edwards only reiterated the Reformed tradition when he said that Christ was the object of the Old Testament saints' faith, but he moves beyond it in terms of the content of this faith. Consider what two of Edwards' most prominent predecessors taught on the subject. In the eighth chapter of *Christologia*, entitled 'The Faith of the Church Under the Old Testament in and Concerning the Person of Christ,' John Owen writes:

> [T]he faith of the saints under the Old Testament did principally respect the person of Christ—both what it was, and what it was to be in the fullness of time, when he was to become the seed of the woman. What his especial work was to be, and the mystery of the redemption of the church thereby, they referred unto his own wisdom and grace;—only, they believed that by him they should be saved from the hand of all their enemies, or all the evil that befell them on the account of the first sin and apostasy from God.[49]

For Owen, the faith of the Old Testament saints was in the person of Christ, though the shadowy nature of their dispensation meant their understanding of the manner of his redemption was slight.

Similarly, Turretin, in arguing for the substantial unity of the covenant of grace in Old and New Testament, notes that he wages 'this most important controversy' against those who hold that 'the fathers of the Old Testament were not saved by the gratuitous mercy of God in Christ, the Mediator ... *through faith in him about to come.*'[50] Turretin argues that since faith and the word are related, in the dispensation of shadows and types faith was similarly obscure. Nevertheless, 'The same thing ... was always known and proposed as the object of faith, but the mode was less clearly discovered before the advent of Christ than after it ...'[51] Christ was ever the object of justifying faith, though the revelation of him was veiled under the Old Testament.

Edwards would of course affirm this mainstream Reformed position in theory, yet in practice it appears that he goes beyond it. His multiplication of the means of grace in the Old Testament through his expanded typology and through his conception of the prophetic corpus as one vast, unified presentation of the person and work of the Messiah seems capable of delivering to the Old Testament saints an understanding of the gospel more commonly associated in his tradition with its New Testament administration.

Conclusion

Jonathan Edwards saw Christ as the true scope and sense of all Scripture. He would, no doubt, have echoed the comment of Richard Sibbes (1577–1635): 'Christ is the object, the centre wherein all ... lines end: take away Christ, what remains? ... all is nothing but Christ.'[52] To Edwards, prophecies were united because they were Messianic. His expanded typology bound the Old and New Testaments Christologically at every moment, more tightly than his heritage had. The saints throughout redemption history trusted Christ, either looking forward to his redemptive work, or looking back to it. To read the Bible aright is to see Christ as its true scope.

This is not without its modern critics. Stephen Stein, responsible perhaps more than any other for attempting to rehabilitate Edwards the biblical scholar, is nonetheless critical of Edwards' Christological interpretation. In his 'Editor's Introduction' to Edwards' 'Blank Bible', he remarks:

> In his commentary on the Pentateuch, Edwards repeatedly spoke of ancient Israel as the 'Jewish Church'. That expression, which occurs eight times in his entries on the five books of Moses, symbolizes the prevailing direction of his exegesis at the same time that it challenges the uniqueness and integrity of the historic Jewish community by imposing a Christian category on it.[53] That construction also diminishes the historical intention and the original integrity of the Hebrew Bible, the scripture of ancient Israel, by transforming it into the Old Testament whose ultimate purpose and meaning depended essentially on the Christian New Testament.[54]

The criticism is perhaps not surprising. Contemporary theological scholarship no longer operates according to Edwards' pre-critical convictions. An 'eclipse of biblical narrative' has occurred, to use the phrase of Hans Frei. Or to change the metaphor, a conceptual chasm has opened that separates Edwards' world from our own.

None of this overturns Edwards' Christological approach to Scripture but rather points us to the pressing need to recover it today. In marked contrast to the fragmented and relativised way the academy has of dealing with Scripture, Edwards offers an account that is breath-taking in its unified scope yet utterly comprehensive in its detail. In particular,

1. In a contemporary academic atmosphere of disciplinary specialisation that often exist in isolation from each other Edwards presents us with something of a 'grand unified theory'

of Scripture, capable of embracing the *minutiae* of Old and New Testaments and able to account for temporally distinct and seemingly-marginal texts as well as more familiar ones.

2. Edwards' approach takes seriously the nature of the Bible as the Scriptures of the Christian church, Scriptures whose scope and meaning is made available to those who profess faith in Jesus the Messiah and are indwelt and illumined by his Holy Spirit.

3. Edwards' conception of the Old and New Testaments as God's grammar book of a typological language offers, at least in principle, a way of connecting the everyday world that the Christian experiences to the eternal things he or she possesses in Christ.

4. By grounding the unity of the Christian Bible on a discrete witness of the Hebrew Scriptures that is Messianic, Edwards offers the possibility of a legitimately evangelical conversation between the church and the synagogue regarding the identity of the Messiah and the object of faith.

Edwards' Bible may seem a 'strange new world' to some. Yet perhaps there is value in its strangeness.[55] Precisely because Edwards' Bible jars with current sensibilities, it challenges us to re-assess our assumptions and question whether our vision of the Scriptures—and their Author—is as wondrously great as it ought to be.

9. Christ in the Song: How Edwards Can Help Us Recover the Song of Solomon

Nicholas T. Batzig

The Song of Songs has long featured as one of the most important texts for preaching and theological reflection in the Reformed church. One could almost say that when the church was in her best condition, her delight in the Song—which she heard as being *her* song—was at its height. Thus, at the high-water mark of the Puritan era, sacramental sermons frequently came from this book of Scripture. In fact, one of the greatest theological treatises of that era was based almost exclusively on the Song of Songs: John Owen's *Communion with the Triune God*.[1]

It is therefore hardly surprising that the Song held a central place in the preaching and writing of Jonathan Edwards. Indeed, the typological features of the Song—particularly that of the bride and groom—loomed so large in Edwards' thinking that they came to summarize his theology of redemption: 'God created the world for his Son, that he might prepare a spouse or bride for him to bestow his love upon; so that the mutual joys between this bride and bridegroom are the end of creation.'[2]

Sadly, such an interest in the Song could hardly be said to prevail in the church today. Far from being a frequent text, many contemporary Christians will live and die without hearing a single sermon on this book! On the few occasions when the Song is preached, it is often preached as if it were merely an ancient Near East love poem. We could spend some time speculating as to the root causes of this sad state of affairs, however, it is clear we need to recover the Song as a text for preaching in the church today. What we need is a guide to show us how it is done, to point out the typological features and the rich theology of this great book of the canon. I believe that Edwards provides us with such a guide. So, without further ado, let us turn to Edwards' thought on the Song of Songs. We first consider the places in Edwards' writings where we find the bulk of this material.

References to the Song in Edwards' Writings

Edwards' fascination with the Song began in his youth, very close to the time of his conversion. In the 'Personal Narrative,' Edwards reflected on the spiritual impact that the Song had on his soul from the earliest days of his Christian experience. In his own words:

> From about that time I began to have a new kind of apprehensions and ideas of Christ, and the work of redemption, and the glorious way of salvation by him. An inward, sweet sense of these things, at times, came into my heart; and my soul was led away in pleasant views and contemplations of them. And my mind was greatly engaged to spend my time in reading and meditating on Christ, on the beauty and excellency of his person,

and the lovely way of salvation by free grace in him. I found no books so delightful to me, as those that treated of these subjects. Those words [of] Canticles ii. 1 used to be abundantly with me, 'I am the rose of Sharon, and the lily of the valleys.' The words seemed to me sweetly to represent the loveliness and beauty of Jesus Christ. The whole book of Canticles used to be pleasant to me, and I used to be much in reading it, about that time; and found from time to time an inward sweetness, that would carry me away in my contemplations.[3]

This autobiographical reflection is proof that the Song was the initial source of Edwards' subsequent preoccupation with the ideas of the 'beauty,' 'sweetness' and 'loveliness' of Christ.

With over 500 references to Canticles scattered throughout his extant writings, Edwards left us with a veritable commentary on the book.[4] In general, we can say that the references to the Song in 'Notes on Scripture,' the 'Miscellanies' and the 'Blank Bible' are more *hermeneutical* in nature, whereas the sermons and Great Awakening writings are more *practical and experimental*. While certainly not mutually exclusive, these two categories can be used to describe all of Edwards' thoughts on the Song.

Edwards was taken up with meditation on the meaning of the Song throughout his life. This is evident from his notebooks, particularly 'Notes on Scripture.' Among the 507 entries in 'Notes,' Edwards referenced the Song of Songs 149 times. However, the most important of these is surely the final entry, no. 507. Indeed, one cannot but wonder whether Edwards deliberately ended the 'Notes' with this masterpiece! In it, Edwards placed the language of Psalm 45 side by side with the language of the Song. Assuming the messianic interpretation of Psalm 45 taught in Hebrews 1:8–10, he insists that:

> ... both these songs treat of these lovers with relation to their espousals one to another, representing their union to that of a bridegroom and bride ... in both the bridegroom is represented as a king, and in both the bride is spoken of as a king's daughter ... In both the bridegroom is represented as greatly delighted with the beauty of the bride ... In both the speech of the bridegroom is represented as exceeding excellent and pleasant ... In both the ornaments of the bride are represented by costly, beautiful, and splendid attire, and in both as adorned with gold ... In both the excellent gifts or qualifications of these lovers, by which they are recommended to each other, and delighted in one another, are compared to such spices as myrrh, aloes, etc .... [and] in both these songs the bride is represented as with a number of virgins that are her companions in her nuptial honors and joys.[5]

The remarkable similarity between the theme and language of Psalm 45 and the Song makes Edwards' conclusion all the more convincing. This section of theological exposition is one of the most substantial (and useful) of all Edwards' observations on the Christology of the Song.

There are also numerous interactions with the Song in Edwards' 'Miscellanies.' 'Miscellanies' no. 1069—which has come to be known by the title, 'Types of the Messiah'—has no less than 73 references. It is here that we find some of the most important biblical-theological observations on the Song. In keeping with the way Edwards habitually used the 'Miscellanies,' these observations fed into his exposition and application of the Song elsewhere.

Edwards' revival writings repeatedly appeal to the Song. Various parts of the Song appear among the seven citations found in *The Distinguishing Marks* (1741). *Some Thoughts on Revival* (1742) has even more references—sixteen by my count—to the Song. In 1746, the publication of *Religious Affections* gave further insight into Edwards' thoughts on the usefulness of the Song. In this work, Edwards appealed to various portions of it a total of thirteen times, nine of which are set in the third and final section, 'Distinguishing Signs of Truly Gracious and Holy Affections.' Not surprisingly given the pastoral context of these writings, the use uses of the Song in *The Distinguishing Marks, Some Thoughts* and *Religious Affections* are mainly experiential and practical rather than theological.

Edwards' Sermons on the Song

From 1724 until 1748, Edwards preached thirteen sermons on various portions of the Song. Of those thirteen sermons, nine remain unpublished.[6] As is true of many of his theological predecessors, Edwards occasionally made use of the Song for sermons on the Lord' Supper. One notable example of this was Edwards' sermon on Canticles 5:1, which Ken Minkema has called 'a rapturous meditation that encourages communicants to put no restraints on their "spiritual appetites" and to "swim in rivers of pleasure."'[7] All of Edwards' sermons on Canticles preached at Northampton contain a short theological exposition of a text from the book. This was, of course, part and parcel with the Puritan plain style of preaching—text, doctrine and application—Edwards adhered to. In his sermons on the Song, the doctrine section always developed particular truths about Christ and/or the church. Edwards brought these messages to a conclusion with an applicatory section, but experiential application featured throughout these expositions.

Ever sensitive to his audience, Edwards sometimes altered sermons that he preached in one context in order to make them suitable for another. Such was the case with his 1728 sermon on Canticles 1:3 which Edwards revised for a 1733 lecture to a more 'sophisticated auditory' in Boston.[8] Most noticeably, Edwards imported his observations regarding Solomon as the author of the book from 'Notes on Scripture' no. 147. Perhaps Edwards felt as though the audience needed to be convinced of a canonical reading of the Song; if so, it is a reminder that worldly approaches towards the Song are nothing new.[9]

Edwards' Use of the Song In Other Sermons

The importance of the Canticles 1:3 sermon can also be seen by Edwards' use of its content in one of his most well known sermons: the sermon on Revelation 5:5–6 that came to be called 'The Excellency of Christ.'[10] This is no insignificant connection. 'The Excellency of Christ'—which was, incidentally, a sacramental sermon—is one of the greatest examples of Edwards' theological genius.[11] The fact that significant elements of it come from the Canticles 1:3 sermon should come as no surprise, as we have already seen the way in which Edwards was captivated by the idea of 'the excellency,' 'sweetness,' 'beauty' and 'satisfaction' of Christ.

One of the earliest sermons in which Edwards incorporated portions of the Song was 'A Spiritual Understanding of Things Denied To The Unregenerate.' Significantly, this was also the first sermon to deal extensively with the 'topic of conversion and divine light.' Thomas Schaeffer has observed that it was this sermon that led 'to the essay on "Excellency" in "The Mind" no. 1 and anticipates in nearly every aspect "A Divine and Supernatural Light," published in 1734.'[12] In this sermon, Edwards made use of the sensory experience language of the Song to explain the nature of saving grace in the life of the believer in the following manner:

> The spiritual illumination of the minds of believers is resembled to tasting. Canticles 2:2–3, 'And his fruit was sweet.' 'Tis no wonder that none can tell how sweetly the fruit of the Tree of Life is but those that have tasted; no wonder that none know that the Lord is gracious so well as they that have tasted and seen ... This spiritual knowledge of the godly is resembled also to smelling a sweet perfume. Thus Christ is called 'a bundle of myrrh,' for the sweetness of it to the smell. Canticles 1:13, 'A bundle of myrrh is my well-beloved unto me.' Thus he is said to be a rose and a lily, in the beginning of the second chapter, because of their odoriferousness. And so Canticles 5:13, 'His lips are like lilies, dropping sweet-smelling myrrh.' Now there are no descriptions, however accurate, of the smell of sweet-smelling myrrh that can give anyone to understand it as those that have actually smelled it.[13]

Dependence on the Song is also seen in Edwards' 'Sweet Harmony of Christ,' a sermon on John 10:4 preached in August, 1735. Here, Edwards emphasizes the wonderful theme of Christ's beauty and loveliness. In the doctrinal section, he wrote:

> Christ is altogether lovely in the eyes of a Christian. There is nothing in Christ, no attribute or qualification, but that he is lovely to him on the account of it. Not only his goodness and grace, but his justice and sovereignty is lovely to the Christian. *Canticles 5:16*, 'He is altogether lovely.' So also the Christian may be said to be wholly lovely in the eyes of Christ; for though there be much remaining deformity, yet 'tis as it were hidden from the eyes of Christ, that he sees it not. He doth not behold iniquity in Jacob, nor see [perverseness in Israel] (*Numbers 23:21*). And

therefore Christ says to his church, *Canticles 4:7*, 'Behold, thou art all fair, my love; there is no spot in thee.'[14]

Throughout this reflections on the Song, Edwards naturally focused more on Christ's beauty, excellency and sweetness. However, this passage reminds us that it was not only the believer's love for Christ but also *Christ's love for the church* that ought to be preached.

Edwards goes on to describe the mutual love that Christ and the church have for one other. He noted:

> Christ and the true Christian have desires after each other. *Canticles 7:10*, 'I am my beloved's, and his desire is towards me.' And the desire of the Christian's soul is after Christ. *Canticles 3:1–2*, 'By night on my bed I sought him whom my soul loveth: I sought him, but I found him not. I will rise now, and go about the city in the streets and broad ways. I will seek him whom my soul loveth.' The true Christian has an admiration of Jesus Christ; he admires his excellencies. *Isaiah 63:1*, 'Who is this that cometh from Edom, with died garments from Bozrah? this that is glorious in his apparel, travelling in the greatness of his strength?' And so Christ is represented as admiring the excellency and beauty of the church *Canticles 6:10* ...[15]

Would that such sentiments would be heard from pulpits today.

Perhaps the most interesting example of Edwards' use of the Song in a sermon is found in 'The Church's Marriage to Her Sons,' an installation sermon that Edwards preached for David Brainerd's friend, Samuel Buell. This sermon was based on the words of Isaiah 62:4–5. Edwards drew on the Song nineteen times in this exposition as he labored to emphasize the point that the minister's primary goal is to promote communion between Christ and the believer. Edwards explained that 'a faithful minister espouses a Christian people, not in his own name, but as Christ's ambassador: he espouses them, that in their being espoused to him, they may be espoused to Christ.'[16] Wilson Kimnach sums up the focus of this sermon when he writes, '"The Church's Marriage" is a celebration not merely of a minister's installation but of the process of redemption through the preaching office in what Edwards clearly intimates are the "latter days" before Christ's heroic return to reclaim his spouse.'[17]

Edwards' Use of Redemptive History and Typology

In order to understand Edwards' interpretation of the Song, we must first take note of the fact that he began from a canonical, covenantal and redemptive-historical approach to reading the Scriptures.[18] With regard to the Song this meant that Edwards sought to understand all of the allusions, symbols, metaphors and types in light of the previous revelation of God in the Old Testament—and, wherever applicable, to do so in the light of the fuller revelation of the New Testament.[19] In short, Edwards viewed the Song as a redemptive-historical addition to God's self-revelation in the books that preceded it. He understood it to be part of the grand narrative of Scripture. Edwards was so committed to this principle that he thought the authorship of the Song—a subject that remains highly controversial in our own day—could be discovered by this approach.

Because Edwards' understanding of redemptive-history held a place of prominence in his hermeneutical process, it comes as no surprise to learn that he mentioned the Song in his redemptive-historical masterpiece—*A History of the Work of Redemption*. In the only reference to the Song in that work, Edwards' explained his understanding of the place that this book held in redemptive history:

> I would here take notice of the additions that were made to the canon of the Scripture in or soon after Solomon's reign. There were considerable additions made by Solomon, who wrote the books of Proverbs and Ecclesiastes, probably near the close of his reign. His writing the Song of Songs, as it is called, is what is especially here to be taken notice; which is wholly on the subject that we are upon, viz. Christ and his redemption, representing the high and glorious relation and union and love there is between Christ and his redeemed church.[20]

Another clear example of Edwards' canonical method is seen in the 1733 version of his sermon on *Canticles* 1:3. In the introductory section of that sermon, Edwards explained that the Song of Songs was 'the most excellent' of Solomon's 1005 songs, 'more than all his other songs.'[21] Furthermore, Edwards noted that the Song of Songs was the only one of Solomon songs 'inserted in the canon of the Scripture.' He wrote:

> We read [in] 1 Kings 4:32 that Solomon's songs were a thousand and five, but this one song of his which is inserted in the canon of the Scripture is distinguished from all the rest by the name of the Song of Songs, or the most excellent of his songs, or more than all his other songs: as the subject of it is transcendently of a more sublime and excellent nature than the rest, treating of the divine love, union, and communion of the most glorious lovers, Christ and his spiritual spouse, of which a marriage union and conjugal love (which, perhaps, many of the rest of his songs treated of) is but a shadow.[22]

In 'Miscellanies' 303, Edwards—with almost a self-reflective appreciation for Solomon—paused to probe the rationale behind Solomon's composition of the *Song*. He writes:

> I imagine that Solomon, when he wrote this song, being a very philosophical, musing man, and a pious man, and of a very loving temper, set himself in his own musings to imagine and to point forth to himself a pure, virtuous, pious and entire love; and represented the musings and feelings of his mind, that in a philosophical and religious frame was carried away in a sort of transport ... God's Spirit made use of his loving inclination, joined with his musing philosophical disposition, and so directed and conducted it in this train of imagination as to represent the love that there is between Christ and his spouse ... The relation that there is between Christ and the church, we know, is very often compared to that that there is between a man [and] his wife—yea, this similitude is abundantly insisted on almost everywhere in the Scripture—and a virtuous and pious and pure love between a man and his spouse is very much of an image of the love between Christ and the church. So that it is not at all strange that the Spirit of God, which is love, should direct a holy amorous disposition after such a manner as to make such a representation, and 'tis very agreeable to other the like representations.[23]

Edwards considered the Song to be the superlative redemptive-historical love song composed by Solomon and the superlative redemptive love song of Scripture. Sean Lucas has rightly concluded that redemptive history 'is at the center' of Edwards' theology.[24]

Israel's History As Background For The Song's Allusions and Types

Edwards guided his interpretation of the Song with the redemptive-historical development of God's dealing with Old Covenant Israel—from the patriarchs to the establishment of the Kingdom. Edwards' consistently channeled his exegesis by means of a canonical approach. We see this in unfold more broadly with regard to the revelation of God's redemptive work in the Old Covenant church prior to the writing of the Song and more narrowly in light of the work of God through Solomon during his reign in redemptive-history. There were essentially four stages in this redemptive-historical interpretive process. Relying heavily on the redemptive revelation of the Old Testament that preceded the Song, Edwards' drew off of things pertaining to the patriarchal narrative at the inception of Israel's formation, Israel's sojourning in the wilderness, conquest of Canaan and the establishment of the Kingdom.

With regard to the meaning of select allusions in the Song, Edwards confined himself to that period of revelation leading up to Solomon and the Kingdom era. He viewed these typological events as fundamental to the interpretation the Song. These Old Testament events were the background upon which the characters of the Song acted out a redemptive drama. Edwards discovered the history of Israel (*i.e.* from its formation to the period of the Solomonic reign and building of the Temple) in the theological symbols and figures in the Song. He then set that conclusion in its prospective biblical-theological context in which Christ's coming into the world to redeem His church was the great, anticipated event.

Edwards drew on the events surrounding God's dealing with Jacob and the formation of Israel in order to interpret the theological significance of certain names of people and places in redemptive-history. In 'Types of the Messiah,' he explained what he believed to be the theological meaning of the name Mahanaim (i.e. 'two camps')—as alluded to by the spouse in the Song. He wrote:

> The church or spouse of the Messiah is spoken of in Canticles 6:13 as being represented by the company of Mahanaim, that we have an account of (Genesis 32:1–2), made up of Jacob's family and the heavenly host that joined them.[25]

Edwards referred to the biblical-theological meaning of 'Mahanaim' in *Notes* on numerous occasions. In entry 85 he wrote:

> *Canticles 6:13.* 'What will ye see in the Shulamite? As it were the company of two armies,' or 'the company of Mahanaim.' The two armies that are the company of Mahanaim are the church of God in earth and in heaven, the company of Jacob and the company of the angels (see *Genesis 32:2*), the church militant and the church triumphant; for both these armies make one spouse of Jesus Christ.[26]

In his lengthiest entry on the Song in 'Notes' no. 460, Edwards again explicated the redemptive-historical meaning of 'Mahanaim' as it is used in the Song. He noted:

> … it greatly confirms that the spouse is a people, and the church of God in particular, that she is compared to an army, an army terrible with banners (*Canticles 6:4*, *Canticles 6:10*), and as a 'company of two armies' [*Canticles 6:13*], or the company of Mahanaim. So the church of God, when brought out of Egypt through the wilderness to Canaan, was by God's direction in the form of an army with banners. So the psalms and prophecies often

represent the church of God as going forth to battle, fighting under an ensign, and gloriously conquering their enemies, and conquering the nations of the world. And the company of Jacob, that was as it were the church of Israel, with the host of angels that met them and joined them, to assist them against Esau's host, was the company of Mahanaim, or 'company of two armies,' so called by Jacob on that account (*Genesis 32:2*).[27]

Then, in one of his strongest affirmations on the redemptive-historical symbolism of the Song, Edwards explained that the language of 'war-horses' and 'chariots,' by which the Shulamite is addressed, could only make sense if it were understood to be applied uniquely to the church:

> So it is a great evidence of the same thing, that the spouse is compared to war horses 'and chariots.' (*Canticles 1:9*), which it is not in the least likely would ever be a comparison used to represent the beauty of a bride in a common epithalamium, or love song. But this is exactly agreeable to a representation elsewhere made of the church of God. *Zechariah 10:3*, 'The Lord of hosts hath visited his flock, the house of Judah, and hath made them as his goodly horse in the battle.[28]

This crucial illustration demonstrates the way in which Edwards sought spiritual meaning in the redemptive-historical names, objects and events referred to in the Song. Edwards applied his understanding of Covenantal typology to the names and events surrounding the lives of the patriarchs and the Old Covenant church—a practice exemplified by Jesus Himself (see John 1:51; 3:).

A further example of this principle is found in Edwards' explanation of the theological significance of 'palm trees' in the Song. He wrote:

The twelve fountains of water and the threescore and ten palm trees that were in Elim (Exodus 15:27) were manifestly types of the twelve patriarchs, the fathers of the tribes, and the threescore and ten elders of the congregation. The paternity of a family, tribe or nation, in the language of the Old Testament, is called a 'fountain.' Deuteronomy 33:28, 'Israel shall dwell in safety alone: the fountain of Jacob shall be upon a land of corn and wine.' Psalms 68:26, 'Bless the Lord, from the fountain of Israel.' Isaiah 48:1, 'Hear ye this, O house of Jacob, which are called by the name of Israel, and are come forth out of the waters of Judah.'[29]

Moving on from the allusions from the patriarchal period, Edwards interpreted the Song's language of the bride as an 'army' in light of Israel's formation into an army during the exodus/wilderness/conquest experience. He noted:

The congregation in the wilderness were in the form of an army, and an army with banners. So the church of the Messiah is often represented as an army. They are represented as being called forth to war and engaged in battle, gloriously conquering and triumphing, in places innumerable, and spoken of as being God's 'goodly horse in the battle' [Zechariah 10:3]; and as 'a company of horses in Pharaoh's chariots' [Canticles 1:9]; and being made as 'the sword of a mighty man' [Zechariah 9:13]; and being gathered to an ensign (Isaiah 11:10, Isaiah 11:12) and standard (Isaiah 49:22 and Isaiah 59:19 and Isaiah 62:10); and having a banner given them (Psalms 60:4); and setting up their banners in God's name (Psalms 20:5), and being terrible as an army with banners (Canticles 6:4, Canticles 6:10).[30]

In addition to interpreting the symbols in the Song that had, as their background, the typological events of the exodus/wilderness/

conquest typology, Edwards explicated the theological meaning of the names of the individuals in the Song who lived during the Kingdom era. He suggested that the name 'Beloved' was a name for Christ under its typical significance in the person of David. He wrote: David was ruddy and of a fair countenance, and goodly to look to (*1 Samuel 16:12* and *1 Samuel 17:42*); agreeable to *Psalms 45:2*, 'Thou art fairer than the children of men.' *Canticles 5:10*, 'My beloved is white and ruddy, the chiefest among ten thousands.'[31] And again:

> David by occupation was a shepherd, and afterwards was made a shepherd to God's Israel. *Psalms 78:70–71*, 'He chose David his servant, and took him from the sheepfolds: From following the ewes great with young he brought him to feed Jacob his people, and Israel his inheritance' ... *Ezekiel 37:24*, 'And David my servant shall be king over them; and they all shall have one shepherd.' *Canticles 1:7*, 'Tell me, O thou whom my soul loveth, where thou feedest, where thou makest thy flock to rest at noon.'[32]

Edwards then compared the use of the name 'Beloved' in Isaiah 5:1–7 and the use of it in the *Song*. 'The figures of speech used in this book, many of them are very agreeable to those used in *Isaiah 5:1–7*.'[33]

Edwards considered the person of Solomon to be pregnant with typological significance as well. He explained, 'the Messiah is called by the name of Solomon (*Canticles 3:7, Canticles 3:11, Canticles 8:11–12*).'[34] Edwards explained the importance of the fact that, in Hebrew, 'Solomon' means the 'peaceable one' when he wrote:

> The things that are said of Solomon fall yet if anything short of those that are said of David, in their remarkable agreement with things said of the Messiah in the prophecies. His name,

'Solomon,' signifies 'peace' or 'peaceable,' and was given him by God himself from respect to the signification, because he should enjoy peace and be a means of peace to God's people. *1 Chronicles 22:9*, 'Behold, a son shall be born to thee, who shall be a man of rest; and I will give him rest from all his enemies round about: for his name shall be Solomon, and I will give peace and quietness unto Israel in his days.' This is agreeable to *Isaiah 9:6–7*, 'For unto us a child is born, unto us a son is given: and the government shall be upon his shoulder: and his name shall be called ... The Prince of Peace. Of the increase of his ... peace there shall be no end.[35]

We see how Edwards' Covenant Theology clearly informed his typological understanding of the Kingdom of God in the days of David and Solomon, and how it was reflective of the fulfillment of that type in the greater Son of David. When considering the theological meaning of the names of David and Solomon, Edwards was employing what we might call an 'etymologico-typological interpretation' of Covenantal types.

In 'Notes' entry 492, Edwards gave us further insight into the process by which he often arrived at a particular spiritual understanding of the imagery of the Song. For Edwards, the spiritual meaning attached to the names of the physical locations that surface in the Song were every bit as relevant as the typological and spiritual significance of allusions to places and events. In Notes 492, Edwards explained what he believed to be the meaning of the 'fishpools of Heshban, by the gates of Bath-Rabbim' in Canticles 7:4.[36] In entry 493, Edwards continued his exploration of theological significance of places mentioned in the Song when he commented on the meaning of 'the tower of Lebanon looking toward Damascus' in Canticles 7:4.[37]

Tabernacle/Temple as Typological of Christ and the Church

While all of the former interpretive observations are essential to understanding Edwards' Christological reading of the _Song_, none are so intriguing as his reflections on the imagery of the _Song_ in the details concerning the Tabernacle in the wilderness and the Temple in Jerusalem. We have already underscored the fact that Edwards' accepted the Solomonic authorship of the Song. We should not, therefore, be surprised to find allusions to typological aspects of the Tabernacle and the Temple in Solomon's superlative _Song_. Not surprisingly, the majority of Edwards' references to the Tabernacle/Temple imagery in the _Song_ are found in his volume on 'Types of the Messiah.' Edwards set out a cluster of types of Christ from the allusions to various aspects of the Tabernacle and Temple mentioned in the _Song_. He wrote:

> Something in the kingdom of the Messiah is spoken of in the prophecies under the name of pomegranates, which were represented in the work of the tabernacle and temple (Canticles 4:3, Canticles 4:13, and Canticles 6:7, Canticles 6:11, and Canticles 7:12 and Canticles 8:2) … The church and people of the Messiah are in the prophecies of the Messiah compared [to] and called a palm tree, or palm trees (Canticles 7:7–8, Psalms 92:12), which is an argument that they were typified by the figures of palm trees in the tabernacle and temple.[38]

Again Edwards highlighted the striking parallels between the language of the Song and the details of the Tabernacle/Temple when he mentioned the 'incense,' 'anointing oils' and 'garments':

> The name of the incense, and the names of the sweet spices that were used in the incense and anointing oil in the sanctuary, are made use of to signify spiritual things appertaining to the

Messiah and his kingdom in the book of Canticles and Psalms 45:8. Something in the Messiah's kingdom is called by the name of the precious stones that adorned the temple. Compare Isaiah 54:11–12 with 1 Chronicles 29:2 and 2 Chronicles 3:8.

And something spiritual in that prophecy, Psalms 45, is called 'needlework,' the name of the work of the hangings and garments of the sanctuary (Exodus 26:36, and Exodus 27:16, and Exodus 36:37, and Exodus 38:18, and Exodus 28:39 and Exodus 39:29). The garments of the church of the Messiah are spoken under the same representation as the curtains of the tabernacle and beautiful garments of the high priest. (See also Canticles 1:5.) Something in the Messiah's kingdom is called by the name of the outward ornaments of the temple (Isaiah 60:13).[39]

Finally, Edwards tied the biblical-theological significance of various ceremonial elements in the Tabernacle and Temple with regard when he wrote, 'The excellencies both of bridegroom and bride are compared to spices ... The same spices were made use of to represent spiritual excellencies in the incense, and anointing oil in the tabernacle and temple, and also in the oil for the light.'[40]

Reflections

Edwards, as with the overwhelming majority of Puritan pastors and theologians, preached the *Song* as a Divine love poem depicting the love between Christ and the church. This feature is often not emulated today because of fear of 'allegorizing.' There may well be an element of truth to such charges in the case of some of the Puritans because they lacked a careful redemptive-historical control. Such charges, however, would simply not stick to Edwards because of the consistent and disciplined manner in which his redemptive-historical methodology guided his grammatical-historical exegesis.

Beyond that, his canonical and covenantal approach to the *Song* enabled Edwards to read it in its full redemptive-historical context.[41] Unlike a number of his Puritan forefathers, the references to the Bride/Bridegroom that permeate Edwards' sermons on *Canticles* are supported by this most important step in his interpretive process—a canonical interpretation of allusions, metaphors, types and symbols in the *Song*.

The highly symbolic and metaphoric language of the Song, the ambiguity surrounding the identification of its characters and the plethora of methodological approaches proposed throughout history have made the interpretation of the Song one of the most difficult hermeneutical tasks for pastors and theologians. The more widely we read commentaries on the *Song*, the more tempted we becomes to throw up the flag of surrender and cast aside any hope of understanding its place within the canon of Scripture. To do so would be to make a mistake of monumental proportion. The *Song* has rightly held a place of prominence in the pulpits and ministries of some of the greatest pastors and theologians in the history of the church. A consideration of the hermeneutical observations of the man who was arguably 'the greatest mind America has ever produced' just might prove to be the key to recovering a Christological and canonical interpretation of the *Song* for the church today.

It would do the church a world of good if her ministers would seek to emulate Edwards and avail themselves of the rich redemptive-historical treasures of the *Song*. It is a matter of great sorrow that the church has neglected this rich inspired source of explicating Christ's love for his church—so sad that many in our churches have never heard the soul-stirring language of Scripture concerning the beauty and glory of the Lord Jesus Christ. Edwards' has handed us the key to help unlock these riches. May we take that key and prayerfully labor to unlock the riches of the superlative redemptive-historical song of Scripture.

10. Our God is an Awesome God: Communicating Jonathan Edwards' Vision of God's Excellencies

Michael Bräutigam

Introduction

As the only native German-speaker among the contributors to this book, I might begin by reminding those in the Anglophone world of one of their many blessings: the theology of Jonathan Edwards. Far more work should be done to rightly *appropriate* his theology, and this is particularly so for the evangelical church. Yet the fact remains that Edwards is at least known among you. Things are otherwise for your German-speaking friends, among whom Jonathan Edwards' theological heritage remains a sadly neglected resource. Along these lines, I thought it might be useful to begin with some remarks about Jonathan Edwards' reception in my native *Deutschland*.

When I discovered Edwards some fifteen years ago as a psychology student in my hometown of Trier, I was surprised to find Edwards' *Works* in the university's philosophy department rather than in the theological library.[1] This turns out to be the norm among German universities. At the University of Tübingen, it is not the theology department but the faculty of 'American Studies' (*Amerikanistik*) which cooperates with Yale Divinity School's Jonathan Edwards Center.[2] Similarly, at the University of Heidelberg, it is the 'American Studies' department which hosts the German 'Jonathan Edwards Center.'[3] Indeed, the centre's website is entirely in English—hardly the ideal way to facilitate an appropriation of Edwards' thought among German-speakers. In general, German scholars are focused primarily on Edwards' political or philosophical ideas.[4] Treatments from a theological perspective are vanishingly few.[5]

Yet there are some encouragements. In addition to the existence of these centres where Edwards is taught—however departmentally misplaced they might be—small evangelical publishers have recently begun selling translations of the *Religious Affections* and *The Life of David Brainerd* as well as Iain H. Murray's biography of Edwards.[6] This is significant, because I think it points to a growing Edwards movement within the German evangelical scene. It is here, it seems, from within the evangelical church, that a discovery of Edwards' thought will be fuelled in the future. I thus welcome the recent translations of Edwards into German and hope that there will be more to come, for I am convinced that an interaction with Jonathan Edwards will be highly beneficial for the German church.

I am not, however, the first to arrive at this opinion. Nearly three hundred years ago, German theologian Johann Adam Steinmetz (1689–1762) realised the significance of Edwards for German theology and, in particular, for the church. Fourteen years Edwards' senior, Steinmetz read with great interest *A Faithful Narrative of the Surprising Work of God* in which the New England minister relates the 'the Conversion of Many Hundred Souls' among his Northampton congregation during the 1734–1736 Connecticut River Valley revival.[7] Published in 1737, *A Faithful Narrative* 'became a key text in the history of revivalism, a manual for other ministers to follow as they sought and guided their own congregations.'[8]

One of these ministers was Steinmetz. He must have acquired a copy fresh from the printing press and he must also have been well-versed in English, for he was able to publish his translation of the *Faithful Narrative* only one year later, in 1738, as *Glaubwürdige Nachricht von dem herrlichen Werck Gottes*.[9] Today, almost three hundred years after Steinmetz' publication, I cannot but reiterate his observation:

> Right at the first perusal of this message [*A Faithful Narrative*] my mind was overwhelmed by delight; and it could well be that my hopes have been raised insofar as one might expect a certain benefit for some souls if it would also be published in our German language.[10]

I share Steinmetz' high expectations. There remains great potential in translating Edwards not only into German, but also into French, Italian, Swedish, Polish etc. The church on the European continent stands to gain much by rediscovering Edwards today.

Jonathan Edwards was primarily a man of the church, a minister who laboured in local churches almost his entire life. I think he would be very disappointed to learn—and if Edwards is right about the nature of our situation in heaven, he has already heard—that he had been transferred to the 'Institute of American Studies' or the philosophy department. Edwards belongs first and foremost to the church. In this essay, I intend to highlight some key aspects that demonstrate Edwards' relevance for the contemporary church throughout the world. In my view, it is particular Edwards' vision of what he called 'God's excellencies,' which could work as a powerful impetus for our community of faith.

This chapter is divided into two major parts. We shall focus, *first*, on Edwards' concept of God as 'a communicative Being,' exploring how Edwards introduces to us a God who enjoys to communicate to us his own love, holiness and joy. We then move, *secondly*, to Edwards' significant emphasis on the minister as God's instrument of divine communication, taking a closer look at how, in his view, pastors communicate knowledge of God and happiness in God to the glory of God.

1. Divine Communicativeness

We turn, first of all, then, to Edwards' fundamental claim that God is a communicative being. This conviction lies at the heart of Jonathan Edwards' theology. In Edwards' view, God communicates *ad intra*, that is, in the communion of the eternal, blessed fellowship of the Godhead: God 'delights in his glory [*ad intra*].'[11] Between the Father, the Son and the Holy Spirit, there is an intimate sharing of knowledge, holiness and joy—God's delight in himself is infinite.[12] According to Edwards, the divine self-communication *ad intra* somewhat flows over *ad extra*. This is Edwards' answer to the question as to why God created the world. Through creation God seeks to be 'diffused, overflowing, and as it were enlarged; or in one word, *existing ad extra*.'[13] Of course, God would surely have remained as glorious, excellent and perfect without creation.[14] Yet creation is almost the necessary consequence of God's exuberant delight in self-communication,[15] it is the result of the 'inclination in God to cause his internal glory to flow out *ad extra*.'[16] Edwards writes:

> The great and universal end of God's creating the world was to communicate himself. God is a communicative being ... God created the world for the shining forth of his excellency and for the flowing forth of his happiness. It don't make God the happier to be praised, but it is a becoming and condecent and worthy thing for infinite and supreme excellency to shine forth: 'tis not his happiness but his excellency so to do.[17]

Human beings now play a crucial part in God's communicative project. We are placed on planet earth to be recipients of God's self-communication. The creatures 'are made,' writes Edwards, 'that God may have in them occasions to fulfil His pleasure in manifesting and communicating Himself.'[18]

Divine Excellency in Creation

This communicativeness is good news for us, Edwards argues, because we are invited to admire the beautiful, altogether glorious, excellent God. Excellence, or excellency, in Edwards' vocabulary 'specifies ultimate good (moral and aesthetic),' it describes 'that which is beautiful and lovely.'[19] ''Tis evident,' Edwards claims, 'that man was made to behold and be delighted with the excellency of God in his works, or in short, to be made happy by beholding God's excellency.'[20] This means that we humans possess our cognitive capacities not in order to (arrogantly) celebrate the competence of our own reason, as Edwards argued time and again in opposition to contemporary Enlightenment thinkers, but in order to (humbly) witness to and participate in God's communication of his excellencies as displayed in creation.[21] Jonathan Edwards was keen to make a case for a holistic, theocentric understanding of reality:[22]

> The immense magnificence of the visible world in inconceivable vastness, the incomprehensible height of the heavens, etc., is but a type of the infinite magnificence, height and glory of God's world in the spiritual world: the most incomprehensible expression of His power, wisdom, holiness and love.[23]

For Edwards, William M. Schweitzer explains, 'all of reality is the harmonious communication of the Triune divine mind.'[24] As Edwards perceived it, the whole of reality was infused with God's beauty, his harmony, and excellency: 'Yea, he is nothing but excellency; and all that he does, nothing but excellent.'[25] He thereby countered any attempts by the Deists to reduce the excellent God to some disinterested deity.[26]

Edwards' passion to perceive and to praise God's excellency in creation is in fact a powerful apologetic tool for us today as we engage critically with the New Atheism movement, with the likes of Richard Dawkins (1941–), who caricatures God as the *Blind Watchmaker*, or Francis Crick (1916–2004), who stated that we are 'just a bundle of neurons.'[27] There is much to learn from the author of the 'Spider-letter,' who, with childlike curiosity inspected and dissected creation in order to trace the fingerprints of his glorious Father in heaven.[28] Edwards helps us to see God's creation with new eyes. I am convinced that it is vital for the spiritual well-being of our congregations today that we rediscover a vision for the glory of creation as a reflection of the divine excellencies.

'No' to Natural Theology, 'Yes' (!) to Natural and Special Revelation

At this point, one needs to take a closer look at the question of natural theology and/or natural revelation in relation to special revelation. My fear is that some might have mistaken Karl Barth's famous 'No' to natural theology for a 'No' to natural revelation as well.[29] This, however, is far from being a well-established argument.[30] At any rate, Jonathan Edwards would have certainly supported Barth's disapproval of natural theology.[31] He countered the deists' claim that one could deduce a natural religion from the 'book of nature.'[32] Still, Edwards emphasised, perhaps more strongly than Barth, his 'Yes' to natural revelation. It is precisely this 'Yes' which deserves to be articulated strongly in the community of faith today: 'The heavens declare the glory of God, and the sky above proclaims his handiwork' (Psalm 19:1).[33]

However, while something of God can be known through the created order, human beings remain blind to God's special self-revelation without the help of divine intervention.[34] In one of his sermons, Edwards reminds his listeners that 'divine things are above man's reason and depend on pure revelation.'[35] He writes:

> The whole of Christian divinity depends on divine revelation; for though there are many truths concerning God and our duty to him that are evident by the light of nature, yet no one truth is taught by the light of nature in that manner in which it is necessary for us to know it.[36]

In order to participate fully in God's self-communication of his knowledge, of his love and joy, we need Scripture, the 'sweet, excellent, life-giving word,' together with 'an immediate infusion or operation of the Divine Being upon the soul.'[37]

A Divine and Supernatural Light

Edwards took the apostle Paul seriously, who explains that the 'god of this world has blinded the minds of the unbelievers, to keep them from seeing the light of the gospel of the glory of Christ, who is the image of God' (2 Corinthians 4:4). Hence, only with divine intervention can the believer participate in the divine communication of excellencies, as he now sees:

> ... things in a new appearance, in quite another view, than ever he saw before: he sees an excellency in God; he sees a sweet loveliness in Christ; he sees an amiableness in holiness and God's commandments; he sees an excellency in a Christian spirit and temper; he sees the wonderfulness of God's designs and a harmony in all his ways, a harmony, excellency and wondrousness in his Word: he sees these things by an eye of faith, and by a new light that was never before let into his mind.[38]

Only God can bring about an 'inward, sweet delight in God and divine things ... a new kind of apprehensions and ideas of Christ, and the work of redemption, and the glorious way of salvation by him.'[39] Edwards compares this spiritual enlightenment to the creation of a 'new sense of the heart' in us.[40] It is about tasting and seeing spiritual things with new eyes: 'Thus it is not he that has heard a long description of the sweetness of honey that can be said to have the greatest understanding of it, but he that has tasted it ... The spiritual illumination of the minds of believers is resembled to that of tasting.[41]

It is only with this new sense that one can see and savour the culmination of God's self-communication in his Son Jesus Christ, who is the 'image of the invisible God' (Colossians 1:15).[42] We need divine, special intervention, in order to see Jesus as who he is, namely, 'an emanation of his [God's] own infinite fullness.'[43]

From Edwards' perspective, congregational worship is the supreme occasion for God's special revelation, his sending of the divine and supernatural light, as Holy Scripture is proclaimed and Christ is magnified. In this context, the minister plays a vital role. The emphasis on the minister's role in God's project of self-communication is a characteristic aspect of Edwards' program and in what follows we shall examine this more closely.

2. Divine Communication and the Role of the Minister

Secondly, according to Edwards, ministers participate in God's communicative project.[44] They are God's instruments through which he communicates himself in a special way to the world and God delights in the preaching of his servants, as they glorify his Son Jesus Christ.[45] The sermon is in this respect central to Edwards and we will focus on this particular aspect in our subsequent considerations. Following Edwards, 'the preaching of the Gospel is the means God has provided for the bringing [of] poor sinners to Christ and salvation by him.'[46] The goal of salvation for Edwards is that human beings would glorify God: 'He [God] commits men's souls to ministers ...' Edwards explains, 'that by their means they may answer their end in glorifying him.'[47]

Yet how do we glorify God? We glorify God, Edwards responds, as we see and savour God's excellency, as we take part in God's enjoyment of himself.[48] To achieve this grand goal, God uses ministers. This seems a daunting task for the preacher. It might be helpful to take a closer look at what Edwards has in mind here.

How are ministers supposed to communicate God's excellencies so that believers would glorify God? We shall focus on three aspects: ministers communicate a) God's knowledge, b) they present an occasion for an encounter with God and c) they communicate God's joy.

a. Communicating Knowledge

Communicating God's excellencies implies for Edwards, first of all, that ministers communicate knowledge of God. Ministers, Edwards claims, are 'not to preach those things which their own wisdom or reason suggests, but the things already dictated to them by the superior wisdom and knowledge of God.'[49] The minister's primary task, then, is to communicate not their own ideas or concepts but God's Word to the congregation. And when it comes to the Word of God, there is nothing, Edwards is keen to point out, the pastor may hold back. The whole counsel of God should be preached. Edwards put it bluntly: 'God does not need to be told by his messengers what message is fit to deliver to those to whom he sends them, but they are to declare his counsel and are not to shun to declare his whole counsels, whether men will hear or whether they will forbear.'[50]

Declaring God's 'whole counsels' implies for Edwards that one does not shy away from studying and teaching difficult and complex doctrines. 'Ministers,' he insists, 'are not only not to reject those doctrines of revelation that are difficult to their reason themselves, but are to teach them to their hearers.'[51] This was important to Edwards. 'God gave man the faculty of understanding,' he contends, 'chiefly, that he might understand divine things.'[52] It was his personal endeavour to test his God-given ability to reason to the very limits—which is perhaps why he rose at around 'four or five in the morning in order to spend thirteen hours in his study.'[53] Yet to Edwards' mind, personal study was not only crucial for the minister himself but also vital for the members of his congregation. Edwards encouraged his fellow brothers and sisters to join him in the task of life-long learning, disciplined prayerful study of the text, in humble reliance on the Holy Spirit. He was convinced that '[d]ivine truths not only concern ministers, but are of infinite importance to all Christians.'[54] 'Every Christian,' Edwards highlights, 'should make a business of endeavouring to grow in knowledge in divinity.'[55]

This is an important reminder for us today. My suspicion is that we are sometimes at risk of dumbing-down our doctrine. To satisfy the consumers in the pew, some might be tempted to offer theological fast food, which cannot ultimately satisfy but leaves the believer malnourished. Mark Noll lamented some time ago that '[t]he scandal of the evangelical mind is that there is not much of an evangelical mind.'[56] This fear might be still justified today. It might be wise to go back to Edwards, adopting his view of the believer as theologian.

While Edwards clearly tested his own cognitive capacities—as those of his congregation—to the limits, he was happy to admit that we stand, ultimately, before divine mysteries. Edwards writes:

> It is their [the ministers'] duty not to reject any doctrine that, by comparing one Scripture with another, appears truly to be held forth by the voice of revelation, though it contains difficulties and seeming inconsistencies that their reason cannot solve. We ought to receive doctrines that thus appear to be taught in Scripture, though they are mysteries—yeah, though they remain mysteries to us.[57]

Thus, Edwards passionately struggled with difficult texts and laboured with seeming contradictions, but he knew about the limits of his own reason and he was happy to stand in awe before mysteries he could not explain. And it was Edwards' stated intention to invite his listeners to join him in his awesome vision of God's mysteries. While Edwards, then, reveals a strong emphasis on theology and teaching, one notes that preaching serves a much higher purpose than mere knowledge transfer as it opens the listeners' vista to the mysteries of God. 'The main benefit that is obtained by preaching,' Edwards writes, 'is by impression made upon the mind in the time of it, and not by the effect that arises afterwards by a remembrance of what was delivered.'[58] Preaching is thus not simply about an accumulation of knowledge, but about an experiential, even mysterious or awe-inspiring encounter.[59]

With this we move to the second aspect of the minister's task in communicating God's excellencies.

b. Presenting the Occasion for an Encounter with the Excellent God

Secondly, the minister communicates God's excellencies as he offers—in and through preaching—an occasion for an encounter with the excellent God. Thus, in preaching, Edwards' intention was to paint a picture of the reality and the glory of God's excellencies, so that his hearers would have a real sense of the divine things. Edwards captivated his listeners, but not with ostentatious rhetoric flourishes or exaggerated gestures. His style was not melodramatic but pragmatic: he simply showed his fellow believers what he saw before his spiritual eyes. And what he saw was 'Christ the Spiritual Sun,'[60] 'The Sweet Harmony of Christ,'[61] and 'The Excellency of Christ.'[62] Edwards carefully explained how in Christ meet 'infinite highness, and infinite condescension,' 'infinite justice, and infinite grace,' 'infinite glory, and the lowest humility,' 'infinite majesty, and transcendent meekness.'[63]

Again, as Edwards describes the excellencies of Jesus Christ, he does not use various techniques of modulation or expression, but what Perry Miller calls a 'rhetoric of sensation,'[64] that is, he uses sensory language, figures of speech, and adjectives that create vivid imagery. Moreover, Edwards was convinced that in order to authentically communicate divine excellencies, he had to be familiar with these excellencies himself. Edwards was keen to get an intimate, heartfelt knowledge of God's excellencies firsthand before he could then, in the context of the worship service, take his congregants by the hand and show them what he saw and experienced. The sermon then provided a platform where he could nurture and cultivate a sense of God's glory, as he demonstrated how he himself was captivated by his vision of an awesome and wonderful God, inviting his listeners to be enthralled by this vision, too.

To arrive at this vision of an excellent God involves, in Edwards' view, a rediscovery of the spiritual disciplines: Scripture reading, prayer, fasting, contemplation and meditation.[65] This is his recommendation: '[M]inisters should be very conversant with the Holy Scriptures; making it very much their business, with the utmost diligence and strictness, to search those holy writings ... [a]nd they should be much in seeking God, and conversing with him by prayer.'[66] Pursuing these spiritual disciplines is probably one of the most essential, yet one of the most endangered aspects of the ministry. The pursuit of spiritual disciplines is in constant danger of being substituted with conflicting, seemingly more efficient tasks. Of course, meetings have to be prepared and budgets need to be set up; still, Edwards encourages us to rethink and to recalibrate our priorities and our time-management. He reminds us that the minister's central task is to contemplate holy things, divine excellencies until one is saturated with a view of the glory of God, so that on a Sunday morning, one is able to guide the congregation through the wardrobe right into the fascinating country of Narnia, exploring with fellow believers the glories of the kingdom of God.

Edwards offers here an important wake-up call for the minister's self-understanding. Communicants in the pew have the right to expect that their minister shepherds them out of the profane and mundane right into the presence of the holy God, the holy of holies. And for this existential encounter to happen it is absolutely essential, in Edwards' view, that the minister has first experienced a close encounter with divine excellencies in the study. If the minister is not captivated by the glory of God as he prepares the sermon in the closet, how can he expect his listeners to be excited about God in church on a Sunday morning. The miracle happens first in the study before it happens in church. Moreover, this experiential encounter with the excellent God is, and this brings us to our third and final point, an intrinsically joyful encounter.

c. Communicating Joy

Thirdly, then, the minister's task is to communicate the joy of experiencing God's excellencies. It is a characteristically Edwardsean tenet that the experience of divine excellencies is a joyful one.[67] God delights in communicating to us not only the knowledge of himself but also his joy. This is the whole point: '[T]he Son created and doth govern the world; seeing that the world was a communication of him, and seeing the communicating of his happiness is the end of the world.'[68] Now it is important to note that for Edwards, knowledge of God and the joyful experience of him belong together. Mind and heart go hand in hand. He writes:

> God made the world that he might communicate, and the creature receive, his glory; but that it might [be] received both by the mind and the heart. He that testifies his having an idea of God's glory [doesn't] glorify God so much as he that testifies also his approbation of it and his delight in it.[69]

Both aspects are essential, and for this reason, Edwards aimed at a rational *and* emotive response in the believer, since he was convinced that God does not only communicate to us his self-knowledge but also his happiness in himself—and the two are intricately connected.

How did Edwards put this into practise? Edwards chose to proceed by working his way through the head right into the heart of his listeners. This sequence was important to him. Knowledge comes before the joyful experience. 'Such is the nature of man,' Edwards writes, 'that no object can come at the heart but through the door of the understanding: and there can be no spiritual knowledge of that of which there is not first a rational knowledge.'[70] True affective experience thus appears in the wake of true spiritual insight. Edwards writes:

> A man cannot see the wonderful excellency and love of Christ in doing such and such things for sinners, unless his understanding be first informed how those things were done. He cannot have a taste of the sweetness and excellency of divine truth, unless he first have a notion that there is such a thing.[71]

Edwards' intention then was to communicate divine truth, aiming at a joyful response in his listeners.

'The preacher,' Edwards claims, 'was not only to inform the understanding but to awaken hearers' hearts and imaginations in an encounter with spiritual realities.'[72] In so doing, Edwards was not afraid to raise his hearers' affections: 'I should think myself in the way of my duty to raise the affections of my hearers as high as possibly I can, provided that they are affected with nothing but truth, and with affections that are not disagreeable to the nature of what they are affected with.'[73]Again, the link between divine truth and affection is explicit. True religious affections are rooted in the divine excellency. '[L]ove or affection to God,' Edwards writes, 'that has no other ground than only some benefit received or hoped for from God without any sense of a delight in the absolute excellency of the divine nature, has nothing divine in it.'[74] In other words, Edwards' goal was to arrive at *admiration* of God—the exquisite combination of love and knowledge. Oliver O'Donovan's reflections are illuminating here: 'This coherence of emotion and cognition we may capture in the term 'admiration,' which is the knowledge of what can only be known in love, and the love of what can only be loved in knowledge.'[75] This is a helpful reminder; adequate admiration of God holds a balance between love and knowledge, it pursues a 'coherence of emotion and cognition.'

One wonders whether there might be some Pentecostal or charismatic denominations today which could learn a great deal from Edwards in this respect. Joyful affections are not to be pursued simply for the sake of an inspiring experience, but they represent the natural effluence of a significant encounter with the divine excellencies. On the other hand, there might be some Reformed movements which might benefit from Edwards' insight that the sermon is more than a cognitive-cerebral exegetical-exercise: '[T]here is a difference between having a right speculative notion of the doctrines contained in the word of God, and having a due sense of them in the heart.'[76] One does not go without the other.

Conclusion

Johann Adam Steinmetz was intrigued by Edwards' *Faithful Narrative of the Surprising Work of God*. He was particularly attracted by the notion of 'surprise.' In his preface to the German translation, Steinmetz laments that some of his Protestant colleagues had somewhat lost their ability to be surprised by God and who 'thus carried out their work ... with a certain sense of despair.'[77] Perhaps this might apply to some of us today, too. We might do well in rediscovering this Edwardsean ability to be surprised by God, or, as C. S. Lewis put it, to be 'surprised by joy.'[78]

Jonathan Edwards encourages us to fan into flame our excitement about the God who continues to take us by surprise with his communicative project. He wants to introduce to us the glorious God who communicates himself in all of reality. Everything is saturated with God's excellency. In a highly creative way, Edwards brings together sovereign divine communicative action and human involvement as he discusses the particular role of the minister in communicating divine excellencies.

Through preaching, the minister communicates the knowledge of God, and this knowledge must be substantial. 'Theology without proclamation is empty,' Gerhard Ebeling writes, 'proclamation without theology is blind.'[79] Edwards would have surely agreed. Yet proclamation for Edwards was more than a lecture, it was an event.[80] For Edwards, the ordinary task of preaching presents an opportunity for extraordinary, surprising things to happen. It is here, where the move from theology to doxology takes place, as God's Word is publicly proclaimed and Christ is magnified and listeners are satisfied with their vision of an excellent God.

Edwards thus sends us back to our study. And he expects us to expect great things from God, to expect to be surprised by God's excellencies, and to communicate this to our fellow pilgrims on the way.

Appendix

Wilt Thou Not Revive Us? A Sermon on Psalm 85:6

William Macleod

Introduction

M y text is Psalm 85:6, 'Wilt thou not revive us again: that thy people may rejoice in thee?' (KJV). Here we have a prayer in which the Psalmist is earnestly pouring out his heart to God for revival. He felt the great need in his day. The question is, do we? We look back over the years and notice a massive decline in church membership. Great preachers we knew in our youth are no longer with us, and lesser men have taken their place. Godly Christians who once were pillars in evangelical churches have been taken home, and too few have replaced them. The church today appears to be dying if not already dead. Worldliness has invaded the church. Christians are sleeping. Spiritual discernment is lacking. The fear of God is missing not just in society in general, but even from the church. Preaching seems to be powerless. Few real conversions are taking place. Things seem to be going from bad to worse. It has been 150 years since the last great revival in our country. What does the future hold? Will things continue to deteriorate? Will the true church die out in Britain? Will God remove His candlestick from its place? We do not know, but surely an urgent pleading for revival should be the great prayer of God's people in our day.

Jonathan Edwards' grandfather Solomon Stoddard was minister of Northampton from 1672 till 1729, almost 60 years. Edwards writes concerning his ministry that he had five 'harvests,' as he called them, when many were added to the church. Some of these times were much more remarkable than others, and the ingathering of souls more plentiful. Yet there seemed to be a great falling away after the last of these, with licentiousness, night walking, frequenting the tavern and lewd practices becoming common. But then in 1734–35 there was the first great revival of Edwards' time. The town was transformed. Everyone became concerned about their souls. Multitudes were saved. The fear of God came down on the community. Edwards gives a full account of this in his 'Faithful Narrative.' The second revival was 1740–42 and is outlined in a 1743 letter to Thomas Prince (WJE 16:115–127). This second revival was part of what we know as the Great Awakening and was much more widespread, covering all New England and the other colonies and with a related movement in the British Isles. Reading what Edwards has written concerning these great movements of God's Spirit should stir our hearts and makes us long for such a mighty revival of God's Spirit in our own times.

1. What is Revival?
Revival is a specific period of increased spiritual interest and renewal in the life of a church or many churches, either regionally or

globally. This should be distinguished from the use of the term
'revival' to refer to an evangelistic meeting or series of meetings.
Revival is when God comes down and works mightily in the church
bringing new life and spiritual interest, prayerfulness, holiness of
life and zeal for the conversion of souls. Communities become
aware of God in a new way and many unbelievers are born again.

I come from the Island of Lewis which has been blessed with
a series of revivals since the gospel first came there with power in
1828. After school, I went to Aberdeen as a student and became
involved in the Christian Union. Hearing where I came from, folk
would say to me that they had heard of the Lewis Revival. Initially,
puzzled, I responded, 'Which one?' They had heard of the Duncan
Campbell revival in 1949. It was just one among a whole series and
certainly not the biggest but the difference in this one was that
an outsider was involved and that after the revival he went to the
Keswick Convention and other places talking about the great work
in which he had been involved. I remember the last general revival
in Lewis which took place in the early 1970s when some hundreds
were converted in the space of a year or so. God used ordinary
preaching and common phrases, accompanied with power, to
deeply convict the ungodly. The Lord's people were roused from
their lethargy. There was no doubting that the work was of God
and many lives were marvellously transformed. Converts from that
movement are the elders in the church there today.

In the history of God's people in the Old Testament there were
several revivals. God visited His people when they were slaves in
the land of Egypt and brought them out with a mighty arm and
made them into a great nation. The book of Judges records several
revivals. The people fell away from God, began to worship idols,

and God punished them by sending some neighbouring king to invade their land and oppress them. After several years of oppression they repented and cried to God and He raised up a deliverer for them, e.g., Gideon, Deborah and Barak, and Jephthah. All was well during the reign of that judge but after he died, they again tended to forget God, fall away into idolatry and judgment came upon them once more. Samuel the prophet was used in a series of revivals which came to their climax in the reign of David and the early days of Solomon. Kings Hezekiah and Josiah also saw wonderful revivals. Led by the king the people as a whole turned from idolatry to the living God. Repentance was followed by joy and gladness and the rich blessing from the Lord.

Essentially, revival is an outpouring of God's Spirit upon the church bringing new spiritual life to God's people, convicting of sin, stirring up repentance, awakening interest in spiritual concerns, increasing zeal for God's glory, burdening with prayer and making Christ and the gospel the centre of life. Revival impacts the unconverted by convicting them of their sin, of God's holiness and justice, of the hell to which they are heading, so that they cry to the Lord for mercy and are unsatisfied till they find peace with God through Jesus Christ. Edwards speaks of the presence of God felt in the community; God's day was a delight, the churches were packed, the worship was earnest and the people listened hungrily to the sermons. Some wept in sorrow for sin, others rejoiced in their salvation and in others being saved. The town, said Edwards, was full of love and joy and distress.

2. We Need Revival

We are not told who was the author of this Psalm and we can only guess when it was written. Many commentators think it was composed some time after the return from the exile in Babylon. Initially on returning to the land of Israel there was great excitement and euphoria. God's promise through Jeremiah had been fulfilled and after 70 years of bondage they were free to return to their own land. They built an altar and started the sacrifices once more. The rubbish was cleared and they proceeded to lay the foundations for the second temple. However, before long, the enthusiasm waned. There were enemies discouraging them. They had to build houses for their own families, clear the land, plant crops and look after their own livelihoods. But in all their work for themselves they were earning money to put it into a bag with holes (Haggai 1:6). They needed revival and Haggai called them back to the work of building the temple of the Lord and the blessing followed.

This situation would certainly fit the Psalm but it may come from another time in Israel's history. Days of declension were not uncommon in the experience of God's people in the Old Testament. The pious Israelite must often have felt the need and longed for revival, for a real, mighty work of God's Spirit. How often down through the centuries would the child of God have prayed prayers like this!

The Psalmist begins by remembering that there were real days of blessing in the past: 'Lord, thou hast been favourable unto thy land: thou hast brought back the captivity of Jacob' (v. 1). God had often been favourable to His people. He had delivered them from captivity and from tyrants who had been given power over them because of their backsliding. God has always been actively training His people. When they go astray after idols, or lust, or violence, He sends prophets to warn them and if they will not give heed He will send His chastisement to bring them back. This had happened in the experience of the Psalmist.

'Thou hast forgiven the iniquity of thy people, thou hast covered all their sin' (v. 2). Praise God for forgiveness of sins, for justification by faith alone. God loves to pardon for Christ's sake. 'Thou hast taken away all thy wrath: thou hast turned thyself from the fierceness of thine anger' (v. 3). Yes, God is angry with sinners. Even His elect feel His anger, though thankfully only for a moment: 'For a small moment have I forsaken thee; but with great mercies will I gather thee. In a little wrath I hid my face from thee for a moment; but with everlasting kindness will I have mercy on thee, saith the Lord thy Redeemer' (Isaiah 54:7–8). The Psalmist is aware that he and his people have again backslidden and turned from the Lord. There is nothing easier than to backslide. Satan is always tempting and the flesh loves sin. Their environment in a sinful world makes sin seem natural and normal. So the Psalmist cried out, 'Turn us, O God of our salvation, and cause thine anger toward us to cease. Wilt thou be angry with us forever? wilt thou draw out thine anger to all generations?' (vv. 4–5).

We too have experienced the favour of God. The Gospel first came to these shores at an early date. Some reckon that it happened in the First Century. Paganism came in again with the invasion of the Angles, Saxons and Jutes from Northern Europe. God once again sent missionaries such as Columba from Ireland. The church again backslid into Medieval darkness but God sent the Reformers of the Sixteenth Century with a mighty revival—Luther, Calvin, Cranmer, Tyndale and Knox. What a revival it was that chased Roman darkness from our shores. Decline followed and then God raised up the Puritans with a new revival. Again there was spiritual backsliding but God raised up Whitefield and the Wesleys and Jonathan Edwards and brought about the Great Awakening of the Eighteenth Century. Decline followed and then once again revival came in the Nineteenth Century 1859–60. Alas, since then there has been a steady decline, one hundred and fifty years of it.

Look at the situation we are in today. Liberalism came in from Germany in the Nineteenth Century and took over the mainline churches. The Bible is no longer received as the infallible, authoritative Word of God. Evolutionary teaching has removed the Creator from the throne, and man no longer feels the need to make his peace with his Maker. Mass evangelism has produced its own man-made revival with its impressive results which must not be searched or examined too closely. The Charismatic Movement has produced signs and wonders and its 'health and wealth' Gospel which promises a heaven in this world, providing you generate your own faith in the movement and its leaders. Fake healings, false prophesies and gobble-de-gook tongue-speaking, as John Macarthur puts it.

Even the Reformed churches have looked longingly across the Atlantic at the mega-churches there and have struggled to follow them and be 'seeker-sensitive,' to entertain and not to offend in the hopes of sharing in their specious success. Church services must first and foremost be entertaining. Intelligent young people are looking for exciting music, trivial choruses repeated ad infinitum and short sermons full of jokes and anecdotes. Sin, holiness, the wrath of God, the judgment day and hell must not be mentioned. The greatest fear in the church today is not worldliness—a word that is scarcely ever heard—but 'legalism', a word to smear anyone who dares to preach personal holiness. But despite all this, the church continues to decline drastically in numbers. Occasionally gifted individuals with teams of helpers and lots of social activities can gather some hundreds together. However the church is making little impact on society and there are few conversions. Such conversions as there are, tend to be superficial and do not last. Growth tends to be by sheep-stealing from smaller congregations as even in Christian circles a crowd draws a crowd and modern Christians show little ability to think for themselves and stand on their own feet.

The fear of God is to be found neither in the world nor in the church. God has, in a sense, turned His back on us. His judgment rests upon the church in our land. Even the best of churches show little true devotion to God, holiness of life, love for deep doctrine, reading of Puritan theology, solid fellowship in the Scriptures, earnestness in secret prayer, compassion for lost souls and zeal for God's glory.

Outside the church, apathy pervades society. To raise the subject of Christ and Christianity, sin and judgment and heaven and hell creates embarrassment. People will happily talk on any other subject. We have the good news of the gospel but no one wants to hear it. Invite folk to a party or a wedding and they will come in droves, but invite them to the gospel wedding feast and they will have all kinds of excuses. There is no sense of spiritual need and so the proclamation of salvation through the blood of Christ is like casting one's pearls before swine.

3. We Need God

'Wilt not thou revive us.' We need God to come. We need Him to act. We can arrange outreach visitation, evangelistic campaigns, conferences, the best visiting preachers, Christianity Explored courses, discipleship programmes, etc., but it is all in vain without the Spirit of God. It is God we need and nothing less. We need the sovereign, powerful, regenerating, reviving work of the Spirit of God. We have a valley full of dead bones, very many and truly dead, indeed whitened by the sun (Ezekiel 37). Can these bones live? There is nothing we can do to revive them. But God gathers the bones, makes the flesh and sinews to grow, but they are still dead corpses. Ezekiel tells us:

> And when I beheld, lo, the sinews and the flesh came up upon them, and the skin covered them above: but there was no breath in them. Then said he unto me, Prophesy unto the wind, prophesy, son of man, and say to the wind, Thus saith the Lord God; Come from the four winds, O breath, and breathe upon these slain, that they may live. So I prophesied as he commanded me, and the breath came into them, and they lived, and stood up upon their feet, an exceeding great army. Then he said unto me, Son of man, these bones are the whole house of Israel: behold, they say, Our bones are dried, and our hope is lost: we are cut off for our parts. Therefore prophesy and say unto them, Thus saith the Lord God; Behold, O my people, I will open your graves, and cause you to come up out of your graves, and bring you into the land of Israel. And ye shall know that I am the Lord, when I have opened your graves, O my people, and brought you up out of your graves, And shall put my spirit in you, and ye shall live, and I shall place you in your own land: then shall ye know that I the Lord have spoken it, and performed it, saith the Lord (Ezekiel 37:8–13).

Christ commanded his disciples 'that they should not depart from Jerusalem, but wait for the promise of the Father, which, saith he, ye have heard of me. For John truly baptised with water; but ye shall be baptised with the Holy Ghost not many days hence' (Acts 1:4–5). The disciples waited in prayer in the upper room. Ten days were to pass before the Spirit came. Now Pentecost was unique; it was a once-for-all historical-redemptive act of God. It was the coming of the Comforter who would abide with the church till Christ came again. Yet Acts 2 also demonstrates how much we need God's Spirit to revive the church and convert sinners. Following the pouring out of the Spirit the disciples had new boldness, an unction from the Holy One which taught them things which before were very unclear to them, power in preaching and, most amazing of all, conviction of sin accompanying the heralding of the gospel and regeneration in the heart by the working of God's Spirit.

Surely if God is teaching us one thing today in Britain, it is that we need Him. He is demonstrating to us over and over again our weakness, inability and helplessness. 'Without me, you can do nothing' (John 15:5). He also encourages us to say, 'I can do all things through Christ which strengtheneth me' (Philippians 4:13). Christ says, 'I will build my church; and the gates of hell shall not prevail against it' (Matthew 16:18). The building is Christ's work and His alone. Yes, Paul plants and Apollos waters, but God gives the increase (1 Corinthians 3:6). No amount of planting and watering produces a harvest without God who gives the increase. The trouble with us is that we want some praise for ourselves but God will not give His glory to another. Oh that we would learn our own helplessness so that we would look to God and depend totally on Him!

4. We Need to Pray

So if it is God's work, then is there nothing that we can do? In a sense that is true. Yet we have human responsibility. We can pray and we can ask for revival. Yet even in this we need God's help to pray earnestly, persistently, humbly and with faith. It is the prayer which comes down from above which will ascend to God and bring down the blessing. When God grants the Spirit of grace and supplications (Zechariah 12:10) effectual, fervent prayers will ascend to heaven (James 5:16). In one sense there is nothing harder to do than to pray—to pray in faith and repentance with the Holy Spirit—and yet we must pray. Satan attacks us more when we pray than at any other time. He tries his hardest to distract us and often succeeds. He floods our minds with worldly thoughts and things we have to do. Yet we must pray for revival. It is our duty and as it has been said we should pray till we pray.

The following points should be noticed with regard to prayer for revival:

1. Identify sin

Isaiah tells us why we are not seeing revival: 'Behold, the Lord's hand is not shortened, that it cannot save; neither his ear heavy, that it cannot hear: but your iniquities have separated between you and your God, and your sins have hid his face from you, that he will not hear' (Isaiah 59:1–2). There is a barrier between us and our God and it is one that we have raised. Let us search our hearts, see our sins, confess, repent, wash in the blood and be clean for God. Let us turn from our sins and be holy and then He will stretch out His mighty arm in revival. Are we asking why His hand in judgment is resting upon us?

2. Mourn and weep over sin

Let us fast and mourn and weep over our sins. Let us have that 'godly sorrow [which] worketh repentance to salvation not to be repented of' (2Corinthians 7:10). Let us remember how Ezra, Nehemiah, Daniel and others fasted before the Lord. Our Saviour expected us to fast, 'But thou, when thou fastest, anoint thine head, and wash thy face' (Matthew 6:17). It's *when* you fast, not *if* you fast.

3. Claim the Blood of Christ

Though we are great sinners, Christ is a great Saviour. 'If we confess our sins, he is faithful and just to forgive us our sins, and to cleanse us from all unrighteousness' (1 John 1:9). And we are assured, 'the blood of Jesus Christ his Son cleanseth us from all sin' (v. 7). We must pray for Christ's sake.

4. Plead the promises

Many promises have been given which can be pleaded in prayer. Think of the words in Isaiah: 'For I will pour water upon him that is thirsty, and floods upon the dry ground: I will pour my Spirit upon thy seed, and my blessing upon thine offspring' (Isaiah 44:3). We are dry and thirsty ground here in Britain. We need the water of life, the Holy Spirit, to be poured out upon us. Yes the Spirit was given in a once-for-all way at Pentecost, but we long for a fresh experience of His power to salvation. He is grieved and hiding Himself. Jesus encourages us, 'If ye then, being evil, know how to give good gifts unto your children: how much more shall your heavenly Father give the Holy Spirit to them that ask him?' (Luke 11:13). We who are sinners love to give gifts to our children, how much more will our loving Father in heaven give us the Holy Spirit when we plead with Him. The Holy Spirit is the one who produces revival.

5. Persevere in prayer

We must persevere in prayer even when it seems we are getting no answer. All Christians should persist in prayer, but especially ministers who are called to be watchmen: 'I have set watchmen upon thy walls, O Jerusalem, which shall never hold their peace day nor night: ye that make mention of the Lord, keep not silence, and give him no rest, till he establish, and till he make Jerusalem a praise in the earth' (Isaiah 62:6–7). Jerusalem is the church and instead of it being a tiny down-trodden minority we long to see it grow and multiply till it become a mighty city set upon a hill for all to see and admire. Persevere in secret pray, family prayer and congregational prayer. Remember how Jacob wrestled with God and said 'I will not let thee go, except thou bless me' (Genesis 32:26).

6. Unite in prayer

Jonathan Edwards wrote his famous book entitled, *An humble attempt to promote explicit agreement and visible union of God's people, in extraordinary prayer for the revival of religion and the advancement of Christ's kingdom on earth.* He wished to see all the churches across America and Britain united in prayer for revival on a set day. He joined with others praying for God's blessing during part of every Saturday night and Sunday morning and kept the first Tuesday in each quarter as a day of special prayer and intercession.

7. Pray expectantly

Along with prayer should be expectation. We are to look for answers. Trusting in the power of God who can do anything and in the mercy of God who will do what is best, we are to look for a glorious answer. Ask and you shall receive for Jesus said: 'Every one that asketh receiveth; and he that seeketh findeth; and to him that knocketh it shall be opened' (Matthew 7:8). He 'is rich unto all that call upon him' (Romans 10:12).

5. We Need to Be Clear on What Revival Does

Many people think of revival as mainly being about the conversion of sinners, and so its main impact (as they see it) is upon the *world*. However, the Psalmist starts with the *church*, the people of God: 'revive us again: that thy people may rejoice in thee.' The *church* has fallen asleep and needs to be awakened and revived. The *church* has become weak and needs a new injection of energy. Edwards speaks of God bestowing a sense of need upon the church and causing God's people to start praying in earnest before a revival as the first step in a revival. When the great revival came to North Korea in 1907, the first impact was upon the church. There was a tremendous conviction of sin causing men and women to fall down weeping and confessing their sins before the church.

Revival brings a new hunger for God. Sadly in the church today we spend money for 'that which is not bread' and our labour for 'that which does not satisfy' (Isaiah 55:2). Christians have their lives taken up with pleasures, parties, sport, entertainment, TV, internet, Facebook, YouTube, etc. It is called 'culture' and relaxation but it swallows up all our spare time, so that there is little reading of solid Christian books, meditating on the Scriptures, serious reflection and self-examination, and prayer. The Psalmist said, 'O God, thou art my God; early will I seek thee: my soul thirsteth for thee, my flesh longeth for thee in a dry and thirsty land, where no water is; to see thy power and thy glory, so as I have seen thee in the sanctuary' (Psalm 63:1–2). He had a passion for God. Do we? When revival comes, the Lord's people will turn from trivia and devote themselves to Him. Holiness of life will become the priority. Witnessing and evangelising will become natural and constant.

Having first impacted the church, revival will then affect the whole of society. The fear of God will come down upon the land. Christianity is shown to be real in the life of believers whom the world typically dismisses as hypocrites. This will shake sinners. Eternity will draw near and the Judgment Day will be seen as inevitable. Evangelism will be easy as people come in droves to church and sit earnestly under the preaching which now has new power. The unbelievers are convicted of sin and of God's wrath upon them and cry for mercy. Real tears are shed in repentance. Sinners are born again, delivered from a state of condemnation and brought to peace with God and assurance of His love, peace of conscience and rejoicing in adoption.

6. We Need Joy

This is a world full of sorrows. Everywhere we look there is pain. Sickness, disability, disappointment, grief, tears and death are universal. Scripture states: 'We know that the whole creation groaneth and travaileth in pain together until now' (Romans 8:22). But the Psalmist prays, 'Wilt thou not revive us again: that thy people may rejoice in thee?' Revival brings joy to a sad and miserable world. Christians ought to be happy, because joy is a fruit of the Holy Spirit who indwells them. But we find it difficult. We have foolishly looked in the wrong place for joy. But a revival will be an occasion of great joy to the Christian. Revival brings heaven close. The Spirit works mightily giving joy unspeakable and full of glory (1Peter 1:8). There is joy in seeing one sinner repent and so when many repent there is overwhelming joy (Luke 15:7). Remember the joy you had when you were first converted and knew that your sins were forgiven and that God loved you and Christ died for you and that the Holy Spirit now lived in your heart and that you were indeed a child of God. The love of God filled your heart. In our lives since then there have been times when God has specially drawn near. Perhaps we were praying, or reading a good book or listening to a sermon and we felt God near and we were stirred to the heart. Revival is a time of overflowing joy in God.

7. We Need to Have Confidence in God

The Psalmist began the Psalm by asserting that God had been good to Israel in the past. He had delivered His people from their captivity (v. 1). He had forgiven their sins (v. 2) and turned from His anger with them (v. 3). The fact of that past deliverance encouraged the Psalmist to hope that God would answer his prayer again. Another encouragement was that God is the God of salvation, the God who loves to save (v. 4). Surely this God will not always be angry with His people (v. 5). He is a merciful God, let Him reveal His salvation (v. 7). I will listen to God for He will speak words of peace to His people. Do not let us return to the foolish ways which brought His anger upon us (v. 8). Salvation is near to us and the God of glory will reveal Himself (v. 9). Through the work of Christ at Calvary, mercy and truth and righteousness and peace have met together. Heaven and earth are joined in Christ who is God and man (v. 11). There is a blessed and prosperous future (v. 12). Many will be justified by faith in Christ (v. 13).

'Wilt thou not revive us again: that thy people may rejoice in thee?' Surely we can pray this prayer with confidence because of who God is and what He has done in the past. We live in dark days but there is no reason to despair. God has not lost His ancient power. The sophisticated sinners of today and the proud atheists who love to dismiss God are not beyond His power to save. It is as easy for Him in 2014 to save a persecutor and blasphemer as it was for Him to save Paul 2,000 years ago. It takes a mighty miracle for God to regenerate anyone. The sinner who is dead in trespasses and sins has to be resurrected. Only God can do it and it takes the same mighty power as created the world and raised Jesus from the dead.

The kingdom of heaven is like the mustard seed which is the smallest of the seeds yet it grows into a great plant in which birds can roost (Matthew 13:31–32). It is like yeast which a woman took and hid in three measures of dough till the whole was leavened. The kingdom, it is promised, will permeate and transform the whole world. King Nebuchadnezzar was given a dream in which the great empires of the world were portrayed as a huge image, the head of gold representing the Babylonian empire, the silver chest and arms representing the Medo-Persian empire, etc. But then God set up a new kingdom different from these, a stone cut out of the mountain not by human hands. This little stone rolled along and smashes the image. 'The God of heaven set up a kingdom, which shall never be destroyed: and the kingdom shall not be left to other people, but it shall break in pieces and consume all these kingdoms, and it shall stand for ever' (Daniel 2:44). We are told that, 'the stone that smote the image became a great mountain, and filled the whole earth' (v. 35).

Edwards was a postmillenarian. He looked forward to great days of Gospel blessing on earth. The Psalmist speaks of Messiah's kingdom: 'He shall have dominion also from sea to sea, and from the river unto the ends of the earth. They that dwell in the wilderness shall bow before him; and his enemies shall lick the dust. The kings of Tarshish and of the isles shall bring presents: the kings of Sheba and Seba shall offer gifts. Yea, all kings shall fall down before him: all nations shall serve him' (Psalm 72:8–11). It is not just a remnant that will be saved. Nothing like this kind of extension of the church has been seen till now.

Let us be optimistic and excited as we view the future of the church. We look forward to seeing the Jews converted as a nation and this being 'life from the dead' for the gentile church (Romans 11:15). We want to see God glorified on earth as well as in heaven. Pray for revival and look with expectation to the Lord to do it. Labour on for the Lord spreading the kingdom and waiting with excitement to see the great things that the Lord will yet do for His church, even on earth. To Abraham it was said, 'in thee shall all families of the earth be blessed' (Genesis 12:3). Blessing is promised for the families not just for a little minority. Moses declared that the earth is going to be full of the glory of God (Numbers 14:21). John related in Revelation how 'the seventh angel sounded; and there were great voices in heaven, saying, The kingdoms of this world are become the kingdoms of our Lord, and of his Christ; and he shall reign for ever and ever' (Revelation 11:15). The best is yet to be and all nations shall bow to King Jesus.

Endnotes

Foreword

1. Ian Breward, 'The Life and Theology of William Perkins, 1558–1602' (PhD dissertation, University of Manchester, 1963), p. 35.

2. Jonathan Edwards, *Christ the Great Example of Gospel Ministers*, in *The Works of Jonathan Edwards, Volume 25, Sermons and Discourses 1743–1758*, ed. Wilson H. Kimnach (New Haven: Yale University Press, 2006), pp. 330–348.

3. Edwards, *Christ the Great Example of Gospel Ministers*, in *The Works of Jonathan Edwards*, 26 volumes (New Haven, CT: Yale University Press, 1957–2008), 25:343–45 (hereafter cited WJE, with volume number followed by the page number)

4. Jonathan Edwards, *The Salvation of Souls: Nine Previously Unpublished Sermons on the Call of Ministry and the Gospel*, ed. Richard A. Bailey and Gregory A. Wills (Wheaton: Crossway, 2002), pp. 128–129. The text may also be found in *The Works of Jonathan Edwards Online* [hereafter cited WJEO], *Volume 55* (Jonathan Edwards Center at Yale University), sermon 553, on 1 Cor. 2:11–13.

5. Edwards, *The Salvation of Souls*, p. 129.

Chapter 1

1. Edwards, 'The True Excellency of a Minister of the Gospel,' WJE 25:87; see also WJE 15:319–321.

2. Edwards, 'The True Excellency of a Minister of the Gospel,' WJE 25:89.

3. Edwards, 'Christ the Great Example of Gospel Ministers,' WJE 25:344; Edwards, in Richard A. Bailey and Gregory A. Wills, eds., *The Salvation of Souls: Nine Previously Unpublished Sermons on the Call of Ministry and the Gospel by Jonathan Edwards* (Wheaton, IL: Crossway, 2002), [hereafter BW] pp. 45–47,49, 50.

4. Edwards, BW 68–69.

5. Edwards, BW 86; WJE 4:175; emphasis added.

6. Edwards, 'One Great End In God's Appointing The Gospel Ministry,' WJE 25:445.

7. Edwards, BW 64, 66.

8. Edwards, 'Christ the Great Example of Gospel Ministers,' WJE 25:336, 94.

9. Edwards, WJE 4:199–205, 148. Tracy, *Jonathan Edwards, Pastor,* p. 112. For attitudes of early American evangelicals toward children, see Philip Greven, *The Protestant Temperament: Patterns of Child-Rearing, Religious Experience, and the Self in Early America* (New York: Knopf, 1977), pp. 21–148. Catherine Brekus observes that Edwards was 'one of the first ministers to treat children as religious equals.' Brekus, 'Remembering Jonathan Edwards' Ministry to Children,' in David W. Kling and Douglas A. Sweeney, eds., *Jonathan Edwards at Home and Abroad: Historical Memories, Cultural Movements, Global Horizons* (Columbia SC: University of South Carolina Press, 2003), p. 48.

10. Alan Heimert, *Religion and the American Mind, from the Great Awakening to the Revolution* (Cambridge, MA: Harvard University Press, 1966), p. 125; E. Brook Holifield, *The Covenant Sealed: The Development of Puritan Sacramental Theology in Old and New England, 1570–1720* (New Haven: Yale University Press, 1974), 228–9; both cited by William J. Danaher, Jr., 'By Sensible Signs Represented: Jonathan Edwards' Sermons on the Lord's Supper,' *Pro Ecclesia* 7 (1998), 285–286.

11. Danaher, 'Sensible Signs,' p. 287.

12. Edwards, WJE 18:85–6,84, 87–88.

13. Danaher, 'Sensible Signs,' pp. 261–287.

14. Thanks to Rhys Bezzant for an email pointing out the importance of Edwards' mentoring of young ministers.

15. Helen Westra's *The Minister's Task and Calling in the Sermons of Jonathan Edwards* (Lewiston, NY: Edwin Mellen Press, 1986) is especially helpful on this score.

16. Edwards, WJE 9:456, 459; on the 'glorious work of God's Spirit,' see Gerald R. McDermott, *One Holy and Happy Society: The Public Theology of Jonathan Edwards* (University Park, PA: Pennsylvania State University, 1992), 37–92; Sermon Notebook 45, Edwards Papers, Beinecke Rare Book and Manuscript Library, Yale University, quoted WJE 25:38; BW 153.

17. Edwards, WJE 22:240; WJE 24:932–933; sermon on Matthew 13:3–4 (a), WJEO (Works of Jonathan Edwards online) 56; WJE 24:340, 619, 944, 356, 1045.

18. Edwards, WJE 10:405–6, emphasis added; WJE 14:201; WJE 13:470.

19. Edwards, 'Preaching the Gospel,' BW 153; WJE 24:256; 'Ministers to Preach Not Their Own Wisdom,' BW 116; WJE 22:95; WJE 4:386.

20. Edwards, WJE 22:84, 87–89,100: WJE 2:266–291.

21. Edwards, WJE 2:266, 365; WJE 25:92, 346, 99–100; original emphasis

22. Northampton's church rivaled the biggest urban churches in New England for size. Holifield reports that the largest had 1500 people (*God's Ambassadors*, 78). On his daily routines, see Marsden, *Jonathan Edwards*, pp. 134–135.

23. For Edwards as for nearly everyone in the eighteenth century, the possibility of women serving as ministers was unthinkable. On the subject of female preachers, see John Punshon, *Portrait in Grey: A Short History of the Quakers* (London: Quaker Books, 1984), pp. 34, 58; and Catherine Brekus, *Strangers and Pilgrims:*

Female Preaching in America, 1740–1845 (Chapel Hill, NC: University of North Carolina Press, 1998).

24. Edwards, BW 91–2; original emphasis.

25. Edwards, 'The True Excellency of a Minister of the Gospel,' WJE 25:100, 336, 346; BW 52.

26. Edwards, WJE 25:68; WJE 22:70, 68, 78, 71–73.

27. Edwards, WJE 22:70, 77, 74–75.

28. Douglas A. Sweeney, 'The Church,' in Sang Hyun Lee, ed., *The Princeton Companion to Jonathan* Edwards (Princeton: Princeton University Press, 2005), 183–184.

29. Rhys Bezzant, *Jonathan Edwards and the* Church (New York: Oxford University Press, 2014), 228–241.

30. In some churches church discipline goes too far, with ministers and elders taking unwarranted liberties and lording it over their flocks in an overbearing way (sometimes called 'heavy shepherding'). But this excess seems to be less common in the Global North than the virtual absence of discipline.

31. Edwards, BW 129–130.

32. Edwards, BW 60–65.

33. Edwards, BW 145; WJE 25:471, emphasis added; WJE 16:130–133.

34. Edwards, WJE 25:339, 337, 339–340.

35. Edwards, WJE 25:475.

36. Wilson Kimnach, 'Edwards as Preacher,' in *The Cambridge Companion*, p. 114; Marsden, *Jonathan Edwards*, p. 158; WJE 4:149–150; Marsden, *Jonathan Edwards*, p. 159; WJE 25:455; Kimnach, 'Edwards as Preacher,' p. 119.

Chapter 2

1. The ministry job titles found on a recent commendation page include 'spiritual entrepreneur,' 'directional leader,' 'transformational architect,' and 'leadership coach'. Rob Wegner and Jack Magruder, *Missional Moves: 15 Tectonic Shifts That Transform Churches, Communities, and the World* (Grand Rapids, MI: Zondervan, 2012), pp. 1–2.

2. I understand that Rob Bell liked to be known as an 'artist.' While some might question whether his creative merits fully justify the title, it is doubtless a more accurate description than 'minister of the Word.'

3. Edwards, 'Sons of Oil, Heavenly Lights,' WJE 25:263.

4. Edwards, 'Miscellany' 332, WJE 13:410.

5. Edwards, *The End for which God Created the World*, WJE 8:432–433.

6. Some have charged Edwards with denying secondary causation. However, Edwards' frequent recourse to speaking of *means* is an important demonstration that he saw no such difficulties himself. Edwards also explicitly affirmed secondary causation: 'God is the creator of men in both soul and body; but their souls are in a special and more immediate manner his workmanship, *wherein less use is made of second causes, instruments or means*, or any thing preexistent.' Edwards, 'The Great Concern of a Watchman of Souls,' WJE 25:64; emphasis added.

7. Westminster Larger Catechism 154.

8. To these (along with others of the Puritan tradition) Edwards might add acts of providence. These are, in essence, startling events that bring us to repentance. Of course, ministers do not cause these events to happen; it is only for them to make judicious use of them as Christ did in Luke 13: 'Or those eighteen on whom the tower in Siloam fell and killed them, do you think that they were worse sinners than all *other* men who dwelt in Jerusalem? I tell you, no; but unless you repent you will all likewise perish' (Luke 13:4–5).

9. Edwards, WJE 8:360.

10. Edwards, 'The Perpetuity and Change of the Sabbath,' WJE 17:245.

11. Edwards, 'The Great Concern of a Watchman of Souls,' WJE 25:68.

12. See Edwards, WJE 8:356. Edwards also preached a sermon on Jeremiah 6:29–30 called 'Living Unconverted Under an Eminent Means of Grace' in reference to his grandfather Solomon Stoddard, WJE 14:359.

13. Edwards, 'The True Excellency of a Minister of the Gospel,' WJE 25:89.

14. Edwards, *Some Thoughts Concerning the Revival,* WJE 4:374.

15. Edwards, 'The Great Concern of a Watchman of Souls,' WJE 25:67.

16. 'Ordinary' because there are, of course, exceptions. See 1 Corinthians 9:6–15.

17. Schweitzer, *God is a Communicative Being,* p. 147; Edwards, 'True Saints are Present with the Lord,' WJE 25:237.

18. Edwards, 'Blank Bible' entry on Genesis 42:23, WJE 24:191; emphasis mine.

19. Edwards, 'Notes on Scripture' 335, WJE 15:319.

20. Edwards, 'Notes on Scripture' 335, WJE 15:320–321.

21. I refer to the portrait that is used on the cover of this book. It was commissioned by Gerald McDermott and the original hangs in his home in Salem, VA.

22. Edwards, 'Sons of Oil, Heavenly Lights,' WJE 25:263.

23. Edwards, 'Sons of Oil, Heavenly Lights,' WJE 25:263.

24. Edwards, 'Sons of Oil, Heavenly Lights,' WJE 25:267.

25. Edwards, 'The True Excellency of a Minister of the Gospel,' WJE 25:100.

26. Edwards, 'Notes on Scripture' 368, WJE 15:359.

27. Edwards, 'Ministers to Preach Not Their Own Wisdom but the Word of God,' in Richard A. Bailey and Gregory A. Wills, eds., *The Salvation of Souls: Nine Previously Unpublished Sermons on the Call of Ministry and the Gospel by Jonathan Edwards* (Wheaton, IL: Crossway Books, 2002), p. 119.

28. Edwards, 'Ministers to Preach Not Their Own Wisdom but the Word of God,' in Richard A. Bailey and Gregory A. Wills, eds., *The Salvation of Souls: Nine Previously Unpublished Sermons on the Call of Ministry and the Gospel by Jonathan Edwards* (Wheaton, IL: Crossway Books, 2002), pp. 128–129.

29. Edwards, 'Sons of Oil, Heavenly Lights,' WJE 25:267–268.

30. Edwards, 'Sons of Oil, Heavenly Lights,' WJE 25:267.

31. Edwards, 'Sons of Oil, Heavenly Lights,' WJE 25:268.

32. Edwards, 'Sons of Oil, Heavenly Lights,' WJE 25:271; emphasis added.

33. Edwards, 'God Glorified in Man's Dependence,' WJE 17:203.

34. Edwards, 'God Glorified in Man's Dependence,' WJE 17:203; emphasis added.

35. Edwards, *Religious Affections*, WJE 2:121–122.

36. Edwards, 'The Great Concern of a Watchman for Souls,' WJE 25:71.

Chapter 3

1. D. Martyn Lloyd Jones, *The Puritans: Their Origins and Successors* (Edinburgh: Banner of Truth Trust, 1987), p. 349.

2. See Edwards, *Narrative of Communion Controversy*, WJE 12:618–619.

3. See David D. Hall, 'Editor's Introduction,' WJE 12:5.

4. Edwards, *Narrative of Communion Controversy*, WJE 13:535.

5. See Edwards, *Narrative of Communion Controversy*, WJE 12:618–619; see also

Edwards' revealing comments, such as how some might regard this conclusion as 'but a proper punishment for my dealing in that manner by Mr. Breck,' WJE 12:555.

6. See George M. Marsden, *Jonathan Edwards: A Life*, chapter 7, pp. 114–132.

7. For interesting details on the Hawleys see George M. Marsden, *Jonathan Edwards: A Life* (New Haven, CT: Yale University Press, 2003), pp. 163–167; 368–369.

8. Edwards, *Faithful Narrative*, WJE 4:150–151.

9. Edwards, *Faithful Narrative*, WJE 4:206.

10. Edwards, 'Letter to Maj. Joseph Hawley,' WJE 16:647–648.

11. Edwards, 'Letter to Maj. Joseph Hawley,' WJE 16:650.

12. Edwards, 'Letter to Maj. Joseph Hawley,' WJE 16:653.

13. Edwards, *Narrative of Communion Controversy*, WJE 13:567.

14. For evidence see especially Edwards, *Religious Affections* in WJE 2:340–341 and 'The Reality of Conversion' in Wilson H. Kinmach, Kenneth P. Minkema and Douglas A. Sweeney, eds., *The Sermons of Jonathan Edwards: A Reader* (New Haven, CT: Yale University Press, 1999), pp. 83–104. See also 'In True Conversion, Men's Bodies are in some respect changed as well as their Souls,' in Michael D. McMullen, ed., *The Blessing of God: Previously Unpublished Sermons of Jonathan Edwards* (Nashville, TN: Broadman & Holman Publishers, 2003), pp. 297–310. In addition, note Edwards' prolific comments on conversion in *A Faithful Narrative*, WJE 4:177–211.

15. See especially Edwards, 'The Church's Marriage to Her Sons and to Her God' (1746) in WJE 4:167–196. See also Douglas A. Sweeney, 'The Church' in Sang Hyun Lee, ed., *The Princeton Companion to Jonathan Edwards* (Princeton, NJ: Princeton University Press, 2005), pp. 167–189. A very recent publication is Rhys S. Bezzant, *Jonathan Edwards and the Church* (New York, NY: Oxford University Press, 2013), see especially pp. 145–212.

16. See especially Jonathan Edwards, *A Treatise Concerning Religious Affections*, WJE

2:383–461. See also Michael J. McClymond and Gerald R. McDermott, *The Theology of Jonathan Edwards*, (New York, Oxford University Press, 2012), especially pp. 384–385. Perceptive and accessible commentary on the subject is also to be found in Gerald R. McDermott, *Seeing God: Jonathan Edwards and Spiritual Discernment* (Vancouver, B.C. Canada: Regent College Publishing, 1995).

17. Jonathan Edwards, 'A Farewell Sermon,' WJE 25:488.

18. Edwards, *A Faithful Narrative*, WJE 4:177.

19. Edwards, *A Faithful Narrative*, WJE 21:159.

20. Edwards, *A Faithful Narrative*, WJE 21: 164.

21. Written about in *Religious Affections*, WJE: 205–7 and also see "The Divine and Supernatural Light "WJE:17:405–426 18. Jonathan Edwards in Miscellanies, "J" & "P" & 1008 in *WJE* 13:170–1 & *WJE*:20:327–8. For a simple explanation of Edwards' use of this term see Josh Moody in *Jonathan Edwards and Justification* (Wheaton, IL. Crossway, 2012), pages 20–24. Jonathan Edwards in Miscellanies, "J" & "P" & 1008 in *WJE* 13:170–1 & *WJE*:20:327–8. For a simple explanation of Edwards' use of this term see Josh Moody in *Jonathan Edwards and Justification* (Wheaton, IL. Crossway, 2012), pages 20–24.

22. Edwards, WJE 20:328.

23. Edwards, WJE 2:206.

24. On this term see Jonathan Edwards in *Religious Affections*, WJE 2:206 and for a good discussion of this term see Gerald R. McDermott in Understanding Jonathan Edwards (New York, Oxford University Press, 2009) pages 185–190.

25. Edwards, 'True Grace, Distinguished for the Experience of Devils,' WJE 25:636.

26. Found in WJE 17:404–426.

27. The best summative book on this "morphology of conversion" and the

'Preparationism' which prevailed is Norman Petit, *The Heart Prepared* (New Haven, CT: Yale University Press, 1996).

28. Edwards, WJE 17:413.

29. Edwards, WJE 17:414.

30. Edwards, WJE 17:413.

31. WJE 12:466; WJE Online Vol. 45: Section 153.

32. Jonathan Edwards in *Religious Affections* WJE 2:307. Jonathan Edwards in *Religious Affections* WJE 2:307.

33. Edwards, WJE 2:266.

34. Edwards, WJE 17:424.

35. Edwards, WJE 12:245–24.

36. 'Definite' and 'dramatic' are hardly the same thing. It is ironic that people charge Edwards with demanding 'dramatic' conversion experiences when his own conversion was anything but dramatic and his agenda in writing on the subject was precisely to undermine artificial expectations about the conversion experience. See William M. Schweitzer, 'An Uncommon Union: Understanding Jonathan Edwards' Experimental Calvinism' (*Puritan Reformed Journal* 2, no. 2 (2010)), pp. 208–19.

37. We should not forget that Stoddard was concerned for conversion no less than Edwards. His introduction of communion as a 'converting ordinance' was actually in continuity (however mistakenly) with his objectives as a preacher of *conversion*. The fact that Edwards quotes extensively from Stoddard in the *Religious Affections* demonstrated his unfeigned admiration for his work, despite obvious areas of disagreement.

38. Found in WJE 12. For an overview of the Controversy see Alan D. Strange in 'Jonathan Edwards and the Communion Controversy in Northampton,' *Mid -American Journal of Theology 14* (2003) pp. 57–97. Also Oliver D. Crisp 'On the

Qualifications for Communion,' *Retrieving Doctrine* (Milton Keynes: Paternoster, 2010), pp. 182–203. Josh Moody in *Jonathan Edwards and the Enlightenment: Knowing the Presence of God* (Lanham, MD: University Press of America, 2005), pp. 33–37.

39. Edwards, 'Narrative of Communion Controversy,' WJE 12:507.

40. Edwards, 'Narrative of Communion Controversy,' WJE 12:508.

41. Edwards, 'Narrative of Communion Controversy,' WJE 12:508–11.

42. Edwards, WJE 25:457–495.

43. Edwards, WJE 25:488.

44. Edwards, WJE 25:477.

45. Edwards, *Humble Inquiry into Rules of the Word of God concerning the Qualifications requisite to a Complete Standing and Full Communion in the Visible Christian Church*, WJE 166–348.

46. Edwards, *An Humble Inquiry*, WJE 12:230.

47. Edwards, *An Humble Inquiry*, WJE 12:228.

48. Edwards, *An Humble Inquiry*, WJE 12:229.

49. There is a massive literature on this. See especially Edmund S. Morgan *Visible Saints* (New York, NY: Cornell University Press,1963), chapter 4; E. Brook Holifield, *The Covenant Sealed* (Eugene, OR: Wipf and Stock Publishers, 2002) chapters 5–6; Rhys S. Bezzant, *Jonathan Edwards and the Church*, (New York, NY: Oxford University Press, 2014) pp. 20–21; 145–212; and David Boorman, 'The Half-Way Covenant,' in *The Puritan Experiment in the New World*, Westminster Conference Papers, (published by The Westminster Conference, 1976).

50. Josh Moody, *Jonathan Edwards and the Enlightenment: Knowing the Presence of God*, (Lanham, MD: University Press of America, 2005), p. 54 n149, also see pp. 33–37.

51. George Marsden calls Edwards' approach 'a High View of the Sacraments, Low Church Style.' Marsden, *Jonathan Edwards: A Life*, p. 352.

52. Edwards, WJE 16:283–284.

53. Edwards, *An Humble Inquiry*, WJE 12:196.

54. See Oliver D. Crisp 'On the Qualifications for Communion,' *Retrieving Doctrine* (Milton Keynes: Paternoster, 2010), pp. 182–203.

55. Edwards, WJE 25:178.

56. Found in WJE 25:164–196. It is interesting that, due to the remarkable success of Samuel Buell's preaching in Northampton, Sarah Edwards was initially jealousy for her husband (WJE 25:164).

57. Edwards, WJE 25:179.

58. Edwards, *Misrepresentations Corrected*, WJE 12:356.

59. Edwards, *Misrepresentations Corrected*, WJE 12:361.

60. See Douglas Winiarski, 'New Perspectives on the Northampton Communion Controversy II: Relations, Professions & Experiences,' 1748–176 in *Jonathan Edwards Studies Online Journal*, Vol 4, No 1 (2014) pp. 110–145.

61. Edwards, *Religious Affections*, WJE 2:414.

62. Edwards, *Religious Affections*, WJE 2:443. See also Gerald McDermott, *Seeing God*, pp. 214–224. For a simple discussion of the 'Sign of Signs' see Sam Storms in *Signs of the Spirit*, (Wheaton, IL: Crossway, 2007) pp. 140–152.

63. Edwards, *An Humble Inquiry*, WJE 4:226–228.

64. Edwards, *An Humble Inquiry*, WJE 4:226–288; note the nine negatives and five positives in this manual of discernment.

65. See Patrick Sherry, *Spirit and Beauty: An Introduction to Theological Aesthetics*

(London, SCM, 2002) 2nd Edition. Sherry astutely pointed out that although Edwards' contribution was unique and original Hans Urs Von Balthasar (Roman Catholic Theologian of some renown) managed to get through all five volumes of his great 14-part work on Theological Aesthetics without mentioning Edwards! See also Roland A. Delatre, *Beauty and Sensibility in the Thought of Jonathan Edwards* (Eugene, OR: Wipf and Stock Publishers, 2006). See also Kin Yip Louie, *The Beauty of the Triune God,* (Eugene, OR: Wipf and Stock Publishers, 2013).

66. Edwards, WJE 25:633.

67. Edwards, WJE 25:639.

68. Edwards, WJE 25:640.

Chapter 4

1. Among many others, see Perry Miller, *Jonathan Edwards* (Westport, CT: Greenwood Press, 1949) and George M. Marsden, *Jonathan Edwards: A Life* (New Haven, CT: Yale University Press, 2003).

2. Douglas A. Sweeney, *Jonathan Edwards and the Ministry of the Word: A Model for Faith and Thought* (Downer's Grove, IL: InterVarsity Press, 2009) and earlier, Patricia Tracey's classic treatment, *Jonathan Edwards, Pastor.* Jonathan Edwards Classic Studies Series (Eugene, OR: Wipf & Stock, 2006).

3. John Gerstner pioneered the field of Edwards as apologist. Some of his main works in this area include, 'An Outline of the Apologetics of Jonathan Edwards,' *Bibliotheca Sacra* 133 (1976) pp. 3–10, 99–107, 195–201, 291–98 and *Reasons for Faith* (New York: Harper & Brothers, 1960). Gerstner also co-authored an apologetics text with R. C. Sproul and Arthur Lindsley where Edwards is used as an exemplar: *Classical Apologetics: A Rational Defense of the Christian Faith and a Critique of Presuppositional Apologetics* (Grand Rapids, MI: Zondervan, 1984). Among others, some more recent contributions include Gerald R. McDermott, *Jonathan Edwards Confronts the Gods: Christian Theology, Enlightenment Religion, and Non-Christian Faiths* (New York, NY: Oxford University Press, 2000); Stephen J. Nichols, *An*

Absolute Sort of Certainty: The Holy Spirit and the Apologetics of Jonathan Edwards (Phillipsburg, NJ: P&R Publishing, 2003) and K. Scott Oliphint, 'Jonathan Edwards: Reformed Apologist,' *WTJ* 57/1 (Spring 1995): 165–86. Finally, see Jeffrey C. Waddington, *The Unified Operations of the Human Soul: Jonathan Edwards' Theological Anthropology and Apologetic* (Ph.D. diss.: Philadelphia, PA: Westminster Theological Seminary, 2013).

4. As a matter of historical fact, Edwards attributed the beginning of the first revival under his watch at Northampton to his defense and articulation of the Protestant doctrine of justification. See Edwards, WJE 19:147–242.

5. Edwards' role in defending the awakening has been ably discussed in Robert Davis Smart's *Jonathan Edwards: Apologist of the Great Awakening* (Grand Rapids, MI: Reformation Heritage Books, 2011) where he discusses Edwards' concept of the 'new sense.'

6. I pass over *Some Thoughts Concerning the Present Revival of Religion* (1743), which appeared fairly soon after *The Distinguishing Marks*.

7. Edwards, *Religious Affections*, WJE 2:383–461.

8. Edwards, *Religious Affections*, WJE 2:272.

9. Edwards, WJE 22:89.

10. Not to state the obvious, but the infernal regions are populated with people possessing historical faith.

11. While we might debate how best to classify Edwards' way of defending the Christian faith, it is certain that he never pretended to occupy the unbeliever's position in order to have some common ground. Indeed, Ava Chamberlain points out that Edwards often assumes the truth of the apologetic point he is making: '… he frequently presupposes not only the existence of God but the truth of the very doctrine that is the object of demonstration.' Ava Chamberlain, Editor's Introduction, WJE 18:28.

12. John Taylor, *The Plain Scripture-Doctrine of Original Sin, Proposed to Free and Candid Examination* (London: N. P., 1738).

13. Edwards, *Original Sin*, WJE 3:228.

14. From Edwards' sermon 'East of Eden,' WJE 17:333–334.

15. Edwards, *Original Sin,* WJE 3:121.

16. See David Lyttle, 'Jonathan Edwards on Personal Identity,' *Early American Literature* 7(2) (1972), pp. 163–71.

17. Edwards' theory of divine constitution depends upon his ideas of continuous creation and occasionalism. Often understood as one idea, these are actually two distinct ideas that frequently occur together. Continuous creationism is the doctrine that God creates the world anew every moment. Occasionalism is the teaching that God is the sole active agent in the universe. Some would argue that these ideas undermine a finished creation and the integrity of secondary causation.

18. Edwards often used the term Arminian, and the ideas represented by this term are in rough theological continuity with historical Arminianism. However, as a point of precision, the 'Arminianism' Edwards responds to can be described as non-Reformed theological influences that may or may not owe their existence the Dutch theologian Jacobus Arminius.

19. See Edwards, *The End for Which God Created the World*, WJE 8:400–536.

20. It should be noted that by reason, Edwards means 'right reason' or reason as it should properly function. He is not arguing that fallen reason would grant the truth of the argument from reason. My assessment about Edwards on this coheres with the work of Paul K. Helseth on the role of 'right reason' at Old Princeton. See his *'Right Reason' and the Princeton Mind* (Phillipsburg, NJ: P&R Publishing, 2010).

21. See William M. Schweitzer, *God is a Communicative Being* (London: T&T Clark, 2012).

22. Edwards, WJE 22:90.

23. See Fiering, *Jonathan Edwards' Moral Thought and Its British Context.*

24. Among others, Michael McClymond and Gerald McDermott make the deist context of Edwards' apologetic abundantly plain.

25. 'The scandal of particularity, then, was an important stimulus to Deism. It was a principal reason why they judged the orthodox God to be a monster in whom they could not believe' (McDermott, *Jonathan Edwards Confronts the Gods*, p. 25).

26. Edwards, 'Miscellany' 837, WJE 20:52–53.

27. Edwards, 'Notes on Scripture' 416, WJE 15:423–469.

28. Edwards, 'Notes on Scripture' 416, WJE 15:430–431.

29. Sans some fairly well delineated 'post-Mosaica', such as the account of Moses' death and burial. See Edwards, 'Notes on Scripture' 416, WJE 15:466–469.

30. Edwards, 'Light in a Dark World, A Dark Heart,' WJE 19:719.

31. This is taken from Edwards' sermon 'Light in a Dark World, A Dark Heart,' WJE 19:719.

32. Edwards held to the so-called 'prisca theologia' or pristine or primitive theology in which certain basic truths have been handed down by tradition from the Noahic patriarchs. See Edwards, 'Miscellany' 1297, WJE 23:244.

33. In the case of Edwards allowing for the possibility of pagan philosophers receiving supernatural revelation, 'Edwards might have solved a minor apologetic annoyance by creating a theological headache.' Schweitzer, *God is a Communicative Being*, (London: T&T Clark, 2012) p. 95. Another more serious case is his giving his imprimatur to Bellamy's *True Religion Delineated* (see Edwards' preface, WJE 4:569–572) in which the governmental theory of the atonement is advanced as an apologetic device. Edwards little supposed that this apologetic would soon supplant

the penal substitutionary doctrine of the atonement among the New Divinity men who claimed Edwards as father.

Chapter 5

1. Edwards, 'The Things That Belong to True Religion,' WJE 25:570–574. This sermon was preached during a three month missionary trial period (Jan-March, 1751).

2. Wilson Kimnach notes that Edwards' sermon 'is made up of remarkably concise statements: packets of ideas successively stating points by which he hoped to establish in the minds of the Indians the essential principles of his religion and the nature of his mission among them.' (WJE 25:566).

3. Edwards, 'The Things That Belong to True Religion,' WJE 25:570.

4. Edwards, 'The Things That Belong to True Religion,' WJE 25:571.

5. 'Accidental' because, of course, the author of *Freedom of the Will* would remind us that there are no true accidents. Edwards' convictions regarding the Indians appear in his Awakening writings as pleas to the church to fulfill her duty and are epitomized in his biography of David Brainerd.

6. Some have criticized Edwards for not learning the Indians' native tongue and spending too much time in his study. However, it should also be noted that Edwards was delighted when his son Timothy was able to master the local Indian language.

7. George M. Marsden, *Jonathan Edwards: A Life* (New Haven, CT: Yale University Press, 2003), p. 369.

8. One of the English (non-native) inhabitants of Stockbridge famously remarked that his land would at least increase in value because of Edwards' presence among them.

9. On the Northampton Lord's Supper controversy see Marsden, *Edwards*, pp. 341–374 and Iain H. Murray, *Jonathan Edwards: A New Biography* (Edinburgh: Banner of Truth, 1987), pp. 311–370. For more on Edwards' theology of the Lord's Supper

see Hughes Oliphant Old, *Holy Communion In the Piety of the Reformed Church* (Powder Springs, GA: Tolle Lege Press, 2013), pp. 605–632.

10. Marsden, *Edwards*, p. 347.

11. Edwards, 'Letter to William McCulloch,' WJE 16:271

12. Marsden, *Edwards*, p. 360.

13. Edwards, 'Letter to John Erskine,' WJE 16:347, 355.

14. Edwards, 'Letter to John Erskine,' WJE, 16:355.

15. Edwards, 'Letter to John Erskine,' WJE 16:355.

16. Jonathan Gibson, 'Jonathan Edwards: A *Missionary?*' in *Themelios* 36.3 (2011), p. 386.

17. There were approximately 250 Indians and 12 English families in the village.

18. Edwards, 'Letter to Thomas Gillespie,' WJE 16:387.

19. Gibson, *Missionary*, pp. 384–385.

20. Jonathan Edwards, *The Works of Jonathan Edwards*, volume 1 (Edinburgh: Banner of Truth, 1992), p. 588.

21. Michael J. McClymond and Gerald R. McDermott, *The Theology of Jonathan Edwards* (Oxford: Oxford University Press, 2012), p. 550

22. See John Thornbury, *David Brainerd: Pioneer Missionary to the American Indians* (Durham, UK: Evangelical Press, 1996); Jonathan Edwards (ed.), *The Life and Diary of David Brainerd* (Grand Rapids: Baker Books, 1989).

23. WJE 7:533.

24. Edwards, 'True Saints are Present with the Lord,' WJE 25:254; see also 'A Sermon Preached on the Day of Brainerd's Funeral,' WJE 7:551.

25. Edwards, 'True Saints are Present with the Lord,' WJE 25:254.

26. 'Contextualization is a popular term in Christian circles today. Basically, contextualization is the attempt to situate particular beliefs and practices in their cultural environment. Migrating from the rarified confines of secular sociology to missiological theory, and then to practical theology departments and ministry programs, the imperative to contextualize the gospel has become something of a mantra among pastors, youth ministers, and evangelists' Michael Horton, *The Gospel Commission* (Grand Rapids: Baker Books, 2011), p. 115.

27. Edwards, WJE 4:73 n.7; regarding Edwards' reception of the Westminster Standards, see also 'Letter to the Reverend John Erskine,' WJE 16:355 and 'Letter to Reverend James Robe,' WJE 16:277, 279.

28. Michael J. McClymond and Gerald R. McDermott, *The Theology of Jonathan Edwards* (Oxford: Oxford University Press, 2012), p. 557.

29. Gideon Hawley, 'A Letter from Rev. Gideon Hawley of Marshpee, Containing an Account of His Services among the Indians ...,' *Collections of the Massachusetts Historical Society*, 1st ser., 4 (Boston, 1794), 51, quoted in George M. Marsden, *Jonathan Edwards: A Life* (New Haven: Yale University Press, 2003), p. 393.

30. In an early letter from Stockbridge Edwards warmly describes John Wauwaumpequunnaunt as 'my interpreter, an extraordinary man on some accounts; understands English well, [is] a good reader and writer and is an excellent interpreter. And perhaps there was never an Indian educated in America that exceeded him in knowledge, in divinity, [and] understanding of the Scriptures.' WJE 16:451–452. It was probably his interpreter's extraordinary abilities that led Edwards to spend time on other things rather than learning the Indian tongue.

31. Edwards, 'Heaven's Dragnet,' WJE 25:575–581.

32. Edwards, 'Heaven's Dragnet,' WJE 25:575.

33. Edwards, 'Heaven's Dragnet,' WJE 25:577.

34. Edwards, 'Heaven's Dragnet,' WJE 25:579.

35. Edwards, 'Heaven's Dragnet,' WJE 25:577.

36. Edwards, 'Heaven's Dragnet,' WJE 25:580.

37. Edwards, 'Christ Is to the Heart Like a River to a Tree,' WJE 25:602–604.

38. Jonathan Gibson, 'Jonathan Edwards: A *Missionary*? in *Themelios* 36.3 (2011), p. 389.

39. Michael Horton, *The Gospel Commission* (Grand Rapids: Baker Books, 2011), p. 116.

40. Jonathan Edwards, *Works of Jonathan Edwards, Volume One* (Edinburgh: Banner of Truth, 1992), 593–594.

41. David F. Wells, *Above All Earthly Powers: Christ in a Postmodern World* (Leicester: Inter-Varsity Press, 2005), p. 9.

42. Sidney H. Rooy, *The Theology of Missions in the Puritan Tradition: A Study of Representative Puritans: Richard Sibbes, Richard Baxter, John Eliot, Cotton Mather & Jonathan Edwards* (Laurel, MS: Audubon Press, 2006), p. 290.

43. Ola Elizabeth Winslow, *Jonathan Edwards 1703–1758* (New York: Collier, 1940), 252. Quoted in Jonathan Gibson, 'Jonathan Edwards: A *Missionary*?' in *Themelios* 36.3 (2011), p. 394.

44. Marsden, *Edwards*, p. 389.

45. Edwards, 'Letter to Sir William Pepperrell,' WJE 16:411.

46. Edwards, 'Letter to Sir William Pepperrell,' WJE 16:411–12.

47. Michael J. McClymond and Gerald R. McDermott, *The Theology of Jonathan Edwards* (Oxford: Oxford University Press, 2012), p. 562.

48. Murray, *Edwards*, p. 393.

49. Edwards, 'History of the Work of Redemption,' WJE 9:120.

50. Edwards, 'History of the Work of Redemption,' WJE 9:458–459.

51. 'We have seen a tendency to confuse these mandates, as if the Great Commandment were the Great Commission and good works were the gospel. There is nothing in the Great Commission about transforming culture. However, the Great Commandment calls every person— believer and unbeliever alike— to works of love and service in our daily lives. If some confuse these mandates, others separate them, as if our high calling in Christ had no connection with responsible stewardship and citizenship in the world.' Michael Horton, *Gospel Commission*, p. 226.

52. Two excellent resources on biblical missions and church planting are (eds.) Daniel R. Hyde and Shane Lems, *Planting, Watering, Growing: Planting Confessionally Reformed Churches in the 21st Century* (Grand Rapids, MI: Reformation Heritage Books, 2011) and Kevin DeYoung and Greg Gilbert, *What is the Mission of the Church?* (Wheaton, IL: Crossway, 2011).

Chapter 6

1. Edwards wrote that '… my main objection against it was that my uncle *Williams* himself never approved of its being put into his book.' Edwards, letter to Coleman of May 19, 1737, WJE 16:69.

2. David W. Kling and Douglas A. Sweeney, *Jonathan Edwards at Home and Abroad* (Columbia, SC: University of South Carolina Press, 2003), p. 298.

3. London, J. Oswald, 1738.

4. Interestingly, two issues of the *Narrative* published later in the same year restored the Guyse and Watts preface in addition to the Boston recommendation and the Hampshire testimony.

5. Iain H. Murray, *Jonathan Edwards: A New Biography* (Edinburgh: Banner of Truth Trust, 1987), p. 122.

6. Iain H. Murray, *Jonathan Edwards*, p. 122.

7. See Arthur Fawcett, *The Cambuslang Revival* (London: Banner of Truth Trust, 1971), p. 92.

8. David W. Kling and Douglas A. Sweeney, *Jonathan Edwards at Home and Abroad* (Columbia, SC: University of South Carolina Press, 2003), p. 224.

9. Edwards, *An Humble Attempt*, in WJE 5:321; also in *The Works of Jonathan Edwards* (1834, Edinburgh, reprinted Banner of Truth, 1974) Vol. 2, p. 282.

10. Gillies, quoted in WJE 5:38.

11. See Edwards, *An Humble Attempt*, 5:320–328

12. Edwards' case in *An Humble Attempt* for instituting a Concert of Prayer was handled in a theological framework, maintaining that the kingdom had not yet reached the world-embracing scope he expected only with the conversion of Israel and 'the latter day glory.' See Edwards, *An Humble Attempt*, WJE 5:329–334, 425–427.

13. The English Presbyterians do not figure among these because they were in theological decline by this point in history.

14. Wesley, in N. Curnock, ed., *The Journal of John Wesley*, pp. 2, 83–84.

15. David W. Kling and Douglas A. Sweeney, *Jonathan Edwards at Home and Abroad* (Columbia, SC: University of South Carolina Press, 2003), p. 205.

16. Edwards, *The Works of Jonathan Edwards* (1834, Edinburgh, reprinted Banner of Truth, 1974) Vol. 1, p. 621; emphasis original; Edwards, *Some Thoughts Concerning the Present Revival*, in WJE 4:503. See also Goen's introduction in WJE 4:19.

17. John Newton, *Sixty-Eight Letters from the Rev John Newton to a Clergyman and his Family* (London, 1841), p. 91.

18. David W. Kling, *Jonathan Edwards at Home and Abroad*, pp. 201–202.

19. G. Smith, *The Life of William Carey* (London, 1887), p. 29.

20. These revivals are documented in Paul E. G. Cook, *Fire from Heaven: Times of Extraordinary Revival* (Darlington: EP, 2009).

21. Iain H. Murray, *Jonathan Edwards*, p. 463.

22. Iain H. Murray, *Jonathan Edwards*, p. 464.

23. A. A. Bonar, *Memoir and Remains of R. M. M'Cheyne* (1892, reprint Edinburgh, Banner of Truth Trust, 1966), pp. 17–18.

24. Iain H. Murray, *The Life of Arthur W. Pink* (Edinburgh: Banner of Truth Trust, 2004), p. 43.

25. Iain H. Murray, D. *Martyn Lloyd-Jones: The Fight of Faith 1939–1981* (Edinburgh: Banner of Truth Trust, 1990), p. 137.

26. Iain H. Murray, D. *Martyn Lloyd-Jones*, p. 208.

27. Iain H. Murray, D. *Martyn Lloyd-Jones*, pp. 253–254.

28. Andrew Atherstone and David Ceri Jones, *Engaging with Martyn Lloyd-Jones* (Nottingham: Inter-Varsity Press, 2011), p. 94.

29. D. M. Lloyd-Jones, *The Puritans: Their Origins and Successors* (Edinburgh: Banner of Truth Trust, 1987), p. 355.

30. D. M. Lloyd-Jones, *The Puritans*, pp. 361–362.

31. Iain H. Murray, *Jonathan Edwards*, p. xii.

32. Quoted in Iain H. Murray, *Jonathan Edwards*, p. 290.

33. Iain H. Murray, *Jonathan Edwards*, p. 471.

Chapter 7

1. William M. Schweitzer, *God Is a Communicative Being: Divine Communicativeness and Harmony in the Theology of Jonathan Edwards*, T & T Clark Studies in Systematic Theology (London: T & T Clark, 2012).

2. Jonathan Edwards, sermon on Luke 10:38–42 (July 1754), Box 7, F. 560, L. 16r., Beinecke; Edwards, 'Personal Narrative,' WJE 16:801; Edwards, 'Life Through Christ Alone,' in WJE 10:526; Edwards, 'The Way of Holiness,' WJE 10:477; Edwards,

'The Duty of Hearkening to God's Voice,' WJE 10:441; Edwards, 'Miscellanies'
No. 6, WJE 13:202–203; Edwards, 'Nothing upon Earth Can Represent the Glories
of Heaven,' WJE 14:139–40; Edwards, 'Divine Love Alone Lasts Eternally,' WJE
8:363; Edwards, sermon on Psalm 119:162, Box 3, F. 189, L. 1r., Beinecke; Edwards,
'The Importance and Advantage of a Thorough Knowledge of Divine Truth,' in
The Sermons of Jonathan Edwards: A Reader, ed. Wilson H. Kimnack, Kenneth P.
Minkema, and Douglas A. Sweeney (New Haven: Yale University Press, 1999),
pp. 38, 35; Edwards, sermon on 1 Cor. 2:11–13, Box 10, F. 719, L. 3v., Beinecke;
Edwards, sermon on Matthew 13:23, Box 6, F. 473, L. 22r., Beinecke; Edwards,
Religious Affections, WJE 2:438; and Edwards, 'Miscellanies' No. 202, WJE 13:202.

3.   See WJE 2:457; 4:228, 380, 481; 15:231, 518; 17:180; 18:236; 19:307; 24:513; Edwards,
     sermon on Luke 10:38–42 (July 1754), Box 7, F. 560, L. 6v., Beinecke; and Edwards,
     sermon on 1 Corinthians 2:11–13 (May 7, 1740, at the 'ordination of Mr. Billing'),
     Box 10, F. 719, L. 3v., Beinecke.

4.   In the 'Blank Bible,' at 2 Timothy 3:16–17, Edwards wrote merely 'See Mastricht,
     pp. 17–18,' a reference to Mastricht on holy Scripture (*'De Sacra Scriptura'*) in
     Theoretico-Practica Theologia, pp. 17–18. See WJE 24:1133.

5.   See Edwards' note at 1 Chronicles 28:19, 'Blank Bible,' WJE 24:410, in which
     he quotes the first of Owen's five volumes on the work of the Holy Spirit,
     ΠΝΕΥΜΑΤΟΛΟΓΙΑ; *or, A Discourse Concerning the Holy Spirit. Wherein an
     Account Is Given of His Name, Nature, Personality, Dispensation, Operations, and
     Effects* (London: J. Darby for Nathaniel Ponder, 1674), 105.

6.   Ames, *The Marrow of Theology*, 186.

7.   WJE 9:365, and 14:265–66.

8.   See the final paragraph of the 'Preface' to *The Bay Psalm Book: A Facsimile Reprint of
     the First Edition of 1640* (Chicago: University of Chicago Press, 1956), unpaginated;
     and Edwards, *Religious Affections*, WJE 2:307. For more on this theme from Calvin
     and other Reformed luminaries, see especially Calvin's *Institutes* (1559), 1.7; and

Henk van den Belt, *The Authority of Scripture in Reformed Theology: Truth and Trust*, Studies in Reformed Theology (Leiden: Brill, 2008). Similar statements may be found in ancient writers such as Justin, Clement of Alexandria, and Origen. See Justin Martyr, *Dialogue with Trypho*, 7.2; Clement of Alexandria, *Stromata*, 2.2, 7.16; and Origen, *Contra Celsus*, 1.2.

9. Edwards, 'Profitable Hearers of the Word,' WJE 14:251–52; Edwards, 'Miscellanies' No. 410, WJE 13:470–71; Edwards, 'Types of the Messiah,' WJE 11:253; and Edwards, sermon on Jeremiah 23:29 (April 1749), Box 5, F. 361, L. 1r., Beinecke.

10. Edwards, 'Yield to God's Word, or Be Broken by His Hand,' WJE 25:211; Edwards, 'Miscellanies' No. 382, WJE 13:451; Edwards, *Religious Affections*, WJE 2:304–306; and Edwards, 'A Spiritual Understanding of Divine Things Denied to the Unregenerate,' WJE 14:78.

11. Edwards, 'Notes on the Apocalypse,' WJE 5:105; Edwards, 'Stupid as Stones,' WJE 17:176; Edwards, 'Heeding the Word and Losing It,' WJE 19:48; and Edwards, 'Gospel Ministers a Savor of Life or of Death,' WJE 22:206–207.

12. Edwards, *Religious Affections*, WJE 2:102–03; Edwards, 'Blank Bible,' WJE 24:1143; and Edwards, sermon on Jeremiah 23:29, L. 13r., L. 15r.

13. Edwards, 'A Spiritual Understanding of Divine Things Denied to the Unregenerate,' WJE 14:82; and Edwards, *Distinguishing Marks of a Work of the Spirit of God*, WJE 4:253.

14. Edwards, *Religious Affections*, WJE 2:115; and Edwards, *Some Thoughts*, WJE 4:397, 386–88.

15. Edwards, *Faithful Narrative*, WJE 4:181, 184; Edwards, *Religious Affections*, WJE 2:292–93; Edwards to the Rev. Benjamin Colman, 30 May 1735, WJE 16:54; and Edwards, *Life of David Brainerd*, WJE 8:474–75.

16. Edwards, 'True Nobleness of Mind,' WJE 14:231–32.

17. Edwards, *The Distinguishing Marks of a Work of the Spirit of God*, WJE 4:240; and Edwards, 'Light in a Dark World, a Dark Heart,' WJE 19:720.

18. Edwards, 'Miscellanies' No. 544, WJE 18:89–90; and Edwards, 'The Importance and Advantage of a Thorough Knowledge of Divine Truth,' *The Sermons of Jonathan Edwards*, 46.

19. Edwards, 'Miscellanies' No. 350, WJE 13:421.

20. Edwards, 'Miscellanies' No. 408, WJE 13:469–70.

21. Edwards, 'Light in a Dark World, a Dark Heart,' WJE 19:724; and Edwards, 'A Spiritual Understanding of Divine Things Denied to the Unregenerate,' WJE 14:77.

22. Edwards, sermon on Luke 11:27–28, Box 14, F. 1065, L. iv., L. 6v.-7r., Beinecke; Edwards, 'The Pure in Heart Blessed,' WJE 17:65–66; and Edwards, 'Treatise on Grace,' WJE 21:178–80.

23. Edwards, sermon on Luke 10:38–42, L. 3r.; Edwards, 'Profitable Hearers of the Word,' WJE 14:266; Edwards, 'Heeding the Word, and Losing It,' WJE 19:47; Edwards, 'Images of Divine Things,' WJE 11:93; and Edwards, sermon on Heb. 6:7, Box 11, F. 820, L. 17r., Beinecke.

24. Edwards, sermon on Jeremiah 8:8 (December 1749), Box 5, F. 353, L. 1r., Beinecke; Edwards, 'A Spiritual Understanding of Divine Things Denied to the Unregenerate,' WJE 14:72, 79; Edwards, 'Profitable Hearers of the Word,' WJE 14:248–49; Edwards, 'Treatise on Grace,' WJE 21:180 (on 'common grace' and 'common illuminations'); and Edwards, 'Miscellanies' No. 123, WJE 13:287.

25. *The Westminster Confession of Faith*, 1.6.

26. Edwards, 'A Spiritual Understanding of Divine Things Denied to the Unregenerate,' WJE 14:81; and Edwards, *Religious Affections*, WJE 2:285.

27. Edwards, *Religious Affections*, WJE 2:296–97; Edwards, 'Miscellanies' No. 239,

WJE 13:354–55; Edwards, 'Miscellanies' No. 123, WJE 13:286–87; and Edwards, 'A Spiritual Understanding of Divine Things Denied to the Unregenerate,' WJE 14:80.

28. Edwards, 'A Spiritual Understanding of Divine Things Denied to the Unregenerate,' WJE 14:94–95; and Edwards, 'Profitable Hearers of the Word,' WJE 14:265, 246–47.

Chapter 8

1. Edwards, 'A History of the Work of Redemption,' WJE 9:289–90.

2. Richard A. Muller, *Post-Reformation Reformed Dogmatics: The Rise and Development of Reformed Orthodoxy, ca. 1520 to ca. 1725*, vols. 1–4 (Grand Rapids, MI: Baker, 2003–06), 2:208.

3. John Owen, *Meditations and Discourses on The Glory of Christ* in His Person, Office and Grace in *The Works of John Owen* 16 vols (London, 1679; repr. Edinburgh: Banner of Truth, 1981), 1:314–15.

4. Ambrose continues: '1. Christ is the truth and substance of all the types and shadows. 2. Christ is the substance and matter of the Covenant of Grace, and all administrations thereof; under the Old Testament Christ is veiled, under the New Covenant revealed. 3. Christ is the centre and meeting place of all the promises for in him the promises of God are yea and Amen. 4. Christ is the thing signified, sealed and exhibited in the Sacraments of the Old and New Testament. 5. Scripture genealogies are to discover to us the time and seasons of Christ. 6. Scripture chronologies are to discover to us the times and seasons of Christ. 7. Scripture-laws are our schoolmasters to bring us to Christ, the moral by correcting, the ceremonial by directing. 8. Scripture-gospel is Christ's light, whereby we are drawn into sweet union and communion with him; yea it is the very power of God for salvation unto all them that believe in Christ Jesus; and therefore think of Christ as the very substance, marrow, soul and scope of the whole Scriptures.' Isaac Ambrose, *Works*, (London, 1701), p. 201, quoted in J. I. Packer, *Quest for Godliness: The Puritan Vision of the Christian Life* (Wheaton, IL: Crossway, 1990), p. 103.

5. Edwards, letter no. 230, WJE 16:728–729.

6. Locke's goal in *The Reasonableness of Christianity* (London, 1695) was to demonstrate that the mere confession of Jesus as 'the Messiah' and not faith in a more detailed creed—say, one that included the doctrine of the Trinity or the divinity of Christ—was sufficient for salvation. On Locke's project, see John Higgins-Biddle's introduction to, John Locke, *The Reasonableness of Christianity as Delivered in the Scriptures*, Edited with an Introduction, by John C. Higgins-Biddle (Oxford: Clarendon, 1999), pp. xv-cxv.

7. Anthony Collins, *The Grounds and Reasons of the Christian Religion* (London, 1724), Pt. I, Ch. VI. Not all of Collins' detractors shared his confidence in the proof from prophecy. James O'Higgins S. J., *Anthony Collins: The Man and His Works* (The Hague: Martinus Nijhoff, 1970), p. 161, notes that it is not clear what prompted Collins to write *Grounds and Reasons*, but it is possible it was the publication in 1722 of a review of the Dutch theologian, William Surenhusius' book, *Βίβλος Καταλλαγῆς in quo secundum veterum Theologorum Hebraeorum Formulas allegandi, et Modos interpretandi conciliantur Loca Ex V. in N. T. Allegata* (Amsterdam, 1713) in which Surenhusius claimed to have discovered twenty-five lost rules by which the Jews of the New Testament times cited and interpreted the Hebrew Scriptures. Collins critiqued Surenhusius' 'rules' which included vowel re-pointing and the substitution of consonants, portraying them as unprincipled 'wire-drawing' in order to force a particular meaning on the Hebrew prophecies, though O'Higgins, *Anthony Collins*, 167–68, argues that Collins' report of Surenhusius is questionable. Another publication that may have animated Collins' pen was the publication of William Whiston, *Essay Towards Restoring the True Text of the Old Testament, and for vindicating the Citations thence made in the New Testament* (London, 1722). Collins accused Whiston of 'clipping and docking' the prophecies in the attempt to recover a pristine Old Testament text. Noting that the citations of the Old Testament in the New are not always verbally identical, Whiston had argued that the text of the Old Testament had been deliberately corrupted by the Jews in an attempt to cast doubt on Jesus' fulfilment of Messianic prophecies. According to Whiston, the corruption of the prophecies forced exegetes 'to go roundly and frequently into that strange notion of the double sense of prophecies, to the great

reproach of the Gospel.' Whiston, *Essay*, p. 92. On the 'double sense' and Edwards' relation to it, see my discussion below. Whiston's work followed his 1707 Boyle Lectures on the interpretation of Scripture's prophecies in which he rejected any interpretation of Scripture's prophecies as types and argued that they had only one referent, the Messiah. William Whiston, *The Accomplishment of Scripture Prophecies* (Cambridge, 1708).

8. Collins' discussion centres on Matt. 1:22–23; 2:15; 2:23; 11:14; 13:14.

9. Collins, *Grounds and Reasons*, pp. 31, 40, 48. Collins does not explicitly conclude that Christianity is groundless, though as this extract demonstrates, his argument certainly tends to that direction. The degree to which Collins' writings cautiously implied atheistical convictions is beyond the scope of the present enquiry, but is debated in the secondary literature. While O'Higgins, *Anthony Collins*, portrays Collins' religious position as 'ambiguous', being 'just on, or just over the fringe of Protestant Christianity' (p. 234), David Berman, *A History of Atheism in Britain from Hobbes to Russell* (London: Routledge (1990), pp. 70–92 argues that it is 'highly probable' that Collins was 'a strong-minded atheist' (p. 71). My concern is simply to highlight the hermeneutical challenge Collins posed to the unity of Old and New Testaments. O'Higgins, *Anthony Collins*, pp. 155–199 offers a detailed exposition of *Grounds and Reasons*.

10. Edwards, 'Miscellanies' no. 851, WJE 20:80–81.

11. William Whiston, *An Essay Towards Restoring the True Text of the Old Testament, and for vindicating the Citations thence made in the New Testament* (London, 1722) and *The Accomplishment of Scripture Prophecies* (Cambridge, 1708).

12. Samuel Chandler, *A Vindication of the Christian Religion*, 2nd ed. 2 vols. (London, 1727–28).

13. Samuel Clarke, *A Discourse concerning the connexion of the Prophecies in the Old Testament and Application of them to Christ* (London, 1725), p. 23.

14. Arthur Ashley Sykes, *An Essay upon the Truth of the Christian Religion* (London, 1725), pp. 178, 204–205.

15. Brown notes that this very question became a subject for discussion at the Hampshire Association of ministers in 1744–45. He conjectures that perhaps Edwards was responsible for pushing the agenda at the Association since he has an extensive entry ['Miscellanies' no. 842, WJE 20:57–64, ca. 1740] on this theme. Edwards raises the subject again ca. 1753 in 'Miscellanies', nos. 1198–99, WJE 23:119–23. Brown, *Edwards and the Bible*, pp. 22, 211 n. 82, 239 n. 55. Edwards' notebooks for his unwritten 'A History of the Work of Redemption' suggest that he intended settling the question there. He notes: 'When Come to MOSES observe how Revelation was given & upheld in the Ch[ur]h of God till that Time. & then observe the Nature of Prophecy. how the Prophet & Persons that had Revelations knew 'em to be Revelations from God how They knew before Moses & how afterword. & how true Prophets were known to others, about the Continuance of Prophecy.' 'A History of the Work of Redemption', Bk. 1, WJE Online vol. 31, http://edwards. yale.edu [accessed 29 January 2009]. Whether or not Edwards was responsible for raising the question at the Association, it was one that he seems to have wrestled with inconclusively.

16. Edwards observes this practice in Jesus' own discourse in John 2:19f where, speaking of His body, He challenged the Jews to 'destroy this temple and in three day I will raise it up.' Edwards reasons that since it was the Spirit of Christ who spoke through the prophets, could not the prophets also have spoken consciously of the antitype in terms of the type? 'Miscellanies' no. 1287, WJE 23:231–32.

17. 'Miscellanies' no. 1308, WJE 23:267–268 comprises an extract from Stapfer, *Institutiones Theologiae Polemicae* 5 vols (Zurich, 1743–47), vol. 2, p. 1088 (trans. by Douglas Sweeney). Stapfer notes that it is not proper that a prophecy's meaning should be perfectly plain: 'For it is not necessary that they are understood before the event; nor is it needed that human industry and wisdom contribute anything to their fulfilment. The latter would certainly occur if human beings knew clearly

beforehand everything by which something ought to happen. Nor, finally, ought divine counsels be returned void from the foreknowledge of human beings.'

18. Edwards, 'Notes on Scripture' no. 118, WJE 15:83.

19. Cotton Mather, *Magnalia Christi Americana* (London, 1702); *Agricola* (Boston, 1727). John Flavel, *Husbandry Spiritualized* (London, 1669).

20. Samuel Mather, *The Figures or Types of the Old Testament* (Dublin, 1683).

21. Mather, *Figures or Types*, p. 52.

22. Mather, *Figures or Types*, pp. 53–55.

23. For an introduction to Edwards' metaphysics see Wallace E. Anderson, 'Editor's Introduction', WJE 6: 1–143.

24. Mather, *Figures of Types*, pp. 55–56.

25. 'Miscellanies', no. 479, WJE 13:523. See also 'Images', no. 8, WJE 11:53. For Edwards the very act of creation was typological so the *protevangelion* was declared in Gen 1:1. The question of Edwards' position regarding the ordering of the divine decrees is beyond the scope of the present enquiry, but discussion may be found in Oliver D. Crisp, *Jonathan Edwards and the Metaphysics of Sin* (Aldershot: Ashgate, 2005), pp. 5–24; John H. Gerstner, *The Rational Biblical Theology of Jonathan Edwards in Three Volumes* (Powhatan, VA: Berea, 1991–93), 2:142–88; Stephen R. Holmes, *God of Grace and God of Glory: An Account of the Theology of Jonathan Edwards* (Edinburgh: T & T Clark, 2000), pp. 126–34.

26. Edwards, 'Types,' WJE 11:150.

27. Edwards, ;Types,' WJE 11:151.

28. Edwards, 'Types,' WJE 11:153.

29. See for example, Wallace E. Anderson, 'Editor's Introduction to "Images of Divine Things" and "Types",' WJE 11:3–48; Mason I. Lowance and David H. Watters,

'Editors' Introduction to "Types of the Messiah",' WJE 11:157–86; John F. Wilson, 'Editor's Introduction,' WJE 9:40–50.

30. Stein, 'Edwards and the Rainbow,' p. 440.

31. For a fuller treatment of this see my discussion in Stephen R. C. Nichols, *Jonathan Edwards' Bible: The Relationship of the Old and New Testaments* (Eugene, OR.: Pickwick Publications, 2013), pp. 85–95.

32. As with prophecy so with types, Edwards notes that although they were given to the Old Testament saints for their instruction, 'yet they were given much more for our instruction under the New Testament; for they understood but little, but we are under vastly greater advantage to understand them than they …. 1 Cor. 9:9–10, 1 Cor. 10:6, 11.' 'Types,' WJE 11:148–49.

33. 'Types,' WJE 11:150. Similarly, Edwards asks: '… how could any of these types be of any manner of instruction to the Jews to whom they were given, if they might judge nothing without interpretation, for the interpretation of none was then given?' However, as with his understanding of prophecy, so Edwards argues that although the types were given to the Old Testament saints for their instruction, 'yet they were given much more for our instruction under the New Testament; for they understood but little, but we are under vastly greater advantage to understand them than they …. 1 Cor. 9:9–10, 1 Cor. 10:6, 11.' 'Types', WJE 11:148–49.

34. 'Miscellanies,' no. 362, WJE 13:435.

35. Miller, *Jonathan Edwards*, pp. 30–32, 76–78; *New England Mind: The Seventeenth Century, passim*; *Errand into the Wilderness*, p. 98.

36. Both Edwards' analysis of the conditionality of the covenant and his own contribution to covenant thought, namely his explanation of the union between Christ and His bride as a 'covenant of grace,' are beyond the present aim which is simply to establish the Christological unity of redemption history in his thought

37. Edwards denominates Turretin thus in *Religious Affections*, WJE 2:289 n. 4; Turretin, *Institutes*, 12:2.5.

38. *Westminster Confession*, 7:5.

39. *Westminster Confession*, 7:6. Similarly, Calvin argues that the covenant made with all the patriarchs is 'so much like ours in substance and reality that the two are actually one and the same. Yet they differ in the mode of dispensation.' Calvin, *Institutes*, 2:10–11 (2:10.2). The distinction between substance and administration is a familiar one in Continental Reformed theology. See for example Turretin, *Institutes*, 12.5.1.45; 12.8.1–25. Heppe, *Reformed Dogmatics*, pp. 371–409. See also the *Westminster Confession*, 7:6. The thorny question of the relationship between Calvin and covenantal theology is beyond the scope of the present enquiry. For an introduction to this see for example, Jens G. Møller, 'The Beginnings of Puritan Covenant Theology,' *Journal of Ecclesiastical History* 14 (1963): 46–67; Holmes Rolston III, 'Responsible Man in Reformed Theology: Calvin versus the Westminster Confession', *Scottish Journal of Theology* 23 (1970): 129–56; John von Rohr, *The Covenant of Grace in Puritan Thought* (Atlanta, GA: Scholars Press, 1986); Everett H. Emerson, 'Calvin and Covenant Theology,' *Church History* 25 (1956): 136–44; R. T. Kendall, *Calvin and English Calvinism to 1649* (Oxford: Oxford University Press, 1979); Paul Helm, *Calvin and the Calvinists* (Edinburgh: Banner of Truth, 1982); R. A. Muller, *Christ and the Decree: Christology and Predestination in Reformed Theology from Calvin to Perkins* (Grand Rapids, MI: Baker, 1988).

40. Edwards, 'Miscellanies' no. 1118, WJE 20:493.

41. Edwards, 'Miscellanies' no. 1353, WJE 23:492–506.

42. Edwards, 'Miscellanies' no. 1353, WJE 23:503; see no. 439, WJE 13:488.

43. Edwards, 'Miscellanies' no. 1353, WJE 23:503.

44. Edwards, 'Christ's Sacrifice,' WJE 10:595.

45. Edwards, 'The Sacrifice of Christ Acceptable,' WJE 14:448.

46. This 'dispositional soteriology' was first advanced in Anri Morimoto, *Jonathan Edwards and the Catholic Vision of Salvation* (University Park, PA: Pennsylvania State University Press, 1995), though others have built upon it. The thesis applies the 'dispositional ontology' account of Edwards' metaphysics championed in Sang Hyun Lee, *The Philosophical Theology of Jonathan Edwards* (Princeton, NJ: Princeton University Press, 2005).

47. Edwards, *A Faithful Narrative*, WJE 2:172–73.

48. Edwards, 'History of the Work of Redemption,' WJE 9:131. See also, among many possible examples, 'Miscellanies,' no. 663, WJE 18:200–201.

49. John Owen, *Christologia: Or, A Declaration of the Glorious Mystery of the Person of Christ*, in *Works*, 1.2–272 (101). See also Edwards' reliance on Owen's commentary on Hebrews in 'Miscellanies', no. 1283, WJE 23:229–30 (229): 'It is manifest that all that ever obtained the pardon of their sins, from the foundation of the world till Christ came (if any at all were pardoned), obtained forgiveness through the sacrifice of Christ, by Heb. 9:26 ... (see Owen on the place ...).'

50. Turretin, *Institutes*, 12.5.1, emphasis added. Turretin names among his opponents, 'the Socinians, Remonstrants, [and] Anabaptists.'

51. Turretin, *Institutes*, 12.5.38.

52. Richard Sibbes, *God Manifested in the Flesh*, in *The Works of Richard Sibbes* (Aberdeen: J. Chalmers, 1809), 1:153.

53. Stein directs attention to a number of entries in the 'Blank Bible', those on: Genesis 16:4; 24:67; Numbers 12:1, 6–8 (2), 9–10; Deut 24:9.

54. Stephen Stein, 'Editor's Introduction,' 'Blank Bible,' WJE 24:30.

55. John Webster's comment regarding theologies of retrieval may be applied to Edwards at this point, namely that such theologies are valuable precisely because they 'de-centre' the accepted norms of critical judgment by trying to stand with the Christian past. John Webster, 'Theologies of Retrieval', in *The Oxford Handbook*

of Systematic Theology, ed. by John Webster, Kathryn Tanner and Iain Torrance (Oxford: Oxford University Press, 2007), pp. 583–99.

Chapter 9

1. For a careful treatment of the history behind Owen's *Communion with the Triune God*, see Kelly Kapic's *Communion with God: The Divine and Human in the Theology of John Owen* (Grand Rapids: Baker Academic, 2007) pp. 147–205.

2. Edwards, 'Miscellany' 271, WJE 13:374.

3. Edwards, 'Personal Narrative,' WJE 16:793.

4. I am exceedingly grateful to Rev. John Franks for passing along his research on Edwards' use of the Song. David S. Lovi and Benjamin Westerhoff are in the process of publishing a commentary on Edwards' references on the Song.

5. Edwards, 'Notes on Scripture' 507, WJE 15:610–613.

6. Two have been published by Yale University Press, a sermon on Canticles 2:3, 'The Believer Hath Rest in Christ,' (WJEO 48) and a sermon on Canticles 6:1, 'That We May Seek Him With Thee' (WJEO 49). Edwards' sacramental sermon on Canticles 5:1, 'Persons need not and ought not to set any bounds to their spiritual and gracious appetites,' was published in the Don Kistler ed. volume, *The Puritan Pulpit*. Edwards' June 1733 sermon on Canticles 1:3 'Thy Name Is Ointment Poured Forth,' has been published in the McMullen, ed., *The Blessing of God* (Michael D. McMullen ed., *The Blessing of God* (Nashville, TN: Broadman & Holdman Publishers, 2003) pp. 163–179).

7. Minkema, 'Editor's Introduction,' WJE 14:39.

8. This revised version has been published in the McMullian, ed., *Blessing of God*.

9. Also, the Boston rendition may have been intended for publication. See Wilson Kimnach's comments in WJE 10:153–156.

10. Mark Valeri observes that the 'sermon on Canticles 1:3 ... bears marked similarities

to the sermon on Revelation 5:5–6, published in 1738 as "The Excellency of Christ."'
Valeri, 'Editor's Introduction,' WJE 17:8.

11. M. X. Lesser notes that 'Aug. 1736 Sacr.' appears on the upper right-hand corner
     of the first leaf, marking the last of the five discourses a sacramental sermon.

12. Schaeffer, quoted in Minkema, ed., WJE 14:67.

13. Edwards, 'A Spiritual Understanding of Things Denied To The Unregenerate,'
     WJE 14:76–77.

14. Edwards, 'Sweet Harmony of Christ,' WJE 19:441.

15. Edwards, 'Sweet Harmony of Christ,' WJE 19:442.

16. Edwards, 'The Church's Marriage to Her Sons, and to Her God,' WJE 25:184.

17. Wilson H. Kimnach, introduction to 'The Church's Marriage to Her Sons, and
     to Her God,' in WJE 25:166.

18. Edwards' believed that the Bible is coherent in all its parts—and is the progressive
     product of one Divine author—we might justly call Edwards' canonical approach,
     a 'Covenantal' or 'Redemptive-historical' approach as there is much overlap in the
     understanding of these terms. When we speak of his approach being 'Covenantal' we
     have in mind what Carl Bogue has so cogently argued in his dissertation *Jonathan
     Edwards and the Covenant of Grace* (Wipf & Stock, 2009). The best in-depth study
     of this principle can be found in Iain D. Campbell's 'The Song of David's Son:
     Interpreting the Song of Solomon in Light of the Davidic Covenant,' *Westminster
     Theological Journal* 62:1 (Spring 2000) p. 18ff. This article is a superb example of
     what a consistent Covenantal approach to the *Song* looks like.

19. If one were to object to this on the grounds of a supposed post-enlightenment
     'grammatical-historical' school of interpretation, I would insist that, on one hand,
     Edwards' method was entirely grammatical-historical (a method that focuses on
     the grammar and historical context of the text), but, on the other hand, it was a
     pre-enlightenment approach by which the more narrow grammatical-historical

context of the book was read in light of the entire theological context of the canon. For a careful treatment of this subject, see Vern Poythress, 'The Presence of God Qualifying Our Notions of the Grammatical-Historical Method: Genesis 3:15 As A Test Case' (*Journal of the Evangelical Theological Society* 50/1. 2007) pp. 87–103. See also Gerhard Ebeling's 'The Significance of the Historical *Critical* Method for the Church and Protestantism' in *Word and Faith* (London: SCM, 1963) pp. 17–61 for an explanation of the shift that occurred in the removal of the 'canonical-theological' element of interpretation in post-enlightenment critical exegesis.

20. Jonathan Edwards, *A History of the Work of Redemption*, WJE 9:233.

21. Jonathan Edwards, 'The Church's Marriage to Her Sons, and to Her God,' WJE 25:184.

22. This sermon was first preached in Northampton in 1728 in and then given as a lecture in Boston in 1733.

23. Jonathan Edwards, 'Miscellany' 303, WJE 13:389–390.

24. Sean Michael Lucas, *God's Grand Design: The Theological Vision of Jonathan Edwards* (Deerfield, IL: Crossway Publishing, 2011) p. 48.

25. Edwards, 'Types of the Messiah,' WJE 11:210.

26. Edwards, 'Notes' no. 85, WJE 15:75.

27. Edwards, 'Notes' no. 460, WJE 15:550.

28. Edwards, 'Notes' no. 460, WJE 15:551.

29. Edwards, 'Types of the Messiah,' WJE 11:210.

30. Edwards, 'Types of the Messiah,' WJE 11:303.

31. Edwards, 'Types of the Messiah,' WJE 11:261.

32. Edwards, 'Types of the Messiah,' WJE 11:261–262.

33. Edwards, *The 'Blank Bible'*, WJE 24:607.

34. Edwards, 'Types of the Messiah,' WJE 11:298–299.

35. Edwards, 'Types of the Messiah,' WJE 11:276.

36. Edwards, 'Notes,' 492, WJE 15:585.

37. Edwards, 'Notes,' 493, WJE 15:586.

38. Edwards, 'Types of the Messiah,' WJE 11:303.

39. Edwards, 'Types of the Messiah,' WJE 11:301.

40. Edwards, 'Notes' 460, WJE 15:548.

41. In recent years, multitudes of attempts have been made to disprove the Christological nature of the Song on the basis of a supposedly universally accepted grammatical-historical approach that places the book within the sphere of Ancient Near Eastern love poetry. Such an approach is thought to be the remedy to an exegetically deficient allegorical method. However, such attempts to correct a perceived interpretive error have striped the Song of its theological significance and have led to interpretations of the Song that functionally make it just like an other Ancient Near Eastern love poem. In fact, most recent commentators who have adopted the stance that Song is merely a human love poem have also tended to strip the book of it's canonical and covenantal background altogether. One interesting exception among recent critical scholars is Ellen Davis. In her commentary on the *Song*, Davis seeks to understand the symbols, allusions and metaphors of the Song in light of what is said in the Hebrew Bible. See Ellen F. Davis, *Proverbs, Ecclesiastes and the Song of Songs* (Louisville, KY: Westminster/John Knox Press, 2000).

Chapter 10

1. *The Works of Jonathan Edwards*, 26 volumes (New Haven, CT: Yale University Press, 1957–2008).

2. The Edwards centre's director is jointly appointed by the faculty of theology, yet

even so, it is not entirely clear as to how the theological department is actually involved in the centre. http://www.uni-tuebingen.de/fakultaeten/philosophische-fakultaet/fachbereiche/neuphilologie/englisches-seminar/abteilungen/amerikanistik/lehr-und-forschungsschwerpunkte.html, accessed March 14, 2014.

3.   http://www.jonathanedwardsgermany.org, accessed March 14, 2014.

4.   Ernest W. Hankamer published on Edwards' political thought; see Hankamer, *Das Politische Denken von Jonathan Edwards* (Ph.D. diss., University of Munich, 1972). Eric Voegelin (1901–85), a German-born American political philosopher, refers to Edwards' philosophy; see for instance his essay, 'A Formal Relationship with Puritan Mysticism,' in *The Collected Works of Voegelin: On the Form of the American Mind*, vol. 1, trans. Ruth Hein, ed. Jürgen Gebhardt and Barry Cooper (Baton Rouge: Lousiana State University Press, 1995), pp.126–143, see especially pp. 131–143. Gustav E. Müller offers an account of Edwards' philosophical thought in *Amerikanische Philosophie* (Stuttgart: Fr. Frommanns Verlag, 1950), 17–38. Two Anglo-Saxon scholars published works on Edwards in German: John Henry McCracken penned a dissertation on Edwards' idealism ('Jonathan Edwards Idealismus, Ph.D. diss., University of Halle, 1899), and William Harder Squires, who studied under Wilhelm Wundt in Leipzig, published on Edwards' doctrine of the will ('Jonathan Edwards und seine Willenslehre,' Ph.D. diss., University of Leipzig, 1901).

5.   I am aware only of Caroline Schröder, *Glaubenswahrnehmung und Selbsterkenntnis: Jonathan Edwards' theologia experimentalis* (Göttingen: Vandhoeck & Ruprecht, 1998).

6.   Edwards, *Sind religiöse Gefühle zuverlässige Anzeichen für wahren Glauben?* (Waldems: 3L-Verlag, 2012); Edwards, *Das Leben von David Brainerd: Tagebuch eines Indianermissionars*, trans. Wilhelm Schneider (Waldems: 3L-Verlag, 2011). Also recently available is a small book with extracts of his works, *Aus Edwards' Schatzkammer* (Hamburg: C. M. Fliss, 2008). Iain H. Murray's Edwards biography

is now also available in German, *Jonathan Edwards: Ein Lehrer der Gnade und die Grosse Erweckung* (Bielefeld: CLV, 2011).

7.   Edwards, 'A Faithful Narrative,' WJE 4:97–211.

8.   Kenneth Minkema, 'Edwards, Jonathan,' in Michael J. McClymond, ed., *Encyclopedia of Religious Revivals in America*, 2 vols. (Westport, CT: Greenwood Press, 2007), I:153.

9.   Edwards, *Glaubwürdige Nachricht von dem herrlichen Werck Gottes, Welches sich in Bekehrung vieler Hundert Seelen zu Northampton, und an anderen Orten in Neu-Engeland geäussert hat etc.*, trans. Johann Adam Steinmetz (Magdeburg: Christian Leberecht Fabern, 1738). I am grateful to Andrew Kloes for directing my attention to this source. Michael J. McClymond recently noted that '[i]n turning to Edwards' revival writings, one is immediately struck by the absence of interest among German-language authors. Beyond a few formulaic references, German sources from the mid-1700s to the mid-1900s seldom mention the theme of revival.' While this might be, broadly speaking, true, he does unfortunately not include Steinmetz' significant translation in his considerations. See Michael J. McClymond, 'A German Professor Dropped into the American Forests,' in *After Jonathan Edwards: The Courses of the New England Theology*, eds. Oliver D. Crisp and Douglas A. Sweeney (Oxford: Oxford University Press, 2012), pp. 209–225, quote on p. 219.

10. 'Mein Gemüthe wurde sogleich bey der ersten Durchlesung dieser Nachricht ... mit einer recht innigen Vergnügung überschüttet; und es kan wohl seyn, daß diese Hofnung dadurch bey mir vergrössert worden: Es sey ein gewisser Nutzen vor manche Seelen daraus zu erwarten, wenn sie auch in unserer Deutschen Sprache bekandt gemacht würde.' Steinmetz, 'Vorrede,' in *Glaubwürdige Nachricht von dem herrlichen Werck Gottes,* p. 2.

11. Edwards, 'Concerning the End for which God Created the World,' WJE 8:452.

12. Edwards, 'Concerning the End for which God Created the World,' WJE 8:432–436. See also 'The Mind,' WJE 6:364–365.

13. Edwards, 'Concerning the End for which God Created the World,' WJE 8:527 (emphasis original), see also p. 433.

14. Edwards writes: 'As to God's excellence, it is evident it consists in the love of himself. For he was as excellent before he created the universe as he is now.' 'The Mind,' WJE 6:364.

15. Scholars debate as to which extent Edwards uses a dispositional ontology. See Sang Hyun Lee, *The Philosophical Theology of Jonathan Edwards* (Princeton: University Press, 1988), pp. 170–210, and by the same author, 'Jonathan Edwards' conception of the Trinity: A Resource for Contemporary Reformed Theology,' in *Toward the Future of Reformed Theology: Tasks, Topics, Traditions*, eds. David Willis and Michael Welker (Grand Rapids, MI: Eerdmans, 1999), pp. 444–455. As a response to Lee, see Stephen R. Holmes, 'Does Jonathan Edwards use a Dispositional Ontology? A Response to Sang Hyun Lee,' in Paul Helm and Oliver D. Crisp, eds., *Jonathan Edwards: Philosophical Theologian* (Aldershot, UK: Ashgate, 2003), pp. 99–114.

16. Edwards, 'Miscellany' 448, WJE 13:496.

17. Edwards, 'Miscellany' 332, WJE 13:410. Elsewhere, Edwards writes: 'And as this fullness is capable of communication or emanation *ad extra*; so it seems a thing amiable and valuable in itself that it should be communicated or flow forth, that this infinite fountain of good should send forth abundant streams, that this infinite fountain of light should, diffusing its excellent fullness, pour forth light all around.' 'Concerning the End for which God Created the World,' WJE 8:433.

18. Edwards, 'Miscellany' 48, WJE 13:496.

19. Edwards, 'The True Excellency of a Minister of the Gospel,' WJE 25:82; Edwards, 'The Mind,' WJE 6:344.

20. Edwards, 'Miscellany' 99, WJE 13:265; cf. 'Miscellany' 106, WJE 13:276–277.

21. Edwards elaborates on this thesis in his treatise, 'Concerning the End for which God Created the World,' WJE 8:403–536.

22. Swiss theologian Adolf Schlatter (1852–1938) shares Edwards' holistic trajectory. Schlatter writes: 'The territory that the theological task has to stride across ranges over the whole revelatory work of God. That endows it with an impetus to the whole [*Richtung auf das Ganze*] … The notion of God [*Gottesgedanke*] contains the clause that all being stands in relation to God and that it visualises in some way his power and will. There is, for that reason, nothing that is unimportant to the one who is faced with the question for God.' Schlatter, *Das Christliche Dogma*, 2nd ed. (Stuttgart: Calwer Vereinsbuchhandlung, 1923), p. 13.

23. Edwards, 'Shadows of Divine Things,' WJE 11:129.

24. Schweitzer, *God is a Communicative Being: Divine Communicativeness and Harmony in the Theology of Jonathan Edwards* (London: T & T Clark, 2012), p. 6.

25. Edwards, 'Miscellany' 87, WJE 13:252.

26. See Gerald McDermott, *Jonathan Edwards confronts the Gods: Christian Theology, Enlightenment Religion, and Non-Christian Faiths* (Oxford: Oxford University Press, 2000).

27. Richard Dawkins, *The Blind Watchmaker: Why the Evidence of Evolution Reveals a Universe without Design* (New York: W. W. Norton & Company, 1986); Francis Crick, *The Astonishing Hypothesis: The Scientific Search for the Soul* (London: Simon and Schuster, 1994), p. 3.

28. See Edwards, 'The "Spider" Papers,' WJE 6:145–169.

29. Barth's 'Nein!', written in the summer of 1934, was originally published in *Theologische Existenz Heute* 14 (1934). For the English translation, see Barth, 'No!,' in *Natural Theology: Comprising 'Nature and Grace' by Professor Dr. Emil Brunner and the Reply 'No!' by Dr. Karl Barth*, trans. Peter Fraenkel, (London: The Centenary Press, 1946), pp. 65–128. For the debate between Karl Barth and Emil Brunner see John W. Hart, *Karl Barth vs. Emil Brunner: The Formation and Dissolution of a Theological Alliance, 1916–1936* (New York: Peter Lang, 2001). Gerrit C. Berkouwer observes that 'Barth has centered his attack more and more upon natural theology as *the*

great enemy of the faith, and general revelation was always involved in this attack as well.' Berkouwer, *General Revelation* (Grand Rapids, MI: Eerdmans, 1955), p. 21 (emphasis original).

30. This is suggested by Kornelius H. Miskotte, 'Natürliche Religion und Theologie,' in *Religion in Geschichte und Gegenwart*, 3rd ed., vol. 4, ed. Kurt Galling (Tübingen: Mohr/Paul Siebeck, 1957), p. 1324.

31. Edwards' strong account of general revelation does not succumb to a full-blown natural theology. See Schweitzer, *God is a Communicative Being*, pp. 55–65.

32. See his sermon, 'Man's Natural Blindness in the Things of Religion,' in *The Works of Jonathan Edwards* (Peabody, MA: Hendrickson, 1998 [1834]), 2:247–256.

33. If not indicated otherwise, Scripture quotations are according to the *English Standard Version* (Wheaton, IL: Crossway, 2001).

34. See Schweitzer,*God is a Communicative Being*, pp. 53–54.

35. Edwards, 'Ministers to Preach no their own Wisdom but the Word of God,' in *The Salvation of Souls: Nine Previously Unpublished Sermons on the Call of Ministry and Gospel by Jonathan Edwards*, eds. Richard A. Bailey and Gregory A. Wills (Wheaton, IL: Crossway Books, 2002), p. 115.

36. Edwards, 'Miscellany' 837, WJE 20:52–53.

37. In his 'Personal Narrative,' Edwards writes: 'I have sometimes had an affecting sense of the excellency of the word of God, as a word of life; as the light of life; a sweet, excellent, life-giving word: accompanied with a thirsting after that word, that it might dwell richly in my heart.' WJE 16:801; Edwards, 'Treatise on Grace,' WJE 21:165. 'The Holy Ghost,' Edwards writes, 'convinces by arguments, he enlightens the reason, and makes use of the gospel.' 'The Threefold Work of the Holy Ghost,' WJE 14:393.

38. Edwards, 'A Spiritual Understanding of Divine Things denied to the Unregenerate,' WJE 14:79.

39. Edwards, 'Personal Narrative,' WJE 16:792–793.

40. On this new 'sense of the heart,' see John E. Smith, 'Religious Affections and the *Sense of the Heart*,' in *The Princeton Companion to Jonathan Edwards*, ed. Sang Hyun Lee (Princeton: Princeton University Press, 2005), pp. 103–114.

41. Edwards, 'A Spiritual Understanding of Divine Things denied to the Unregenerate,' WJE 14:76.

42. Edwards here reveals his clear Christocentric focus. God glorifies himself, Edwards insists, by making himself known in his Son Jesus Christ, the 'one grand medium.' He writes: 'The one grand medium by which he glorifies himself in all is Jesus Christ, God-man … 'Tis by this one grand medium that God communicates himself to all his elect creatures in heaven and on earth: all fullness dwells [in Christ], a fullness not only to fill man but to fill angels … Jesus Christ and that as God-man is the grand medium by which God attains his end, both in communicating himself to the creature and [in] glorifying himself by the creation.' 'Approaching the End of God's Grand Design,' WJE 25:116–117.

43. Edwards, 'Concerning the End for which God Created the World,' WJE 8:435.

44. Edwards, 'The True Excellency of a Minister of the Gospel,' WJE 25:82–102.

45. 'The name of Christ is ever delightful to God; and the preaching of Christ in the world … is acceptable to God, as he delights in having the name of his Son glorified.' Edwards, 'Notes on Scripture' 363, WJE 15:349.

46. Edwards, 1000. Sermon on Acts 16:9 (Aug. 1751), WJE *Online*, vol. 69, accessed February 21, 2014.

47. Edwards, 'The Great Concern of a Watchman for Souls' WJE 25:66. This points to Edwards very high view of the ministry. Elsewhere, Edwards writes: 'There are two kinds of persons that are given to Christ, and appointed and devoted of God to be his servants, to be employed with Christ, and under him, in his great work of the salvation of the souls of men; and they are *angels* and *ministers*.' Edwards,

'Christ the Example of Gospel Ministers' WJE 25:344 (emphasis original). See also 'Types' entry 53, WJE 11:65–66. In Edwards' view, ministers are then in some respect 'subordinate saviours' (Schweitzer, *God is a Communicative Being*, p. 149), and they also play a distinct role in heaven (see Edwards, 'Exposition of the Apocalypse' entry for Revelation 21:12 WJE 5:154–155). One wonders whether Edwards has sufficient biblical warrant to justify this high view of the ministry; this, however, is not the place to engage in a more elaborate discussion of Edwards' high view of the ministry.

48. As the believers are united with Christ, Edwards argues, 'they are partakers of his [Jesus'] relation to the Father, or of his sonship … So they are in their measure partakers of the Son's enjoyment of his Father.' 'Miscellany' 571, WJE 18:109, see also 'Miscellany' 741, WJE 18:366–367.

49. Edwards, 'Ministers to Preach not their own Wisdom but the Word of God,' *The Salvation of Souls*, p. 116.

50. Edwards, 'Ministers to Preach no their own Wisdom but the Word of God,' in *The Salvation of Souls*, p. 126.

51. Edwards, 'Ministers to Preach no their own Wisdom but the Word of God,' in *The Salvation of Souls*, pp. 125–126.

52. Edwards, 'Christian Knowledge,' in *Jonathan Edwards on Knowing Christ* (Edinburgh: Banner of Truth Trust, 1990), p. 17.

53. George M. Marsden, *Jonathan Edwards: A Life* (New Haven: Yale University Press, 2004), p. 133.

54. Edwards, 'Christian Knowledge,' in *Jonathan Edwards on Knowing Christ*, p. 18.

55. Edwards, 'Christian Knowledge,' in *Jonathan Edwards on Knowing Christ*, p. 11.

56. Mark A. Noll, *The Scandal of the Evangelical Mind* (Grand Rapids, MI: Eerdmans, 1995), p. 3. See also Marva J. Dawn, *Reaching Out Without Dumbing Down: A Theology of Worship for This Urgent Time* (Grand Rapids, MI: Eerdmans, 1995).

57. Edwards, 'Ministers to Preach no their own Wisdom but the Word of God,' in *The Salvation of Souls*, p. 119.

58. Edwards, 'Some Thoughts Concerning the Present Revival of Religion in New England,' WJE 4:397.

59. What Rudolf Otto called the *mysterium tremendum*, an 'unheimlich-furchtbares Gefühl.' Otto, *Das Heilige* (München: Biederstein, 1947), p. 13, cf. p. 18.

60. Edwards, 'Christ the Spiritual Sun,' WJE 22:48–63.

61. Edwards, 'The Sweet Harmony of Christ,' WJE 19:435–450.

62. Edwards, 'The Excellency of Christ,' WJE 19:560–594.

63. Edwards, 'The Excellency of Christ,' WJE 19:565, 567, 568.

64. Michael J. McClymond and Gerald R. McDermott, *The Theology of Jonathan Edwards* (New York: Oxford University Press, US, 2012), p. 20.

65. See Donald S. Whitney, 'Pursuing a Passion for God Through Spiritual Disciplines: Learning from Jonathan Edwards,' in *A God Entranced Vision of All Things: The Legacy of Jonathan Edwards*, eds. John Piper and Justin Taylor (Wheaton, IL: Crossway Books, 2004), pp. 109–128.

66. Edwards, 'The True Excellency of a Minister of the Gospel,' WJE 25:100.

67. Edwards argues that 'where there is a kind of light without heat, a head stored with notions and speculations, with a cold and unaffected heart, there can be nothing divine in that light, that knowledge is no true spiritual knowledge of divine things.' *The Religious Affections*, WJE 2:120.

68. Edwards, 'Miscellany' 104, WJE 13:273.

69. Edwards, 'Miscellany' 448, WJE 13:495.

70. Edwards, 'Christian Knowledge,' p. 15.

71. Edwards, 'Christian Knowledge,' p. 15.

72. McClymond and McDermott, *The Theology of Jonathan Edwards*, p. 20.

73. Edwards, 'Some Thoughts Concerning the Revival, The Great Awakening,' WJE 4:387.

74. Edwards, 'Treatise on Grace,' WJE 21:175.

75. Oliver O' Donovan, *Self, World, and Time: Ethics as Theology*, vol. 1 (Grand Rapids, MI: Eerdmans, 2013), p. 113.

76. Edwards, 'Christian Knowledge,' p. 13.

77. Steinmetz, 'Vorrede,' p. 2.

78. C. S. Lewis, *Surprised by Joy: The Shape of My Early Life* (New York: Harcourt Brace & Co., 1955).

79. Gerhard Ebeling, *Theology and Proclamation* (London: Wm. Collins Son and Co., 1966), p. 20.

80. Based on his reading of Edwards, Samuel T. Logan coined the term of 'preaching phenomenologically, *eventfully*.' Samuel T. Logan Jr., 'The Phenomenology of Preaching,' in *The Preacher and Preaching: Reviving the Art in the Twentieth Century*, ed. Samuel T. Logan Jr. (Phillipsburg, NJ: Presbyterian and Reformed, 1986), p. 160 (emphasis original).